Corporate Acquisitions and Mergers in the United States

Corporate Acquisitions and Mergers in the United States

Vijay Sekhon

Sidley Austin LLP

This book was originally published as a chapter in Corporate Acquisitions and Mergers.

General Editor: Peter Begg

Wolters Kluwer

Published by:
Kluwer Law International B.V.
P.O. Box 316
2400 AH Alphen aan den Rijn
The Netherlands
Website: lrus.wolterskluwer.com

Sold and distributed in North, Central and South America by:
Wolters Kluwer Legal & Regulatory U.S.
7201 McKinney Circle
Frederick, MD 21704
United States of America
Email: customer.service@wolterskluwer.com

Sold and distributed in all other countries by:
Air Business Subscriptions
Rockwood House
Haywards Heath
West Sussex
RH16 3DH
United Kingdom
Email: international-customerservice@wolterskluwer.com

Printed on acid-free paper

ISBN 978-94-035-0080-5

e-Book: ISBN 978-94-035-0081-2
web-PDF: ISBN 978-94-035-0082-9

This title is available on www.kluwerlawonline.com

Printed in the United Kingdom.

SIDLEY AUSTIN LLP

Sidley Austin LLP ("Sidley" or the "Firm") is a premier law firm with a practice highly attuned to the ever-changing international landscape. The firm advises clients around the globe, with more than 2,000 lawyers in 20 offices worldwide.

Sidley maintains a commitment to providing quality legal services and to offering advice in litigation, transactional and regulatory matters spanning virtually every area of law. The firm's lawyers have wide-reaching legal backgrounds and are dedicated to teamwork, collaboration and superior client service.

Sidley received 48 first-tier national rankings, the most of any U.S. law firm, in the 2018 *U.S. News – Best Lawyers®* "Best Law Firms" survey. In addition, the firm received 149 first-tier regional rankings. Such recognition is a result of the firm's unwavering commitment to successfully representing clients on complex matters spanning a range of legal areas.

Sidley has offices in Beijing, Boston, Brussels, Century City, Chicago, Dallas, Geneva, Hong Kong, Houston, London, Los Angeles, Munich, New York, Palo Alto, San Francisco, Shanghai, Singapore, Sydney, Tokyo and Washington D.C.

Author

Vijay Sekhon is a partner in Sidley's Century City office and a member of the M&A, Private Equity, Capital Markets and Corporate Reorganization and Bankruptcy practice groups. His practice focuses on mergers, purchases, sales and reorganizations of businesses for companies and private equity and hedge funds. Vijay also focuses on public debt and equity offerings, private placements and purchases and sales of debt and equity, and general corporate and securities law, including advising companies and private equity and hedge funds on their disclosure obligations under the federal securities laws.

He has represented Goldman Sachs; JPMorgan Chase Bank, N.A.; The Blackstone Group, L.P.; TPG Capital; Cerberus Capital Management, L.P.; Canyon Partners; Franklin Templeton Investments; Pine River Capital Management, L.P.; The Yucaipa Companies, LLC; Levine Leichtman Capital Partners Inc.; Fast Retailing Co., Ltd.; Universal Studios Japan; Z Capital Partners, LLC; Siris Capital Group, LLC; QVT Financial; JHL Capital Group; Glendon Capital Management LP; Tribune Publishing Company and Castle Creek Capital LLC.

Vijay served as senior counsel in the Office of the General Counsel of the U.S. Securities and Exchange Commission from 2009 to 2011, and an adjunct professor at the University of Southern California Gould School of Law from 2014 to 2017. He was a judicial intern for former Chief Justice William H. Rehnquist in the United States Supreme Court and the Honorable Ellen Segal Huvelle in the United States District Court for the District of Columbia. Vijay has published numerous articles related to law, business and finance in respected academic and practitioner journals, including the *Stanford Journal of Law, Business & Finance*, the *Berkeley Business Law Journal*, the *Securities Regulation Law Journal*, the *Real Estate Finance Journal*, and *Pratt's Journal of Bankruptcy Law*. He has been recognized as a "Next Generation Lawyer" for Private Equity Buyouts by *The Legal 500* and a "Rising Star" for Private Equity by *Law360*.

Vijay earned his J.D. from Stanford Law School, and received his B.A., *summa cum laude*, from the University of California at Berkeley. Vijay is also a member of the Financial Lawyers Conference.

1999 Avenue of the Stars
17th Floor
Los Angeles, California, U.S.A.

Email: vsekhon@sidley.com
Tel.: 1-310-595-9507
Fax: 1-310-595-9501

Contents

OVERVIEW OF TRANSACTION STRUCTURE, ISSUES AND DOCUMENTATION

[01] The structure, complexity and timing of an acquisition of a U.S. business by a foreign acquirer will depend upon a number of factors, including whether the acquisition is a purchase of assets or shares or a merger; whether the target business is publicly or privately held; whether the deal is negotiated or "hostile"; whether the acquirer is acquiring a parent company or a division, segment or subsidiary of a company; whether the acquirer is acquiring control or merely making a strategic or minority investment; the form of consideration; the type of business to be acquired; and the regulatory framework within which the target business operates. This section reviews structural and other considerations primarily relevant to the negotiated acquisition of a privately held U.S. business. Additional considerations relevant to negotiated and hostile acquisitions of U.S. public companies are discussed in paragraphs 85–200 below.

FORM OF ACQUISITION

[02] Negotiated acquisitions of U.S. businesses are typically accomplished in one of the following three ways: (i) by purchasing the assets of the target business; (ii) by acquiring the shares of the target business; or (iii) by effecting a statutory merger (in most cases, with a newly formed subsidiary of the acquirer). Each method is discussed below.

Asset Acquisition

[03] In an asset acquisition, the acquirer purchases all or substantially all of the assets of a company—or of a division, segment or subsidiary of the company. Because the liabilities of the seller's business generally do not automatically transfer in an asset acquisition, the acquirer only assumes those liabilities that it specifically agrees to assume. However, an acquirer may be responsible for certain liabilities, by operation of law, most notably environmental liabilities, product liability claims, certain tax liabilities and certain pension liabilities relating to employees of the acquired business particularly in connection with a sale of all or substantially all of the seller's assets. An acquirer may mitigate successor liability concerns by excluding certain assets from the transaction, or by acquiring the assets through a newly formed shell subsidiary, thereby protecting the acquirer's other assets.

[04] The sale of all or substantially all of the assets of the seller usually requires shareholder approval with respect to the seller under applicable state law. Approval by the acquirer's shareholders is typically not required, however. In addition, each party's board of directors typically must approve the transaction.

[05] In an asset acquisition, instruments transferring title must be prepared for each asset or category of assets, whether real estate or tangible or intangible personal property. The transaction may also be subject to transfer or sales tax, and deciding which party will bear the economic burden of such taxes is often an important aspect of the overall negotiation. There are generally no stamp duties in the United States, although some states and local governments impose documentary or recording taxes in connection with the recordation of deeds or mortgages.

[06] Because licenses and other qualifications to operate the acquired business do not automatically transfer in an asset acquisition, they must be either assigned to the acquirer (which may require counterparty consent) or be issued or renewed in the name of the acquirer. Further, various approvals and consents to the transfer of the assets may be required by governmental and regulatory agencies and/or by other third parties with whom the seller has a contractual relationship (including customers, vendors, lenders, landlords and others).

[07] Representations and warranties made by the seller in the purchase agreement can provide meaningful protection to the acquirer after the closing. If the seller has few or no assets after the transaction, however, the acquirer should consider (i) requiring that the seller's parent company or principal shareholders indemnify the acquirer (directly or through a guarantee) for breaches of those representations and warranties, and/or (ii) holding back or placing in escrow a portion of the purchase price for a specified length of time following the closing, against which claims for breaches of the seller's representations and warranties may be offset. Representations and warranties insurance has also become a common source of post-closing recourse for buyers in private asset and share acquisitions in lieu of or in addition to recourse to the seller's parent company or an escrow.

Share Acquisition

[08] In a share acquisition in which the shares of the target are closely held, the acquirer (or, in many cases, a subsidiary of the acquirer) typically seeks to purchase all of the outstanding equity of the target (or in some cases, simply a controlling interest) from the target's shareholders. This is customarily effected by entering into one or a series of share purchase agreements with the target's shareholders. If the acquirer is able to acquire a majority, but not all, of the target's outstanding shares, the acquirer may nevertheless be able to effect a second-step merger between the target and the acquiring subsidiary to eliminate the minority shareholders. Because of appraisal rights and the possibility of litigation by minority shareholders, however, acquirers typically do not rely on a back-end merger to eliminate minority shareholders of a closely held target if alternatives (including a "two-step" merger as described in paragraphs 09 and 89–92 below) are available. Where a controlling stockholder wishes to "squeeze out" the minority shareholders of a corporation, the court will apply either the "entire fairness standard" (requiring the applicable party to prove that the transaction is, or is not, fair and reasonable to the corporation and its stockholders) or "business judgment rule" (as described in paragraph 152 below) in determining whether the controlling stockholder satisfied its fiduciary duties to the corporation and its stockholders.[1] If the transaction is approved by: (i) neither a special committee of the board of directors nor a majority of the disinterested stockholders of the corporation, the "entire fairness" standard applies with the burden of proof on the defendant; (ii) either a special committee of the board of directors or a majority of the disinterested stockholders of the corporation, the "entire fairness" standard applies with the burden of proof on the plaintiff; or (iii) both a special committee of the board of directors and a majority of the disinterested stockholders of the corporation, the "business judgment" rule applies with the burden of proof on the plaintiff.

[09] In a share acquisition in which the shares of the target are widely held, on the other hand, the acquiring company might make a friendly tender offer (*i.e.*, an offer recommended by the target company's board) to purchase any and all shares of the target, with the intention of effecting a second-step merger to eliminate the shareholders who do not tender their shares.

[10] The target's liabilities remain with the target after its shares are transferred. No instruments of transfer are necessary for the transfer of specific assets and, generally, no transfer or sales taxes are imposed, although certain states have unique requirements.

[11] In a share acquisition, an acquirer generally seeks representations, warranties and indemnification from the target's selling shareholders secured by an escrow of a portion of the purchase price (except indemnification is not customary or practical in the case of a target whose shares are publicly traded or widely held). As described in paragraph 07 above, representations and warranties insurance has also become a common source of post-closing recourse for buyers in private asset and share acquisitions in lieu of or in addition to such indemnification and escrow.

Merger or Consolidation

[12] In a merger, two or more corporations combine with one of the constituent corporations surviving. In a consolidation, on the other hand, two or more corporations combine to form a *new* corporation. The surviving corporation (in the case of a merger) or the new corporation (in the case of a consolidation) has all the rights, obligations, assets, and liabilities of the constituent corporations. Upon effectiveness of the merger or consolidation, the legal existence of the non-surviving corporation(s) ceases, and former shareholders of such corporation(s) receive cash, shares of the new or surviving corporation, or some other form of consideration for their shares.

[13] Mergers and consolidations generally require approval of the shareholders and the boards of directors of all constituent corporations, and dissenting shareholders of the constituent corporations often have appraisal rights (that is, the right to file an action to receive the "fair value" of their shares) that are often not available in other acquisition methods. A publicly held acquirer will often affect the merger through a

[1] Kahn v. M&F Worldwide Corp., 88 A.3d 635 (Del. 2014).

wholly owned subsidiary that merges with and into the target company (also known as a "reverse triangular merger") to avoid the need to obtain approval of its shareholders and consents of third parties under the non-surviving company's contracts.

[14] Mergers are often the most tax-efficient acquisition structure for sellers in the United States, as mergers avoid the "double tax" inherent in an asset sale and, in many cases where cash or debt instruments are not the principal merger consideration, may be treated as a tax-free reorganization. In addition, a merger may be the only way of gaining 100% ownership of a public company. Consolidations are less common than mergers in part due to the fact that, similar to asset acquisitions, various approvals and consents by third parties to the transfer of contracts (including with customers, vendors, lenders, landlords and others) may be required in connection with a consolidation.

FORM OF CONSIDERATION

[15] Consideration for the acquired business may be any combination of cash, shares, promissory notes or other debt instruments. An acquisition effected by the exchange of securities of the acquiring corporation for shares of the target might require registration of the acquirer's securities with the U.S. Securities and Exchange Commission (the "SEC") if the target's shares are widely held or if the target's shareholders insist on receiving securities that are freely tradable. As discussed in more detail in paragraphs 201–372, registration of securities entails detailed disclosures about the issuer of the securities and, compared with cash consideration, can result in additional expense and longer periods between deal announcement and closing. Payment in the form of securities may also require approval of the acquirer's shareholders, either under applicable state law or under the listing standards of a stock exchange (or both).

[16] Because the acquirer and the seller may not be able to agree on the value of the target business, the parties may agree to certain post-closing adjustments to the purchase price. For example, if the purchase price is based, in part, on the net asset value of the target, the parties may agree to adjust the purchase price based upon a closing date balance sheet prepared after closing. In addition, in a so-called earn-out provision, adjustments to the purchase price may be based on the target's performance during a designated time period, either before or after the closing date. Furthermore, acquirers in certain transactions offer the target's shareholders "contingent value rights" that require the acquirer to pay an additional amount to the target's shareholders upon the occurrence (or nonoccurrence) of a certain event. If the final purchase price will not be determined until after closing, the acquirer will typically seek to withhold a portion of the purchase price or deposit it into an escrow account at closing with payment or disbursement to be made to the appropriate parties following final adjustments in accordance with agreed procedures.

ACQUISITION VEHICLE

[17] Acquisitions are often undertaken by a newly formed subsidiary of the acquirer rather than the acquirer itself. There are several reasons why many foreign acquirers buy U.S. companies through a newly formed U.S. subsidiary. A newly formed U.S. subsidiary may be more appropriate when more than one U.S. acquisition is contemplated and subsequent acquisitions should not be subsidiaries of earlier acquired U.S. companies. In addition, if intercompany loans are used to finance the U.S. acquisition or ongoing operations, interest on such loans can be paid to a number of countries free of U.S. withholding taxes (if the lender is a tax resident of a country that has a bilateral tax treaty with the U.S. and the lender is entitled to the benefits of such tax treaty). It is important in the case of such intercompany loans, however, that the U.S. company is adequately capitalized and that corporate formalities are observed to minimize the possibility of the loan being re-characterized as capital contributions and repayments as a dividend subject to U.S. withholding taxes (although some bilateral tax treaties reduce the withholding tax on dividends to relatively low rates). In addition, interest payments would also be re-characterized as dividends, resulting in a loss of the interest deduction and a possible increase in the rate of withholding tax (as certain treaties provide a lower withholding rate for interest than dividends).

[18] Many newly formed acquisition companies are organized in Delaware. A Delaware company that does not engage in an operating business is not subject to Delaware corporate income tax, and similarly may also not be subject to state income taxes imposed by other states if it has no operations in any other state. Delaware's corporate statutes are designed to make corporate governance simple and flexible. Delaware courts are familiar with corporate law matters because a large number of U.S. companies are incorporated there. The well-developed body of Delaware corporate case law and a knowledgeable judiciary add a certainty to the Delaware court systems that other states may lack.

TAKEOVER CONTESTS FOR PUBLIC COMPANIES

[19] If an acquirer fails to open—or complete—negotiations with the board of directors of a publicly traded target regarding a takeover, several means are available to increase pressure on the target's board of directors to consider a bona fide acquisition proposal, including "bear hugs," proxy fights and hostile tender offers. While such actions will likely strain relations between an acquirer and the target's board of directors, the fiduciary duties of the target's board of directors generally preclude it from ignoring entirely a proposal that can increase value for its shareholders.

[20] Although hostile takeovers of U.S. publicly traded companies are complicated, a well-prepared and dedicated acquirer willing to pay a premium stands a good chance of success. To succeed, an acquirer must deal with the target's takeover defenses. The tender offer rules, target defenses, and takeover strategies are discussed in more detail in paragraphs 84–200 below.

USING SECURITIES TO PAY FOR ACQUISITION

[21] A foreign acquirer can acquire U.S. businesses using its own securities in several ways. For example, it can offer its shares in exchange for the shares held by a target's shareholders, whether directly in an exchange offer or as the consideration payable following a merger of the target with the foreign acquirer's acquisition subsidiary. Alternatively, foreign issuers can raise cash through U.S. securities offerings that can then be used to acquire either privately held companies or public companies.

Securities Act and Securities Exchange Act Registration

[22] The two primary sources of U.S. securities law are the Securities Act of 1933, as amended (the "Securities Act"), and the Securities Exchange Act of 1934, as amended (the "Exchange Act"), together with the regulations issued under each by the SEC. All offers or sales of securities in the United States must either be registered under the Securities Act or qualify for one of the available exemptions.

[23] Once an issuer has registered securities for public sale in the United States, the issuer becomes subject to the ongoing public reporting requirements under the Exchange Act. This reporting obligation continues indefinitely so long as the issuer's securities are held of record by 300 or more persons or come to be listed on one or more U.S. stock exchanges, such as the New York Stock Exchange (the "NYSE") or quoted on The Nasdaq Stock Market ("NASDAQ"). A reporting issuer also becomes subject to other rules requiring continuing compliance, including the Sarbanes-Oxley Act of 2002 and various other standards relating to accounting controls and audit requirements. The NYSE and NASDAQ also impose on listed companies rules that address a broad range of matters relating to, among other things, the issuance of securities, the disclosure of corporate developments, corporate governance, and the rights of shareholders.

ACQUISITION FINANCING

[24] The U.S. market for senior and subordinated acquisition financing remains robust, providing an acquirer the possibility to generate tax deductions at the target level and increase its overall return on capital deployed in the acquisition. There has been a shift in the identity of the lenders since early 2013 when, in the wake of the debt crisis in 2008, U.S. regulators published an updated Interagency Guidance on Leveraged Lending (the "Guidance") and signaled an unfavorable view of the involvement of regulated financial institutions in leveraged lending activities. As a result, many regulated banks have since curtailed their leveraged lending and non-bank "direct" lenders have become more active in the leveraged lending market. While the Guidance did not specifically define what constitutes leveraged lending, both the Guidance and subsequent commentary have identified certain factors for regulated financial institutions to consider in establishing their own policies and underwriting criteria for loans, including whether a borrower's total gross debt divided by EBITDA exceeds 4.0x or senior gross debt divided by EBITDA exceeds 3.0x.

[25] For an acquirer with sufficient resources, financing an all-cash tender offer on the basis of its own assets and cash flows can be simple and rapid. In contrast, financing a U.S. acquisition on the basis (in whole or part) of the assets and cash flows of a target is significantly more complex, time-consuming, and expensive because lenders face several distinct legal and structural issues when providing such financing. If an acquirer requires target-based acquisition financing, proof of such financing's availability or limited conditionality is a critical badge of the acquirer's credibility to be analyzed by the target's advisors and shown to a target's board and stockholders. In the U.S., such availability is reflected in a very specific—and limited—set of "certain funds" conditions, which focus on the requirement that (i) a finite subset of representations and warranties relating to the target must be true, (ii) there not having occurred a material adverse effect in respect of the target, and (iii) the delivery of certain limited types of collateral (usually only collateral that can be perfected by filing financing statements and, if received from the target, certain stock collateral). With one exception, U.S. style conditionality does not significantly differ from the European-style "certain funds" conditions given that the availability of funding in limited condition U.S.-style financings are closely tied to the conditions precedent in the underlying acquisition / merger agreement which give the acquirer the right to terminate its obligations to acquire, or to decline to acquire, the target. U.S. style conditionality differs from European-style "certain funds" in that lenders and borrowers agree to a commitment letter and detailed term sheet, but not full documentation. The detailed term sheet will contain the material terms of the new debt (type and amount of facilities, fees and interest rates, maturity, amortization, optional and mandatory prepayment terms, guarantors, collateral, and the definitive list of representations and warranties, covenants (affirmative, negative and financial) and events of default and parameters of voting mechanics, amendments and assignment/participations) and documentation principles with respect to the drafting of the definitive documentation, which usually includes a specific identified precedent as a starting point for the loan documentation. Such structures make it unlikely that an acquirer would be required to close the acquisition but have no funding to do so.

Central Structural Issue

[26] The paramount concern for both senior and subordinated lenders providing target-based acquisition financing is the certainty of obtaining prompt and direct access to the assets and cash flows of the target's business. In the case of private company acquisitions, access to a target's assets and cash flows can be provided immediately if all or most of the target's businesses are held in the company being acquired. The same is generally true for acquisitions of public companies structured as a typical one-step merger transaction. Two-step public company acquisitions, however, are always more difficult for lenders to finance, for both business and legal reasons. First, in a two-step transaction, there is an inherent delay between the first-step tender offer acquisition of less than all of the target's shares and the second-step merger squeezing out the target's remaining minority stockholders.

In addition, if a target's shares continue to be traded on a national stock exchange (which will typically be the case until the squeeze-out merger occurs), lenders will need to satisfy special margin stock lending rules (*see* below) and the target will need to satisfy its ongoing reporting and other obligations under the Exchange Act. These concerns have been substantially eliminated with respect to Delaware target companies following the adoption of Section 251(h) of the Delaware General Corporate Law ("DGCL"). The structural alternatives for, and the special rules applicable to, acquisitions of public companies are discussed in more detail in paragraphs 84–200 below.

[27] As a result, lenders providing target-based acquisition financing for public companies in a two-step transaction may prefer not to make available any funds until all of the impediments to the squeeze-out merger have been eliminated. However, because too much conditionality will undermine the competitiveness of an acquirer's bid (and without a successful bid there is no need to provide financing), lenders and acquirers in practice tend to work out compromises on the key issues. Negotiations between lenders and acquirers tend to focus on the following issues.

Fraudulent Conveyances

[28] If lenders require credit support from post-acquisition subsidiaries of a borrower, fraudulent conveyance issues arise. A fraudulent conveyance may be found to exist under state or, in the event of a bankruptcy, federal law if the incurrence of an obligation or the transfer of an interest in property (a) is either made with actual fraudulent intent with respect to other creditors (b) or constitutes constructive fraud on other creditors. Individual state laws are typically modeled after either the Uniform Fraudulent Conveyance Act or the Uniform Fraudulent Transfer Act; for purposes hereof, there is not a significant substantive difference except to note that each state's laws may differ in respect of the details. In acquisition financing, the debate focuses on the constructive fraud test which requires that two components be satisfied: (i) the entity incurring the obligation or transferring the interest must not have received "fair" or "reasonably equivalent" value therefor, and (ii) the entity was either insolvent or had unreasonably small capital at the time of such incurrence or transfer, or it became insolvent or was left with unreasonably small capital as a result thereof, or the entity intended to incur, or believed that it would incur, debts beyond its ability to pay when due. Under state law, both the terms "transfer" and "conveyance" include the granting of liens or the incurrence of debt and the payment of money.

[29] Whenever the proceeds of an acquisition financing end up entirely in the hands of selling stockholders, the prevailing view is that the first prong of the constructive fraud test has been satisfied (because the value of the financing was paid over to the selling shareholders and not the company itself). Thus, lenders concentrate their efforts on establishing that the second prong of the test has not been satisfied—that is, that a subsidiary's guarantees and security in support of acquisition financing did not render it insolvent or leave it with unreasonably small capital. Notwithstanding the foregoing, lenders do not often require independent cash flow analyses from third-party appraisers or from the acquirer's accountants or investment bankers in order to provide objective evidence of solvency at the time of closing, and will instead in many instances perform their own due diligence and rely on their own analyses. In certain cases lenders may request receipt of any internal solvency analyses and reports that are performed by the corporation for of its own benefit, however, lenders will typically require the target to certify to its own solvency (on a pro forma basis after giving effect to the funding of the loans and the acquisition) as a condition of funding.

Target Stockholder Approvals

[30] Lenders will ask an acquirer to condition its offer on the tender of a sufficient number of target shares which, if purchased, permits the acquiring subsidiary to complete the second-step merger as a "short-form merger" or a merger that satisfies DGCL Section 251(h) (for Delaware target companies), but will often settle for the acquirer purchasing at least the number of target shares necessary to guarantee approval of the second-step merger after a stockholders' meeting. In the latter circumstance, interest on the tender offer debt can be either rolled up into principal or become payable after the 60–90 days necessary to call a target stockholder meeting and obtain the required approval.

Margin Stock Lending Rules

[31] The U.S. Federal Reserve Board (the "Board") has issued a series of regulations preventing "the excessive use of credit" for the purchase of certain publicly traded securities. For example, pursuant to Regulation U of the Board, a "lender" is not permitted to extend a "purpose credit" secured directly or "indirectly," in whole or in part, by any "margin stock" (*i.e.*, stock listed on a national securities exchange) in an amount exceeding the maximum "loan value" of all of the collateral. Regulation U does not apply to credit extended to certain "exempted borrowers," including registered brokers and dealers and members of national securities exchanges.

[32] One-step acquisitions of public companies, and two-step acquisitions effectuated pursuant to a "short-form merger" or DGCL Section 251(h), are generally not directly or indirectly secured by margin stock, and therefore do not need to comply with the margin rules. However, the first step of a two-step transaction may be subject to the margin rules if the lender either requires the loans to be secured by the target stock purchased in the tender offer or restricts the borrower's right to sell, pledge or otherwise dispose of such stock. In the case of loans incurred to fund a tender offer, Regulation U in effect requires that the principal amount of such loans not exceed 50% of the total purchase price of the tendered stock unless (i) Regulation U can be made inapplicable to the credit using one of the methods described below, or (ii) other collateral is concurrently provided to make up for the shortfall in the loan value of the acquired stock. One common method of avoiding the indirect applicability of Regulation U is to "strip" the credit by eliminating restrictions (typically contained in the negative covenants) on borrower's ability to sell or encumber the acquired margin stock. "Stripping" is not available, however, for borrowers that are shell corporations unless certain conditions are met. In limited circumstances, the applicability of Regulation U may be avoided by making loans offshore; however, the rules permitting such exceptions are very complex and should be discussed with counsel.

Subordinated Debt

[33] Payment subordinated debt can play an important role in financings, in part given the manner in which it is treated by different investors in the capital structure. To the senior lender (to whom the subordinated debt is subordinated), payment subordinated debt may be viewed as a substitute for equity, requiring that payments to subordinated lenders be blocked under certain negotiated circumstances, including if the borrower is in default with respect to some or all of its obligations under the senior loan documents, and obligating the subordinated lenders to turn over to the senior lenders any amounts the former may have received following acceleration of the senior debt or the borrower's bankruptcy. Note that payment subordination should be distinguished from lien subordination, whereby junior creditors agree to subordinate their priority and other rights in certain collateral to the priority and rights of senior creditors. References to subordinated debt in this section refer only to payment-subordinated debt.

[34] To the borrower, subordinated debt is debt, although its higher coupon rate will compensate subordinated lenders for taking risks that senior lenders do not. Subordinated debt will, by virtue of having interest payments that may be tax deductible (*see* below), be less expensive for the borrower than equity. Subordinated debt is not equity, and thus should have no right to control management decisions through electing directors or to benefit from appreciation in the value of the business; however, the subordinated lenders often negotiate for and receive board observation rights.

[35] To the subordinated lenders, the nature of subordinated debt will depend significantly on the circumstances in which they acquire it. Underwriters attempting to place public or broadly offered subordinated debt will press for whatever provisions they believe are necessary under the current market conditions to place the subordinated debt. Selling stockholders who take subordinated debt to obtain a slightly higher selling price and do not invest new money (and whose rights to payment may be subject to offset for warranty breaches in the sale agreement) may accept minimal protections and rights in exchange for shorter repayment periods. Subordinated bridge lenders, on the other hand, will demand significant rights of acceleration and covenant protection during the short maturity of the bridge financing and are probably only willing to accept payment subordination in the event of the borrower's bankruptcy or a payment default on the senior debt.

[36] The key area of negotiation between senior and subordinated lenders involves the circumstances giving subordinated lenders the right to demand and retain repayments of their subordinated loans.

GENERAL TAX CONSIDERATIONS

[37] At a high level, an acquisition generally can be structured either as a stock acquisition or as an asset acquisition. The tax consequences of each can vary considerably to both the buyer and the seller and can play a large part in the negotiation of any deal.

Asset Acquisition

[38] An asset acquisition offers two main potential advantages over a stock acquisition for a foreign investor: (i) a step-up in basis of the acquired assets to their fair market value up to the purchase price (assuming that the acquisition does not qualify as a "reorganization" for income tax purposes), which will generally result in increased future tax deductions, and (ii) additional post-acquisition flexibility for organizational tax planning. However, these tax advantages may come at the cost of the seller. Depending on the seller, the seller's tax considerations may mandate a stock acquisition.

[39] The main disadvantage of an asset acquisition from a seller's perspective is that if the seller is a "Subchapter C" corporation and the acquisition does not qualify as a "reorganization," it can be exposed to two levels of tax on the transaction: first, at the corporate level, as the assets are sold and, second, at the shareholder level, as the sale proceeds are distributed to the shareholders. The overall transaction, therefore, can be subject to a higher overall tax burden for the seller than if it had been structured as a stock acquisition.

Stock Acquisition

[40] In a stock acquisition, U.S. persons[2] pay only one level of tax on the gain on sale. Generally, non-U.S. persons do not pay any U.S. federal income tax relating to the sale of stock. In the case of an individual, its capital gain is currently taxed at a top preferential rate of 20% (plus 3.8% for certain individuals) for capital assets held for more than one year as opposed to a maximum federal rate of 39.6% on ordinary income. Conversely, the buyer will generally not be able to fully depreciate the target's underlying assets to the extent of the purchase price (and thereby reduce its taxable income on a going-forward basis) since the buyer's historic tax basis in the assets will carry over in the acquisition. Other elements of the target's tax history would also carry over unaffected by the acquisition. The purchaser would have exposure

[2] **For individuals**, the term "U.S. person" means any U.S. citizen or U.S. resident (in each case, as set forth in the Code and the underlying Treasury Regulations).
For persons other than individuals, "U.S. person" means, in each of the following cases, as set forth in the Code and Treasury Regulations: (a) any domestic partnership or domestic corporation; (b) any estate other than a foreign estate; or (c) any trust with respect to which: (i) a court within the United States is able to exercise primary supervision over the trust's administration; and (ii) one or more U.S. persons have authority to control all substantial decisions of trust.

with respect to any tax deficiencies of the target for pre-closing years. This exposure, however, can be mitigated through the negotiation of representations and warranties and indemnification for the breach of such representations and warranties and for pre-closing taxes.

Section 338 Election

[41] In certain circumstances, an acquirer may be able to obtain some of the benefits of an asset acquisition even though shares of the target have been purchased by making one of two elections under Section 338 of the Internal Revenue Code of 1986, as amended (the "Code"). These elections permit a purchaser of stock to treat the transactions as an asset purchase even if they are documented as a stock purchase. Any gain inherent in the target's assets (including goodwill and going-concern value) is recognized, and the tax basis in such assets is stepped-up to their fair market value to the extent of the purchase price. However, the tax on the gain is imposed on either the seller or the buyer, depending on which Section 338 election is made. Thus, a Section 338 election is only desirable in limited circumstances. For example, the election can be desirable (a) when the target is a member of a consolidated group, (b) when the target has net operating loss or credit carry-forwards that are not expected to be able to be fully utilized, (c) when the selling shareholder's basis in its shares is not substantially higher than the target's basis in its underlying assets, or (d) when the entity is foreign, is not considered to be a "controlled foreign corporation" or engaged in a U.S. trade or business for U.S. federal income tax purposes.

Post-transaction Taxation

[42] The foreign acquirer should also consider what measure of its income is subject to tax in the United States and in which manner after the acquisition of the target. Its taxation will depend on various factors, including, but not limited to, the entity that is chosen to make the acquisition, which investments are held by, or through, the U.S. target and the residence of the acquirer. For example, a foreign acquirer's ownership of foreign operations through a U.S. subsidiary (which would result if a U.S. target has operations outside the United States) will generally increase the effective tax rate on the non-U.S. operations because of the extra layers of tax on the repatriation of profits. Therefore, the tax considerations in any acquisition, especially in the international context, may require more complicated structuring than simply determining whether to acquire assets or shares.

[43] The general tax considerations summarized above are discussed in more detail in paragraphs 373–420 below.

ANTITRUST AND OTHER REGULATORY APPROVALS

[44] Each foreign acquirer may need to make the antitrust and foreign investment filings described below. Additional filings, hearings and/or clearances may be required if the target's business is subject to additional regulatory supervision (such as banking, broadcasting, energy, transportation and defense).

Antitrust Clearance

[45] For transactions exceeding certain thresholds, the Hart-Scott Rodino Antitrust Improvements Act of 1976 (the "HSR Act") requires parties to notify U.S. antitrust authorities and observe a waiting period prior to closing the transaction. The HSR Act applies when two tests are satisfied. First, under the "size of transaction" test, the transaction must result in the acquirer holding nonexempt voting securities, noncorporate interests, or assets of the target with a value greater than US$80.8m. Second, for transactions with value greater than US$80.8m and not more than US$323m, a "size of persons" test also applies—one person involved in the transaction must have annual net sales or total assets of at least US$161.5m, and another person must have annual net sales or total assets of at least US$16.2m. The measurement of transaction value, annual net sales, and total assets and the identification of the entity to be measured are subject to complex regulations. The HSR Act and related regulations provide for numerous exemptions, including specific exemptions that may be available when a transaction involves a foreign company lacking sufficient nexus to U.S. commerce. The HSR Act imposes a waiting period of 30 days after notification by the acquirer and the target before the acquisition may be completed; in a cash tender offer context, the waiting period is 15 days after notification by the acquirer. The waiting period is automatically extended if antitrust authorities issue a formal request for additional information; when they do so, the transaction may not be completed until 30 days from completion of submission of additional requested information (10 days in the context of a cash tender offer). As a practical matter, the HSR Act will not impede acquisition of a U.S. company by a foreign acquirer where the acquirer does not have other significant business in the United States. In that situation, antitrust authorities often grant early termination of the statutory waiting periods if requested by the parties (although the granting of such early termination is made publicly available by the antitrust authorities).

[46] The general considerations summarized above are discussed in more detail in paragraphs 421–462 below.

Regulatory and National Security Issues

[47] Regulatory obstacles may exist with respect to acquisitions in certain industries, such as defense, manufacturing, banking, insurance, telecommunications, high-tech, utilities, broadcasting, energy, transportation and shipping. In addition, the Foreign Investment and National Security Act of 2007 (FINSA) empowers the President of the

United States to block (or unwind) any transaction that results in foreign control over a U.S. business and may threaten to impair U.S. national security. The inter-agency Committee on Foreign Investment in the United States (CFIUS) conducts reviews and investigations under FINSA, and makes recommendations to the President. While the statute has only occasionally been used to block transactions, parties have also terminated transactions when it is clear that CFIUS has serious concerns. Reviews and investigations under FINSA can take several months. Notifications to CFIUS are voluntary. However, if the parties do not notify a transaction to CFIUS, CFIUS has the authority to initiate transactions without a formal notice and may do so even after a transaction has closed. CFIUS is particularly, but not exclusively, focused on transactions involving critical infrastructure; foreign government-controlled investors; and U.S. businesses that are government contractors, possess security clearances, have access to export-controlled or other sensitive technology or products, or have access to personal information. Other national security regulations and other reporting requirements might also apply, including in situations where the U.S. business has access to export-controlled products, services, or technology, or when the U.S. business or its personnel possess security clearances.

INTELLECTUAL PROPERTY

[48] Intellectual property (or "IP") drives many mergers, acquisitions and other strategic transactions, making IP diligence and the allocation of IP risks critical to these matters. To safeguard each side's deal value, both parties must understand the strengths and limitations of the target's intellectual property and the role that IP plays in the target's business. The buyer (or both parties in collaboration or other partnering agreement) must also consider how any limitations on the use of that intellectual property may impact their post-closing business strategies.

[49] IP diligence done right is customized to the needs of the party conducting it. Diligence varies depending on the type or structure of a transaction (*e.g.*, acquisition of an entire company vs. a carve-out, asset purchase vs. a merger, or collaboration), the materiality of intellectual property to the transaction, the transaction size and the industry or geographic scope of the business, as well as deal dynamics. A buyer in a bidding war often chooses to review less, while a buyer of a troubled company or its assets may undertake a more thorough analysis.

IP diligence begins by asking questions like:

(i) What intellectual property does the target own or license from others? For intellectual property licensed to the target, are there any restrictions that adversely affect the target now or in the future?

(ii) What is the status of registered intellectual property before the relevant governmental offices?

(iii) Has the target taken appropriate steps to protect its intellectual property?

(iv) Are there existing or potential barriers to the transfer of intellectual property?

(v) What interests do others have, by license, ownership or otherwise, in any of the target's intellectual property?

(vi) Is the target involved in any pending or threatened intellectual property disputes?
(vii) If the target is in a regulated industry, are there any issues affecting its intellectual property that are unique to that industry (*e.g.*, the Hatch-Waxman Act in the pharmaceutical industry)?

[50] Other inquiries, as appropriate, might address the target's software (including open source software usage), IT systems and data rights. The information gathered in response to these questions must be put into context to assess it properly. Diligence should reveal which individual items of intellectual property are important, and how they will be used post-closing.

[51] The definitive agreements of the transaction should address any intellectual property issues discovered during diligence. Parties most commonly allocate intellectual property risks through representations and warranties. The respective leverage of the parties prompts what these representations and warranties say, but they often address key intellectual property, ownership, license and other third-party rights, validity and noninfringement. A party can also address intellectual property issues through closing conditions, special termination rights, extended survival of some or all of the representations and warranties, special damages limits and special indemnities.

ENVIRONMENTAL

[52] Environmental issues have a significant impact on many U.S. business acquisitions, particularly if the seller is a manufacturer or if it owns real property. Operating businesses such as manufacturers are subject to a wide range of federal, state and local environmental permitting, operating and reporting requirements which can create significant liabilities. Both federal and state laws impose liability on corporate successors (including those that purchase all or substantially all of the assets, as opposed to the stock, of the seller); impose liability strictly, so that compliance with law is not a defense; and impose liability on the basis of status, as well as conduct, so that mere passive ownership of previously contaminated land may give rise to cleanup obligations. The primary U.S. cleanup statute of concern is the Comprehensive Environmental Response, Compensation, and Liability Act ("CERCLA"), with comparable legislation in nearly every state.

[53] CERCLA, and many state equivalents, includes some defenses against liability for historic releases that current owners or operators did not cause or for which they are otherwise not responsible. The initial step toward seeking to gain the protection of those defenses includes conducting an "all appropriate inquiry" ("AAI") before the acquisition or leasing of property. To satisfy the AAI requirement, a prospective purchaser or lessee must obtain a Phase I environmental site assessment report ("ESA") meeting the standards set forth by ASTM International ("ASTM") in the *Standard Practice for Environmental Site Assessments: Phase I Environmental Site Assessment Process,* E1527-05 ("Phase I standard"). Although the performance of diligence meeting the Phase I standard is designated to assist a potential purchaser or lessee qualify for a defense of CERCLA liability, stock purchasers often perform diligence meeting the

Phase I standard because of the useful information such diligence can provide. The Phase I standard requires, among other things, investigations into the current and past uses of property, inquiry into government environmental records concerning potential contamination and environmental liens, and visual inspections of the subject property and adjoining sites. The AAI investigation must be performed by an environmental consultant who meets certain education or experience requirements. While the Phase I standard does not require sampling, the results of an ESA may indicate that sampling should be considered as part of diligence.

[54] Although the Phase I standard sets out diligence requirements, these requirements are fairly generic and focus on identifying contamination. Environmental risks vary depending on the type of business operations and the type of transaction. Therefore, the scope of environmental diligence should be tailored to the specifics of the transaction. For example, where development is planned, diligence should include a review of development-related environmental risks such as wetlands, threatened and endangered species, and cultural resources. For environmentally sensitive businesses subject to regulatory requirements governing air emissions, water discharges, waste handling and/or chemical usage, it may be prudent to conduct an environmental compliance review ("ECR") of the prospective business to assess potential liabilities regarding permitting, operations and reporting. Violations of environmental regulatory requirements can result in penalties and, in some cases the need to modify or cease certain operations or incur capital expenditures for pollution control devices. Performance of an ECR often requires the technical expertise of an environmental professional knowledgeable about the compliance issues associated with a particular business.

[55] While environmental risks are most prevalent in transactions involving manufacturing or other environmentally sensitive operations involving the transfer of real property, they should not be overlooked in other transactions or leasehold situations. The strict liability schemes of various remediation statutes impose liability upon current owners *and* operators of a facility for contamination, regardless of whether the source was historic activity unrelated to current operations.

[56] Once environmental risks are appropriately identified during diligence, numerous options exist for addressing them. Those options include purchase price reductions, indemnifications, escrows, covenants requiring post-closing remediation, environmental insurance, and entry of contaminated sites into Voluntary Cleanup or Brownfields Programs. Such Programs are designed to facilitate the redevelopment, sale, and reuse of commercial and industrial properties by providing a process for property owners, operators and potential purchasers to voluntarily address potentially contaminated property through investigation, and if necessary, remediation.

[57] The acquisition market in the United States is sufficiently sensitive to environmental issues that an environmentally troubled company may sell at a disproportionate discount to value or, in extreme circumstances, not be marketable at all. The best way to manage environmental risks in an acquisition is through careful and thorough investigation and constant attention during structuring and negotiations.

EMPLOYEE BENEFIT PLANS

[58] A target's employee benefit plans can be a source of major liabilities for a buyer and, depending on the magnitude of the liabilities, employee benefit considerations may significantly impact the structure or the purchase price of an acquisition. In addition, the future of and other matters regarding the benefit plans are very visible and sensitive because employees will keenly focus on the form and future of their benefits after the acquisition. Likewise, subject to the terms of the target's equity compensation programs, the treatment of equity awards held by target service providers in connection with the transaction must be determined. Some arrangements provide for automatic acceleration, while others permit a buyer to assume or replace target awards on the original vesting schedules. The latter approach may afford the buyer some built-in retention value from the target's equity compensation awards. Therefore, significant consideration must be given to such arrangements in the context of an acquisition and a buyer must understand the target's liability and alternatives with respect to various employee benefit arrangements.

Types of Plans

[59] U.S. benefit programs are generally divided into three major categories—retirement plans (*e.g.*, defined benefit, profit sharing, 401(k) plans and both qualified and nonqualified arrangements), welfare plans (*e.g.*, health, life and disability insurance and severance arrangements) and executive compensation arrangements (*e.g.*, employment agreements and equity compensation programs). In an acquisition, tax-qualified retirement plans (*i.e.*, plans that qualify under Section 401(a) of the Code) typically receive a significant amount of attention as they are associated with very large liabilities. Executive compensation arrangements are also scrutinized due to their high profile. Given the current state of health care reform in the U.S., welfare benefits are becoming more of a priority for review in the context of transactions. Accordingly, it is important to consider that all arrangement types may present significant liabilities and/or planning opportunities. The extent to which employee benefit liabilities transfer to a buyer in an acquisition will largely depend on the transaction form (asset purchase, share purchase or merger) and whether the buyer assumes seller's plans.

Asset Purchase

[60] In general, in an asset purchase, the buyer only becomes liable for the target's employee benefit obligations that the buyer specifically assumes in connection with the transaction. However, a buyer may be liable for certain obligations of the target or the target's affiliates if a principal purpose of the transaction is to evade liability with respect to defined benefit pension or multiemployer plans. The buyer may also have liability for continuing health coverage (*i.e.*, "COBRA coverage") for target employees even though such liability is not expressly assumed.

[61] Typically, a buyer would try to negotiate a downward purchase price adjustment if the buyer is expected to assume the target's benefit liabilities in connection with unfunded plans. In certain cases, the target or seller may argue that the plans represent assets of the target (*e.g.*, an over-funded defined benefit plan) and, therefore, an upward price adjustment is appropriate.

Share Purchase

[62] In a share purchase, all of the target's employee benefit obligations remain with the acquired company. Generally, employee benefit plans continue after the transaction unless they are specifically terminated or other affirmative actions are taken with respect to the arrangements. Special considerations apply if the target is a subsidiary of a parent and where the target's employees participate in the parent's employee benefit plans (or another parent-subsidiary).

[63] Under the Code and the Employee Retirement Income Security Act of 1974, as amended ("ERISA"), an employer and all of its affiliates are jointly and severally liable for certain employee benefit liabilities, particularly liabilities with respect to qualified defined benefit plans. Accordingly, in a share purchase transaction, it is important to take into account liabilities and benefit plans maintained by both the target and the target's affiliates.

Merger

[64] From an employee benefits perspective, a merger is substantially the same as a share purchase in that the surviving company becomes liable for all of the target's benefit obligations and the target's benefit arrangements continue by the surviving company unless they are specifically terminated or merged with other plans of the surviving company.

CONTRACTS WITH MANAGEMENT AND EMPLOYEES

Union Contracts

[65] In an asset acquisition, if a majority of the bargaining unit employees of the company formed to acquire the assets of the target were employed by the seller, the new company is obligated to recognize and bargain with the union, but the seller's labor contract does not stay in effect unless the acquirer has assumed the agreement. Some union contracts contain a clause requiring an acquirer of the assets of the business to assume the union agreement, or for the seller to provide notice of the intended transaction to the union within a certain timeframe before the sale. If a majority of the new company's employees were not employed by the seller, the new company does not have any bargaining obligations based on the transaction.

[66] In a share acquisition, all labor contracts continue in effect, and the acquired business continues to be the employer under such labor contracts.

Employment Agreements

[67] In an asset acquisition, the status of employment agreements generally depends upon the agreement of the parties to the acquisition and upon whether the acquirer continues to use the services of the employees. In a share acquisition, employment agreements continue to be binding upon the acquired company unless the agreements specifically provide for termination upon a change in control of the corporation, which they seldom do. Executive service agreements, however, sometimes give the executive the right to terminate his or her employment upon a change of control and, in this context, often provide the executive with large severance payments.

[68] If the acquirer desires to keep existing management in place after the acquisition, it may want employment agreements with key employees as part of the acquisition. More often, it is the employees of the acquired business who insist on new employment agreements. The important provisions of an employment agreement are those governing compensation (including benefits and perquisites), the term of the agreement, the termination notice period, and the noncompetition covenants. Noncompetition agreements are especially important in service businesses, where customers of the business may be more loyal to individuals than to the company that employs them. Due to U.S. tax rules relating to nonqualified deferred compensation (Section 409A of the Code), care needs to be taken in negotiating new agreements with employees in the context of a transaction to ensure that adverse tax consequences do not result from inadvertent changes in terms of payment under re-negotiated agreements.

[69] Enforceability of noncompetition agreements is problematic and disfavored in certain U.S. states, such as in California. However, most state laws (including California) recognize a purchaser's right to protect its investment by restricting the competitive activities of the principals whose business is acquired. In particular, states are generally willing to recognize an employer's right to protect trade secrets and confidential business information. If the executive sells shares in connection with the transaction there is usually more flexibility in terms of the noncompetition provisions.

DOCUMENTING THE DEAL

[70] Corporate acquisitions of any size, even straightforward ones, involve considerable legal documentation and negotiation. The major tasks for the acquirer, its lawyers and its accountants are: (i) reaching agreement with a financial adviser, if one is to be used; (ii) negotiating a confidentiality agreement and the basic terms of the acquisition (and sometimes formalizing them in a letter of intent); (iii) conducting a due diligence investigation of the target; (iv) negotiating and drafting the definitive purchase agreement and, in the U.S., commitment papers in the event of

an acquisition financing; and (v) negotiating and drafting supporting documents, including the financing documents, most significantly, the credit agreement and the applicable collateral documents.

Agreement with Financial Adviser

[71] In reaching agreement with a financial advisor, the issues most commonly subject to negotiation are compensation and indemnification. Typically, the investment banker receives a success fee if the transaction is completed (and sometimes a periodic advisory fee and an opinion fee). The investment banker also typically receives broad indemnification except for liabilities caused by the investment banker's fraud, willful misconduct or gross negligence.

[72] The engagement of an investment bank is a particularly good idea if the acquirer is entering the U.S. market for the first time, the available targets are not known, the acquirer needs advice on price, or the target itself is represented by an investment bank.

Confidentiality Agreement and Letter of Intent

[73] Once a target company has been identified and approached, the parties generally enter into a confidentiality agreement with respect to the information to be shared by the parties. These confidentiality agreements often contain non-solicitation agreements with respect to employees of the target company and, with respect to public company targets, a "standstill" prohibiting the potential acquirer from acquiring shares of the target on the open market. After the execution of a confidentiality agreement, the parties generally negotiate the essential terms of the transaction and often negotiate and execute a letter of intent. The letter of intent is usually not binding as to the ultimate consummation of the acquisition. The letter of intent, or a separate exclusivity agreement, can contain a binding exclusivity provision restricting the seller from soliciting or negotiating a similar deal with another acquirer for an agreed period of time.

Due Diligence

[74] Once a letter of intent and/or confidentiality agreement is signed, the acquirer often conducts a legal and financial investigation (known as "due diligence") of the target's business.

[75] In connection with due diligence, the acquirer generally creates a due diligence request list asking the seller to provide it with information about the target's business (including detailed information about its operations, real property, personal property (including intellectual property), environmental matters, employee benefit plans, financial condition, litigation and tax filings) and to provide it with copies of the relevant material documents (including corporate and organizational records, insurance policies, supply contracts, employment and labor contracts, employee benefit plans, leases, debt agreements, licenses, tax returns and informational filings). The acquirer, its lawyers and its accountants review these documents and information, as well as any other information they can obtain about the company or business, to determine if there are any legal, financial or other problems with the company or business and to learn as much about the target company as possible. In certain environmentally sensitive industries, specialist environmental consultants may be retained to conduct at least a Phase I audit (review of environmental records) and, in certain situations, a Phase II audit (soil and groundwater testing).

[76] Due diligence need not precede the execution of a definitive purchase agreement. Rather, the satisfactory completion of due diligence could be a condition to the acquirer's obligations under the purchase agreement. The seller often resists such a condition since it provides the acquirer with a one-sided, subjective option to terminate the deal or renegotiate the price. The seller might instead offer the acquirer an opportunity to conduct its investigation before the agreement is signed or within a specified period of time thereafter.

Purchase Agreement

[77] The purchase agreement sets forth the basic terms of the transaction (*i.e.*, what is to be sold and the price to be paid). Particularly in an asset sale, it should specifically and carefully describe the assets to be transferred and the liabilities to be assumed and should also set forth how the purchase price will be allocated among the assets. In the U.S., if the acquirer is purchasing the target (or its assets) with third-party financing, the seller will require executed commitment papers, which include a commitment letter provided by a lender (or a group of lenders) pursuant to which such lenders have committed to provide the necessary financing, subject only to certain customary limited conditions described above (*see* paragraph 27). Such limited conditionality will in large part track the conditions to closing provided to the purchaser in the purchase agreement. A complete set of commitment papers also includes a fee letter, which includes the fees each lead arranger and the lenders will receive and permit the lead arrangers to make changes to certain of the business terms reflected in the commitment letter in the event of a difficult syndication of the facility. Given the interconnected nature of the purchase agreement and the commitment papers, committed lenders in the U.S. now require that "Xerox" protections be included in the purchase agreement pursuant to which the committed lenders receive certain protections from the seller, particularly in the event the deal does not close due to unavailability of the financing.

Representations and Warranties

[78] Typically, the seller makes extensive representations and warranties to the acquirer regarding the target company, including with respect to:

(i) the due incorporation and valid existence of the target company,
(ii) the seller's authority to enter into the transaction,
(iii) the capitalization of the target company,

(iv) the accuracy and completeness of the financial statements and other documents given to the acquirer by the seller,
(v) undisclosed liabilities of the target company,
(vi) the target company's valid title to its assets,
(vii) its taxes,
(viii) the absence of litigation and governmental investigations of the target company,
(ix) environmental matters,
(x) the target company's compliance with ERISA and related employee benefit and labor matters,
(xi) necessity for consents to the transaction,
(xii) the absence of defaults under material agreements involving the target company, and
(xiii) intellectual property matters.

[79] Other representations and warranties may be required, depending on the nature of the target's business and other facts unique to the transaction. The parent company or principal shareholders of the target company also may be asked to make or stand behind at least some of these representations and warranties. If the acquirer is paying for the acquired business with its own shares, it may make representations and warranties as to its financial condition comparable to those of the seller; otherwise, its representations and warranties are minimal.

Covenants

[80] The purchase agreement sets forth various covenants between the seller and the acquirer. The seller generally agrees to conduct the target company's operations in the usual course and to maintain the assets of the company and not to take any action that would have a material adverse effect on the business or engage in material transactions without the acquirer's approval during the period between signing and closing, if there is such a period (*i.e.*, the transaction could be a "sign and close" transaction, in which there is no time between the signing of the purchase agreement and the closing of the transaction).

Conditions

[81] The purchase agreement sets forth conditions to the obligations of the parties to complete the transaction. Acquirers customarily make their obligation to proceed with the acquisition contingent on receipt of applicable regulatory, governmental and (for public or widely held companies) shareholder approvals, the truth and accuracy of the seller's representations and warranties (subject to negotiated materiality thresholds), the performance of the seller's covenants in all material respects, and the absence of material adverse changes in the seller's financial condition. Moreover, the conditionality included in an executed set of commitment papers will tie to, and in large part mirror, certain of the conditions included in the purchase agreement such that, with certain exceptions, a committed lender will be required to fund the acquisition if the acquirer is prepared to close an acquisition.

Additional Documentation

[82] Other documents required to complete an acquisition can be extensive and may include voting and/or support agreements by major shareholders; debt and equity commitment letters and guarantees (in connection with leveraged buyouts) (*see* paragraphs 77 and 78) and definitive credit documentation, including the credit agreements and ancillary collateral agreements; agreements with key employees, customers and suppliers; noncompetition agreements; related transaction agreements; deeds, assignments and other transfer documents in the case of an asset sale; consents of major suppliers, governmental agencies, major creditors, landlords and others; resolutions of the boards of directors of the corporations and their shareholders; an escrow agreement if any of the purchase price is placed in escrow; receipts for money paid at the closing; and promissory notes representing a portion of the purchase price. A significant portion of the effort included in the documentation of the acquisition is the drafting and negotiation of the credit agreement and the other collateral documentation.

[83] With respect to the acquisition of a U.S. public company, additional documentation required may include tender offer documents, proxy statements, registration statements and other reports that might need to be filed with the SEC and/or submitted to the target's shareholders.

ACQUISITIONS OF PUBLIC COMPANIES

[84] Acquisitions of publicly traded U.S. corporations raise a host of unique legal issues for non-U.S. acquirers. This section highlights many of these issues and provides guidance to non-U.S. parties considering making an acquisition of a U.S. public company. It also touches upon some U.S. regulatory issues that may arise in connection with acquisitions of foreign companies that have a significant number of U.S. shareholders.

STRUCTURING ISSUES

[85] Although transaction structures vary based on the particular facts of the transaction, as described below, there are two primary processes that are used in acquisitions of U.S. public companies.

One-Step Transaction

[86] In a "one-step" transaction, the two companies negotiate a merger agreement and, at the effective time of the merger, the target's shares are automatically converted into the right to receive the consideration specified in the merger agreement. Under U.S. state law, a company generally needs to obtain the approval of its shareholders in order to merge in a transaction other than one in which the shareholders' rights

are unaffected. Thus, the target's shareholders will have to approve the transaction. If the acquirer itself (rather than a merger subsidiary) is merging with the target, the approval of the acquirer's shareholders will also be required under state law. If the acquirer uses a merger subsidiary, only the approval of the acquirer, as the sole shareholder of its subsidiary, will be required. Approval of the acquirer's shareholders may also be required under the rules of the stock exchange on which the acquirer's shares are listed if the acquirer is issuing a substantial percentage of its shares in connection with the merger.

[87] Under SEC rules, the proxy statement that must be sent to shareholders before the shareholders vote on a matter must be filed in advance with the SEC and may be subject to a review process by the SEC's staff. If securities of the acquirer will be issued as consideration in the merger, a registration statement generally also must be filed with and reviewed by the SEC, although in these circumstances the registration statement and proxy statement are typically combined into one document.

[88] This straightforward arrangement is most often the structure of choice for negotiated combinations in which the consideration to be paid to the target's shareholders consists of stock or other securities of the acquirer.

Two-Step Transaction

[89] In a "two-step" transaction, the parties first negotiate a merger agreement and then, upon the execution of the merger agreement, the acquiring company makes a tender or exchange offer for some or all of the target's stock followed by a "second-step" or "squeeze-out" merger of the nontendering shareholders, usually for the same consideration.

[90] If cash will be used as some or all of the consideration, the use of a tender offer may allow the acquirer to gain control of the target more quickly than with a one-step merger. A cash tender offer does not require prior review by the SEC and, barring competition law or regulatory, financing or other constraints; the tender offer can be closed as early as 20 business days after being commenced. At that time, the acquirer usually purchases at least enough stock in the target to be able to effectively control the target and assure the acquirer's ability to approve the second-step merger. If the acquirer can acquire more than 90% of the outstanding stock of the target in the tender offer, it will usually have the power under state law to approve the second-step merger immediately and without a shareholder meeting. Thus, the entire acquisition—from initial discussions to closing—can be consummated in 60 days in the best case scenario. If the acquirer is not able to achieve this 90% threshold, it will need to go through the same proxy statement/shareholder meeting process as with the one-step merger.

[91] The need for so called top-up options, which allow the bidder to purchase an additional number of shares from the target upon the closing of the tender offer in order to reach the 90% threshold have been obviated in Delaware by the enactment of DGCL Section 251(h), which states that stockholders of a public corporation do not have to approve certain mergers if, after the tender or exchange offer, the acquirer holds enough stock to approve a merger under DGCL Section 251(h) (usually a simple majority). Only target corporations with stock listed on a national securities exchange or held of record by more than 2 000 stockholders immediately prior to the execution of the merger agreement are eligible to take advantage of DGCL 251(h). DGCL 251(h) may not be used if a corporation's certificate of incorporation expressly requires stockholders to vote on a merger.

[92] If the acquirer will be using stock or other securities as some or all of the consideration, an exchange offer can be used, but the registration process can take 60 to 90 days, giving an exchange offer only a modest timing advantage, if any, over a one-step merger.

Structuring the Merger

[93] An acquisition through merger in a one-step transaction can be structured in a variety of different ways. The simplest is a transaction in which the target and the acquirer merge. However, this structure is often not available in cross-border transactions where the target and the acquirer exist under the laws of different countries.

[94] The most common alternative is for the target to be merged with a subsidiary of the acquirer that is formed under the target's jurisdiction expressly for that purpose (this is often referred to as a "merger sub").

[95] The most common type of merger is known as a "reverse triangular merger," in which the newly formed subsidiary merges into the target, with the target as the surviving corporation. One reason that this is common is that some courts have held that a merger can be deemed to be an "assignment," thereby requiring the consent of the counterparty to those agreements, but a reverse triangular merger is generally not considered an "assignment"[3] Having the target be the surviving corporation in the merger may also reduce issues associated with regulatory permits and licenses, and with maintaining proper title to property and equipment. Tax structuring and planning considerations are also relevant to this decision in many cases.

[3] *See PPG Industries, Inc. v. Guardian Industries Corporation*, 597 F.2d 1090 (6th Cir. 1979). At least one court has found an impermissible assignment even where the contracting party was the surviving corporation in the merger. *SQL Solutions, Inc. v. Oracle Corporation*, No. C-91–1079 MHP 1991 WL 626458 (N.D. Cal. Dec. 18, 1991). In particular, intellectual property licenses may be closely scrutinized in this way.

ADVANTAGES AND DISADVANTAGES OF USING SECURITIES TO PAY FOR THE ACQUISITION

Advantages

[96] The use of stock or other securities to pay for acquisitions can have several advantages over cash. The use of stock or other securities to pay for acquisitions minimizes or eliminates the need for the acquiring company to use cash or incur debt to finance the transaction. Shareholders of a target company who receive stock in exchange for their existing stock may be able to defer the recognition of gain for tax purposes if the acquisition meets certain requirements, although special rules applicable to exchanges of stock of foreign corporations (discussed in paragraphs 421–463 below) may prevent a tax-free exchange.

[97] Another potential advantage of a stock-for-stock merger is that it may be easier to defend against interference from unwanted bidders. For example, Delaware courts have held that *Revlon* duties do not apply to stock-for-stock mergers between non-controlled entities (although such courts are less settled with respect to situations in which the consideration is mixed). *See* the discussion set forth below under *Legal Duties of Target's Board in Acquisitions—Revlon Duties.* Further, the use of stock consideration offers the shareholders of the target company the chance to participate in the potential upside and synergies (while also bearing potential risks) arising from the transaction, allowing the acquirer to justify a smaller premium in certain situations.

Disadvantages

[98] The use of stock or other securities to pay for acquisitions can have several disadvantages as well. First, registration of an acquirer's securities with the SEC takes time, giving more time to competitors to make competing bids or "jump" a signed deal, and, in a hostile context, more time for the target to put together its defense. Second, given the choice, shareholders may prefer to receive cash due to uncertainty about how much the securities will be worth, at the closing of the transaction. Third, the public offering of securities in the United States gives rise to more onerous and extensive U.S. securities law disclosure, compliance and liability issues, and will subject a foreign acquirer to at least portions of the Sarbanes-Oxley Act of 2002[4] (*see* paragraphs 201–372 below for a detailed discussion of these matters).

Exchange Ratios

[99] The simplest form of exchange ratio is a fixed ratio (*e.g.*, 1.5 shares of acquirer stock for each share of target stock) that does not vary with changes in stock prices. With a fixed exchange ratio, the target's shareholders assume the risk that the acquirer's stock

[4] Pub. L. 107–204, 116 Stat. 745 (2002).

will lose significant value before the merger closes and the acquirer and its shareholders assume the risk that the acquirer will overpay if its stock significantly gains in value.

[100] Another option is a floating exchange ratio that provides for a variable number of acquirer shares based on a fixed value (*e.g.*, US$75 worth of acquirer's stock for each share of target stock). While a floating exchange ratio provides value certainty to the target's shareholders, the acquirer would bear the risk that a large decline in the acquirer's stock price would increase the amount of acquirer's stock paid to the target's shareholders.

[101] A pricing "collar" is a highly customizable mechanic that can be used to mitigate the risk of price fluctuations in the acquirer's stock. A "collar" on a fixed exchange ratio typically leaves the exchange ratio fixed until the stock price of the acquirer drops below a predetermined price (a "floor") or rises above a predetermined price (a "ceiling" or "cap"). Once the price goes below the floor or above the cap, the merger agreement would provide either that the transaction can be abandoned at the acquirer's election or that the exchange ratio would begin to "float." A "collar" on a floating exchange ratio can set a minimum and a maximum number of shares the acquirer is obligated to issue, or establish a termination right or another pricing mechanism in the event of extreme price fluctuation. There are many variations which the acquirer and target can adapt to the circumstances of the transaction.

LEAVING IN PUBLIC MINORITIES

[102] Acquisitions may be made cheaper by acquiring less than 100% of a target's shares and in turn leaving a public minority in place, but in the U.S. the bargain may be illusory for a number of reasons. A public minority may make the economies that are the main purpose of the acquisition difficult or impossible to achieve. The target will remain a public company subject to the disclosure and governance requirements of the U.S. securities laws, which are burdensome and costly. In addition, the continued presence of minority shareholders may make it significantly more difficult for an acquirer to combine and restructure its and the target's businesses, assets and liabilities in an optimal way, because of potential claims by the minority shareholders of conflict of interest (including breach of fiduciary duty or usurpation of corporate opportunity). The costs of subsequently buying out the minority may also be high.

SECURITIES REGULATIONS

[103] Federal securities laws apply to the acquisition of public companies through the regulation of tender offers, proxy solicitations and offers and sales of securities under the Securities Act of 1933, as amended (the "Securities Act"),[5] and the Securities Exchange Act of 1934, as amended (the "Exchange Act").[6]

TENDER OFFERS

[104] Tender offers Conducted in the United States are subject to U.S. federal securities laws even when such tender offers are primarily conducted outside of the United States or conducted with respect to both public and private securities. The term "tender offer" is not defined in the statute or regulations, but it is generally understood to be an offer to purchase securities of a company directly from the holders of such securities if certain conditions are met. While often occurring with respect to publicly traded equity securities, certain tender offer regulation extend to offers to purchase unregistered equity securities as well as debt securities.

[105] In *Wellman v. Dickinson (1979)*, a leading judicial decision in the area, a U.S. District Court established an eight part test to determine whether a series of actions constitutes a tender offer subject to the Exchange Act: (i) active and widespread solicitation of public shareholders for the shares of an issuer; (ii) solicitation is made for a substantial percentage of the issuer's stock; (iii) offer to purchase stock at a premium over prevailing market price; (iv) terms of the offer are firm rather than negotiable; (v) offer is contingent on the tender of a fixed number of shares, often subject to a fixed maximum number to be purchased; (vi) offer is open for only a limited period of time; (vii) offeree is subjected to pressure to sell her stock; and (viii) public announcements of a purchasing program concerning the target company precede or accompany rapid accumulation of large amounts of the target company's securities.[7] Not all factors need to be present to find that the acquirer made a tender offer subject to the Exchange Act.

[106] While the "Wellman Test" factors are commonly considered in determining whether a "tender offer" has occurred, their presence or absence is not determinative. Courts have held that a "tender offer" exists when, viewing the transaction in the light of the totality of circumstances, there appears to be a likelihood that unless the tender offer rules are followed, there will be substantial risk that solicitees will lack information needed to make carefully considered appraisal of the proposal put before them.[8] The ambiguity of that standard leaves open the possibility that a "tender offer" will be found under circumstances where the acquirer never had an intention to make one.

[107] Two sections of the Exchange Act govern third-party tender offers. Section 14(d) and Regulation 14D apply to tender offers for "equity securities" (defined in the Exchange Act to include convertible debt and certain other securities) that are

[5] 15 U.S.C. §77a et seq.
[6] 15 U.S.C. §78a et seq.
[7] *Wellman v. Dickinson*, 475 F.Supp. 783 (S.D.N.Y. 1979) *aff'd on other grounds*, 682 F.2d 355 (2d Cir. 1982), *cert. denied sub nom. Dickinson v. SE*, 460 U.S. 1069.
[8] *Hanson Trust PLC v. SCM Corp.*, 774 F.2d 47 (2d Cir. 1985).

registered under the Exchange Act. These regulations apply to: (i) any offer where the acquirer would, after consummation of the offer, be the beneficial owner of more than 5% of the class of equity securities that is subject to the offer (including any securities already held by the acquirer); and (ii) any offer where the acquirer acquires beneficial ownership of more than 2% of the class of equity securities during any 12-month period.[9] Section 14(e) and Regulation 14E set forth certain general anti-fraud provisions and govern tender offers for any securities, including debt securities and securities that are not registered under the Exchange Act.

The Tender Offer Process

[108] The following discussion deals with tender offers for the stock of public companies made in the United States only. Cross-border tender offers are discussed separately below under the heading "Cross-Border Tender Offers."

Commencement

[109] Under SEC rules, a tender offer legally commences when the bidder first publishes, sends or gives security holders the means to tender the securities identified in the offer. This is the time at which security holders must be supplied with the formal disclosures required by the tender offer rules. A bidder making a tender offer only needs to have an intention to commence and complete an offer and a reasonable belief that it will have the means to complete the offer (and not be acting with the intention to manipulate the price of the bidder's or target's securities).[10] Most bidders and targets in negotiated transactions agree that the tender offer will commence within a specified number of days (*e.g.*, 10 business days) after signing the definitive agreement.

[110] A tender offer typically commences by simultaneously placing a "tombstone" advertisement in a newspaper of national circulation (usually The Wall Street Journal) and mailing an offer to purchase, letter of transmittal and other related documents to the target's shareholders. Under the SEC rules, the bidder must file a "Schedule TO" Tender Offer Statement with the SEC "as soon as practicable" on the date of commencement.[11]

[111] The tender offer materials must: (i) include certain disclosures as required by this Schedule TO, (ii) remain open for at least 20 days from the date from which the bidder files a Schedule TO and (ii) offer all stockholders who sell to the bidder the highest consideration offered to a stockholder during the tender offer. During the offering period, tendering shareholders have the absolute right to withdraw any shares tendered. Once the tender offer expires, the bidder is obligated to take-up

[9] *See* § 14(d) of the Exchange Act.
[10] 17 C.F.R. 240.14e-8.
[11] 17 C.F.R. 240.14d-3.

and pay for the shares tendered "promptly" or else return the shares. If the bidder has not purchased the shares tendered after 60 calendar days from the date of commencement, tendering shareholders will have the absolute right to withdraw any shares tendered.

[112] In the United States, it is permissible to make tender offers subject to obtaining financing. This contrasts with the U.K. practice of financial advisors requiring committed financing to be in place before confirming publicly that sufficient resources are available.

Target Response

[113] Within 10 days of the tender offer's commencement, the target's board of directors must send its shareholders a recommendation regarding the tender offer.[12] At that time, the target must file Schedule 14D-9 Solicitation/Recommendation Statement with the SEC containing the recommendation and an explanation of the reasons therefor. In a friendly tender offer, the board recommendation is usually made on the date the tender offer commences, whereas in a hostile tender offer, the target company will usually need additional time to evaluate the offer.

[114] Prior to filing the Schedule 14D-9, the target company is permitted to make only a "stop, look and listen" communication regarding the offer to its shareholders advising the shareholders that they should not tender any shares until the target company's board of directors has had an opportunity to evaluate and respond to the tender offer.[13]

Subsequent Offering Period

[115] The SEC's rules allow third-party bidders to use a subsequent offering period, without withdrawal rights, if certain conditions are satisfied.[14] A subsequent offering period must be at least three business days and must be commenced on the day following the expiration of the initial offering period.

[116] The SEC does not require advance notice of a subsequent offering period so long as a bidder discloses up front that it may have a subsequent offering period. As a result, bidders often reserve the right to provide a subsequent offering period to preserve optionality to provide one if all conditions have been satisfied but less than 90% of the target's shares have been tendered (public tender offers generally require the tender of at least 90% of the target's shares to allow for a Delaware short-form merger following the closing of the tender offer). However, so-called top-up options, which allow the bidder to purchase an additional number of shares from the target upon the closing of the tender offer in order to reach the 90% threshold, have

[12] 17 C.F.R. 240.14e-2.
[13] 17 C.F.R. 240.14d-9.
[14] 17 C.F.R. 240.14d-11.

become common in negotiated tender offers (other than in Delaware as a result of DGCL 251(h)), making subsequent offering periods less important.

Exchange Offers

[117] A tender offer in which the target's stockholders receive partial or full consideration for their shares in the form of stock is often called an "exchange offer." Exchange offers can commence immediately upon the SEC declaring the registration statement to be effective.

[118] A party desiring to commence an exchange offer before the registration statement is declared effective must file a registration statement for the securities to be offered containing a preliminary prospectus with all information about the transaction that shareholders would find necessary in making a decision on the tender offer. Once the registration statement has been filed and the preliminary prospectus has been distributed to shareholders, the exchange offer may commence.

[119] Bidders are required to update shareholders with supplements if there are any material changes in the information disclosed in the preliminary prospectus. After a supplement is sent to shareholders, exchange offers must remain open for a specified minimum period of time so shareholders can consider the new or revised information. Rule 14d-4 specifies the minimum number of days an offer must be kept open after the dissemination of a supplement:

- Five business days for a supplement containing a material change other than price or share levels.
- Ten business days for a supplement containing a change in price, the amount of securities sought, the dealer's soliciting fee or other similarly significant change.
- Ten business days for a supplement included as part of a post-effective amendment.
- Twenty business days for a revised prospectus where the initial prospectus was materially deficient.

Cross-Border Tender Offers

[120] The U.S. tender offer rules apply to tender offers made "directly or indirectly, by use of the mails or by any means or instrumentality of interstate commerce or of any facility of a national securities exchange or otherwise."[15] As a result, tender offers for targets that are located outside the United States can be subject to U.S. regulation, which may conflict and/or be more stringent than foreign regulations.

[121] To encourage bidders to include U.S. shareholders in cross-border tender offers, the SEC made significant changes to its tender offer regulations in 1999

[15] *See* s. 14(d)(1) of the Exchange Act.

and 2008.[16] The rules establish two different "tiers" of regulation depending on whether U.S. persons hold 10% or less (Tier I) or 40% or less (Tier II) of the target's securities. Transactions that fall under Tier I are exempt from most U.S. tender offer regulations and U.S. registration requirements for securities issued in cross-border exchange offers. Transactions that fall under Tier II are exempt from certain U.S. tender offer regulations but not from U.S. registration requirements.

Determining Percentage of U.S. Holders

[122] To determine the percentage of securities held by U.S. residents, the rules require the bidder to "look through" the record ownership of brokers, dealers, banks and other nominees to determine the residence of their customer accounts. This must be done for nominees that are located in the United States, the jurisdiction of organization of the target and the bidder, and the principal trading market for the securities. In order to make this determination, bidders in negotiated transactions are required to ask nominee record holders about the domicile of their customer accounts. If the information cannot be obtained after making such inquiry, the bidder may assume that the beneficial holders have the same domicile as the nominee's principal place of business. A hostile bidder is permitted to presume that the U.S. ownership levels are not exceeded based on the relative levels of average daily trading volumes in the U.S. and abroad in the last 12 months unless the target's most recent annual report or other publicly available information indicates, or the bidder knows or has reason to know, that U.S. ownership exceeds the threshold. A bidder in a negotiated transaction may also rely on this presumption if it is unable to conduct the look-through analysis so long as the primary trading market for the securities that are subject to the tender offer is outside the United States. The calculation of U.S. ownership excludes securities held by the bidder itself.

[123] If a second bidder commences a tender offer during an ongoing tender offer for which a Tier I or Tier II exemption is available, the second bidder is eligible for the same exemption even if U.S. security holders hold more than the specified percentage of the class of securities, assuming the second bidder meets the other requirements for the Tier I or Tier II exemption. Thus, any movement of securities into the United States following the initial offer will not disadvantage the second bidder.

---

[16] "Cross-Border Tender and Exchange Offers, Business Combinations and Rights Offerings," SEC Rel. No. 33-7759 (October 22, 1999) and amended in 2008 in a release entitled "Commission Guidance and Revisions to the Cross-Border Tender Offer, Exchange Offer, Rights Offerings, and Business Combination Rules and Beneficial Ownership Reporting Rules for Certain Foreign Institutions," SEC Rel. No. 33-8957 (September 19, 2008).

Tier I Exemption

[124] A tender offer that qualifies under Tier I is exempt from: (i) the filing, dissemination and procedural requirements of the U.S. tender offer regulations set forth in section 14(d)(1) through (7) of the Exchange Act, Regulation 14D and Rules 14e-1 and 14e-2, (ii) the heightened disclosure requirements of the SEC's "going private" rules[17]and (iii) the registration requirements under the Securities Act.[18]

[125] Tier I transactions remain subject to certain of the U.S. anti-fraud rules, including prohibitions on purchases while in possession of material nonpublic information and prohibitions on purchases outside of the tender offer.

[126] Bidders may rely on the Tier I exemption if the following conditions are satisfied:

- (i) the target is a "foreign private issuer";[19]
- (ii) U.S. security holders hold 10% or less of the class of securities sought in the tender offer;
- (iii) U.S. security holders are permitted to participate in the offer on terms at least as favorable as those offered to any other holder;
- (iv) the bidder provides U.S. security holders with an English language translation of any tender offer documents provided to security holders in the target's home jurisdiction (which includes both its place of organization and the principal foreign market where its securities are traded);
- (v) if the bidder disseminates the offer by publication in the target's home jurisdiction, it must publish the information in the United States as well as in a manner reasonably calculated to inform U.S. security holders of the offer; and
- (vi) if the class of securities that is the subject of the offer is registered under the Exchange Act, the bidder must submit any informational documents provided to security holders, in English, to the SEC on a Form CB via the SEC's EDGAR system within one business day after publication or dissemination, and, if the bidder is a foreign company, appoint an agent for service of legal process in the United States by submitting a Form F-X with the SEC via EDGAR at the same time.

[127] Additionally, bidders relying on the Tier I exemption must provide U.S. investors with procedural[20] and substantive terms equivalent to those offered to any other holders of the subject securities. Exceptions to this equal treatment requirement include: (i) if the bidder is offering securities that are exempt from registration under

[17] 17 C.F.R. 240.14d-1(c); 240.13e-3(g)(6).
[18] 17 C.F.R. 230.802.
[19] A "foreign private issuer" is generally any foreign issuer other than a foreign government or an issuer that meets the following two conditions: (i) more than 50% of its voting securities are held by U.S. persons, and (ii) either (a) a majority of its directors or executive officers are U.S. citizens or residents, (b) more than 50% of its assets are located in the United States or (c) its business is administered principally in the United States. *See* 17 C.F.R. 240.3b-4.
[20] *E.g.*, duration and withdrawal rights.

the Securities Act, it can offer cash instead of securities to U.S. security holders in any U.S. states that would require the securities to be registered or (ii) if the cash is substantially equivalent in value to the securities offered to non-U.S. holders and certain additional conditions are met, a bidder can offer U.S. security holders cash instead of securities.

[128] In addition, bidders may offer loan notes to non-U.S. security holders without offering them to U.S. security holders without violating the SEC's "all holders/best price" rule (Rule 14d-10).[21]

Tier II Exemption

[129] A tender offer that qualifies under Tier II is eligible for more limited relief from the U.S. tender offer regulations. Bidders may rely on the Tier II exemption if the following conditions are satisfied:

(i) the target is a foreign private issuer; and
(ii) U.S. security holders hold 40% or less of the class of securities sought in the tender offer.

[130] Under the Tier II exemption, the following will be exempted from U.S. tender offer regulations:

(i) *Loan Notes*—Bidders may offer loan notes to non-U.S. security holders without offering them to U.S. security holders without violating the SEC's "all holders/best price" rule.[22]
(ii) *Multiple Offers*—Bidders may conduct multiple offers, one to U.S. holders (which may include all holders of American Depository Receipts ("ADRs"), even non-U.S. holders) and one or more offers to non-U.S. holders, without violating Rule 14d-10 (although for partial tender offers, the use of separate proration pools may not be permitted under section 14(d)(6)) so long as the offer to U.S. holders is on terms at least as favorable as those offered to any other holders.
(iii) *Notice of Extensions; Prompt Payment*—Bidders may provide notices of extensions and comply with the obligation to promptly pay for securities accepted in the offer in accordance with home jurisdiction law or practice rather than in accordance with the requirements of Rule 14e-1.
(iv) *Subsequent Offering Period; Withdrawal Rights*—Bidders may satisfy the announcement and prompt payment requirements for a subsequent offering period by complying with home jurisdiction law or practice rather than in accordance with the requirements of Rule 14d-11; and bidders do not have to extend withdrawal rights following the close of the offer and prior to the commencement of a subsequent offering period.

---

[21] Loan notes, or promissory notes issued in connection with business combination transactions in lieu of cash consideration, qualify for tax deferrals in many countries. Because loan notes do not offer U.S. investors similar tax savings, a bidder need not offer them to U.S. security holders.

[22] Rule 14d-10.

(v) *Payment of Interest*—Bidders may pay interest on securities tendered during a subsequent offering period if required under applicable foreign law notwithstanding Rule 14d-11(f) (which requires the same consideration to be paid in the subsequent offering period as was paid during the initial offer) and Rule 14d-10.

(vi) *Suspension of Withdrawal Rights During Counting of Securities*—Bidders may suspend withdrawal rights at the end of the offer while the securities are being counted as long as:
   a. the bidder has provided an offer period including withdrawal rights of at least 20 U.S. business days;
   b. all conditions to the offer have been satisfied or waived; and
   c. withdrawal rights are reinstated (if otherwise required by section 14(d)(5)) when the counting is complete;

(vii) *Mix and Match Elections*—Bidders may offer holders the ability to elect various forms of consideration that are subject to limits or caps and use separate proration pools for the initial offer period and a subsequent offering period.

(viii) *Early Termination of Initial Offering Period*—Bidders may terminate an initial offer period if, at the time the initial offer period and withdrawal rights terminate:
   a. the initial offer period has been open for at least 20 U.S. business days;
   b. the bidder has disclosed the possibility and impact of an early termination in the original offer materials;
   c. the bidder provides a subsequent offering period;
   d. all offer conditions are satisfied; and
   e. the bidder does not terminate during any mandatory extension required by U.S. tender offer rules.

[131] In addition, according to an SEC interpretive position, the SEC will not object if a bidder in a cross-border tender offer that satisfies the conditions of Tier II waives or reduces the minimum acceptance condition without extending withdrawal rights as long as:

(i) the bidder announces that it may waive or reduce the minimum acceptance condition at least five business days before it actually does so;

(ii) the bidder disseminates the announcement through a press release and other methods reasonably calculated to inform U.S. security holders;

(iii) the press release states the exact percentage to which the minimum acceptance condition may be reduced (or if it will be waived rather than reduced), and the bidder announces its actual intentions regarding the waiver or reduction as soon as required under home country rules;

(iv) security holders have withdrawal rights during the five-day period following the announcement of a possible waiver or reduction;

(v) the press release advises security holders to withdraw their tenders immediately if their willingness to tender would be affected by the waiver or reduction of the minimum acceptance condition;

(vi) the procedure for waiving or reducing the minimum acceptance condition must be described in the offering materials;

(vii) the offer must remain open for at least five business days after the waiver or reduction;

(viii) all offer conditions are satisfied or waived when withdrawal rights are terminated;
(ix) the potential impact of the waiver or reduction is fully discussed in the initial offering materials or any supplemental materials; and
(x) the bidder may not waive or reduce the minimum acceptance condition below the percentage required for the bidder to control the target after the tender offer under applicable foreign law and, in any case, may not waive or reduce the minimum tender condition below a majority of the outstanding securities of the class.[23]

Purchases Outside of a Tender Offer

[132] The SEC's Rule 14e-5 prohibits a covered person from purchasing subject or related securities in connection with a tender offer for the securities except as part of such tender offer. The SEC has provided several exceptions to Rule 14e-5 in cross-border situations. In a Tier I tender offer, the Rule 14e-5 prohibition will not apply if:

(i) the offering documents provided to U.S. security holders prominently disclose the possibility of, arrangement for or intent to make such a purchase;
(ii) the offering documents disclose the manner in which any information about such purchases will be disclosed;
(iii) the bidder discloses purchase information in the United States in a manner equivalent to disclosures in the target's home jurisdiction; and
(iv) the purchases comply with the applicable tender offer laws of the target's home jurisdiction. There is also an exception under certain circumstances for purchases made by "connected exempt market makers" and "connected exempt principal traders" as defined in the City Code.

[133] In a Tier II tender offer, the Rule 14e-5 prohibition will not apply to:

(i) purchases pursuant to concurrent non-U.S. tender offers as long as:
  a. the Tier II conditions are met;
  b. the economic terms and consideration in the U.S. offer and the non-U.S. offer are the same (although foreign currencies can be converted into U.S. dollars at an exchange rate disclosed in the offering documents);
  c. the procedural terms of the U.S. offer are at least as favorable as the terms of the non-U.S. offer;
  d. the intention to make purchases pursuant to the non-U.S. offer is disclosed in the U.S. offering documents; and
  e. the purchases in the non-U.S. offer are made solely pursuant to the offer and not in an open market, private or other transaction; or

[23] *See* Commission Guidance and Revisions to the Cross-Border Tender Offer, Exchange Offer, Rights Offerings, and Business Combination Rules and Beneficial Ownership Reporting Rules for Certain Foreign Institutions, SEC Release No. 33–8957; 34–58597 (Sep. 19, 2008).

(ii) purchases by the bidder and its affiliates and affiliates of a financial advisor that are permitted under and conducted in accordance with applicable law in the target's home jurisdiction as long as:
  a. the target is a foreign private issuer,
  b. the purchaser reasonably expects that the Tier II conditions are met;
  c. no purchases otherwise than pursuant to the tender offer are made in the United States;
  d. the U.S. offering materials disclose prominently the possibility of such purchases outside of the tender offer, and if there will be public disclosure of purchases, the manner in which information regarding such purchases will be disseminated;
  e. there is public disclosure in the United States of information regarding all purchases otherwise than pursuant to the tender offer from the time of public announcement of the tender offer until the tender offer expires to the extent that such information is made public in the target's home jurisdiction;
  f. in the case of purchases by a bidder and its affiliates, the tender offer price is increased to match any consideration paid outside of the tender offer that is greater than the tender offer price; and
  g. in the case of purchases by an affiliate of a financial advisor, the financial advisor has an affiliate that is registered under the Exchange Act, the purchases are not made to facilitate the tender offer and the financial advisor and certain additional requirements are met.

Other Sources of Relief for Conflicting Regulatory Requirements

[134] Many of the remaining inconsistencies between U.S. regulations and those of other jurisdictions can be dealt with through seeking interpretive relief from the SEC on a case-by-case basis. This is usually done through the process of submitting a letter called a "no action request" asking the SEC's staff to concur with an interpretation of regulatory requirements and agree not to recommend enforcement to the SEC if certain actions are taken. Where specific rules must be waived, the Commissioners are sometimes called upon to take formal exemptive action in the form of an interpretive release. In either case, lengthy discussions between the interested party's counsel and SEC attorneys are often required. While the SEC makes a special effort to respond efficiently to inquiries regarding international tender offers and securities offerings the SEC may take several weeks or more to grant relief.

Multi-Jurisdictional Disclosure System

[135] The "Multi-jurisdictional Disclosure System" was designed to help alleviate conflicts between U.S. and Canadian securities law regulations. To minimize the compliance difficulties that arise with two systems with such overlapping jurisdictional claims, special rules have been adopted in the United States and Canada to coordinate the regulation of tender offers where shareholders of the target reside in both jurisdictions. Under this system, both cash tender offers and exchange offers for the securities of companies organized under Canadian law that qualify as "foreign private issuers" are exempt from many U.S. regulations so long as:

(i) less than 40% of the class of securities subject to the tender offer is held by U.S. holders,
(ii) the offer otherwise complies with the applicable Canadian rules and
(iii) the Canadian offering documents are filed with the SEC and provided to U.S. security holders.[24]

[136] Similar Canadian rules exempt offerings for U.S. companies whose shareholders are not primarily Canadian persons. Some difficulties remain in the relatively rare situation where the bulk of the shareholders of a company organized in Canada are U.S. persons or vice versa.

Proxy Solicitations

[137] Solicitations of proxies to vote securities registered under the Exchange Act are regulated under section 14(a) of the Exchange Act and SEC Regulations 14A and 14C. The term "proxy" is broadly defined to include any proxy, consent or authorization, which can also take the form of failure to object or dissent.[25] Similarly, the term "solicitation" is broadly defined to include: (i) any request for a proxy, even if no proxy form is included, (ii) a request to execute, not to execute or to revoke a proxy or (iii) furnishing a proxy form or other communication to shareholders under circumstances reasonably calculated to lead to the procurement, withholding or revocation of a proxy (except furnishing a proxy form in response to an unsolicited request).[26] Under this broad definition, preliminary communications from the acquirer may be treated as part of a proxy solicitation, even if such communications do not request a proxy, and could include communications with the press designed to influence shareholders' votes.

[138] Before soliciting proxies with respect to securities registered under the Exchange Act, the person making the solicitation generally must file a detailed proxy statement with the SEC. Except in the case of proxy statements used by management for annual meetings at which only routine matters will be considered, proxy statements generally must be submitted to the SEC in preliminary form. The SEC staff may review the materials and provide comments to the filer. After receiving the SEC's comments, the filer must respond as appropriate before definitive proxy materials may be mailed to shareholders.

[139] Notwithstanding this process, SEC rules allow preliminary proxy materials to be distributed to shareholders as soon as they are filed with the SEC, so long as no form of proxy is included.[27] Parties may also solicit shareholders without the benefit of even a preliminary proxy statement, so long as such materials are filed with the SEC and

[24] 17 C.F.R. 240.14d-1(b).
[25] 17 C.F.R. 240.14a-1(f).
[26] 17 C.F.R. 240.14a-1(l).
[27] 17 C.F.R. 240.14a-3(a)(1).

a complete proxy statement is delivered to shareholders before or at the same time as the forms of proxy, consent or authorization are furnished to, or requested from, shareholders.[28]

[140] As is the case with hostile tender offers, the proxy rules include a requirement for the target company to either mail the bidder's proxy materials to the target's shareholders or provide the bidder with a current shareholder list so that it can make its own mailings.[29] Under federal law, the choice between mailing and providing a shareholder list resides with the target company. However, state corporate laws generally allow any shareholder to obtain a copy of the shareholder list directly from the issuer.

[141] Solicitation of proxies to approve a merger in which shareholders will receive securities as some or all of the consideration is subject to the registration requirements of the Securities Act as well.[30] The registration process is described in greater detail in paragraphs 201–372 below.

[142] Unlike tender offers, cross-border regulatory coordination is generally not an issue with proxy solicitations involving U.S. shareholders of non-U.S. companies because securities issued by "foreign private issuers" enjoy a blanket exemption from the SEC's proxy rules, whether or not they are held by U.S. persons or are traded in the United States.[31]

Tender Offer May Constitute a Proxy Solicitation

[143] When a proxy solicitation accompanies a tender offer, additional disclosures may be required. Tender offer materials may be considered proxy solicitations if they contain information relating to proxies beyond the information required to be disclosed under Schedule TO. The tender offer and proxy materials must fully disclose the interrelationship of the tender offer and the proxy solicitation, and both the tender offer and the proxy solicitation must disclose the acquirer's expected course of action if the solicitation is unsuccessful.

[144] Additionally, the target's response to Schedule 14D-9 or a competing bidder's communication to shareholders may constitute a proxy solicitation requiring compliance with the proxy rules. In some cases it may be desirable to submit materials that are to be communicated to shareholders during a proxy contest to the SEC in advance to prevent an inadvertent violation of the proxy rules.

[145] Materials that recommend acceptance or rejection of a tender offer may be required to be filed as an amended Schedule TO or 14D-9. If a target makes an early response to a proxy contest initiated in connection with a tender offer, the target may be required to file Schedule 14D-9 prior to the expiration of the normal 14D-9 deadline of 10 business days from the commencement of the tender offer.

[28] 17 C.F.R. 240.14a-12.
[29] 17 C.F.R. 240.14a-7.
[30] Pursuant to Rule 145 under the Securities Act.
[31] 17 C.F.R. 240.3a12-3.

Information Statements

[146] The proxy disclosure rules can apply in some circumstances even if no proxy is being solicited. The organizational documents of companies in the United States may provide that their respective shareholders are entitled to take action without a meeting. In that case, a majority shareholder of a company that is subject to the federal proxy rules may be able to approve a merger or other corporate action by signing a written consent to the action. No meeting would need to be held and no proxies would need to be solicited from the other shareholders. Even if a meeting is requested, if the majority shareholder does not need any other votes to assure success, it may choose not to solicit proxies from other shareholders.

[147] In either case, even though no proxies are solicited, the Exchange Act generally requires that an "information statement" on Schedule 14C containing substantially the same disclosure as a proxy statement on Schedule 14A be filed with the SEC and be made available to its shareholders.[32]

[148] Despite this general requirement, the SEC has determined that certain "short-form" mergers between parent companies and their subsidiaries do not require an information statement.

Private Tender Offers

[149] As seen above, the Wellman Test can be satisfied even in the case of the securities of nonpublic companies. Thus, a company or third party may also conduct a private tender offer for outstanding shares of its stock. The private tender offer may be structured as an issuer repurchase, where the company repurchases its own shares, or a third-party purchase. In doing so, the company can control the information provided to the parties to the transaction and the timing and price of the transaction, and must be careful to comply with the restrictions of the insider trading restrictions of Rule 10b-5. While SEC rules do not require specific disclosure for private tender offers, compliance with the anti-fraud and insider trading provisions of Rule 10b-5 is aided by the preparation of a formal disclosure document setting forth material nonpublic information in connection with a private tender offer.

[150] Because Section 14(d) of the Exchange Act and Regulation 14D apply only tender offers for Exchange Act registered securities, the requirements of Exchange Act Section 14(d) do not apply to private tender offers. However, the requirements of Section 14(e), Rule 10b-5 and Rule 14e-3 (discussed previously) do apply to private tender offers and thus such tender offers should be analyzed as set forth above, excluding the requirements of Section 14(d) and Regulation 14D.

[32] *See* s. 14(c) of the Exchange Act and Regulation 14C promulgated thereunder (17 C.F.R. 240.14c-1 et seq.).

LEGAL DUTIES OF TARGET'S BOARD IN ACQUISITIONS

Business Judgment Rule

[151] The directors of a target company that receives a takeover proposal have no absolute legal duty to negotiate or accept an offer (even if it represents a substantial premium over the target's current market price) if the company has not already committed to a break-up or sale of control of the company, and the directors are disinterested and acting on a generally informed basis. The decision in *Paramount v. Time*,[33] as clarified by *Arnold v. Society for Savings Bancorp*,[34] has settled that point. Directors' only obligations in such situations are governed by the "business judgment rule"—they must act in what they reasonably believe, in good faith and after appropriate consideration, to be the best interests of the target and its shareholders. In order for the business judgment rule to apply, the directors must be fully informed, careful, disinterested and independent. As courts are reluctant to substitute their business judgment for the directors', directors actions are protected by the presumptions of the business judgment rule unless the board's decision cannot be attributed to any rational business purpose.[35]

Revlon Duties

[152] In contrast to the business judgment rule standard described above, once a board of directors decides to pursue a course of action that will result in the sale of control or the break-up of a company, the Delaware courts have imposed upon the directors so-called Revlon duties, which are heightened duties to obtain the best price reasonably available for the shareholders.[36] If Revlon duties apply, the directors are charged with conducting a sale of the company or its assets with the objective of maximizing the value to the shareholders.

[153] Generally, a stock-for-stock merger where neither company has concentrated share ownership will not trigger Revlon duties if the post-merger entity remains in a "large, fluid, changeable and changing public market."[37] In such a transaction, "control" of the target simply transfers from one widely dispersed group of public shareholders to another widely dispersed group of public shareholders that still has no controlling shareholder. For that reason, the selling shareholders would retain their opportunity to receive a control premium in a future sale of control.

---

[33] *Paramount Communications, Inc. v. Time Inc.*, 571 A.2d 1140 (Del. 1989).
[34] *Arnold v. Society for Savings Bancorp, Inc.*, 650 A.2d 1270 (Del. 1994).
[35] *Sinclair Oil Corp. v. Levien*, 280 A.2d 717, 720 (Del.1971).
[36] *See Revlon, Inc. v. MacAndrews & Forbes Holdings, Inc.*, 506 A.2d 173, 182 (Del. 1986).
[37] *Paramount* 571 A.2d at 1150.

[154] In transactions in which shareholders of the target are to receive part cash and part stock, Revlon duties may apply depending on the mix of stock and cash, but Delaware courts are still in the process of clarifying the precise bounds of when Revlon duties apply to mixed consideration situations.[38]

[155] Once it is established that Revlon duties apply, the target's directors have a duty to secure the transaction offering the best value reasonably available for the shareholders. Delaware courts have consistently held that there is "no single blueprint" or standard methodology pursuant to which a board of directors must run a sale process to satisfy its Revlon duties; instead, what must be done to satisfy Revlon duties depends on the specific facts and circumstances of the transaction at issue.[39] Furthermore, boards of directors have considerable control over when Revlon duties begin to apply because such duties apply "only when a company embarks on a transaction—on its own initiative or in response to an unsolicited offer—that will result in a change of control."[40] In other words, Revlon duties will not be triggered simply because a company arguably is put "in play" by the actions of outsiders.[41]

PROTECTING THE DEAL FROM OTHER BIDDERS

[156] Competition is always a possibility in acquisitions of public companies. This is because the target's shareholders will either vote against a negotiated merger if a better offer has been announced or, in a two-step transaction, will not tender their shares if they anticipate a better deal. There is inevitably a delay between the public announcement of the negotiated deal and its consummation, which provides time and free education to competing bidders—two crucial ingredients to their potential success.

[157] An acquirer can adopt several strategies to improve its ability to enforce its negotiated acquisition agreement with the target.

[38] Delaware courts have found that Revlon duties do not apply in a transaction in which the consideration is 33% cash (*In re Santa Fe Pacific Corporation Shareholder Litigation*, 669 A.2d 59 (Del. 1995)) but do apply in transactions in which the consideration is 62% cash (*In re Lukens Inc. Shareholders Litigation*, 757 A.2d 720 (Del. Ch. 1999) (757 A. 2d 1278, Del. 2000, affirmed without opinion)). And, more recently, the Delaware Chancery Court held that Revlon duties were triggered by a transaction in which the consideration was approximately 50% cash and 50% stock because a significant portion "of the stockholders' investment would be converted to cash and thereby deprived of its long-run potential" (*In re Smurfit-Stone Container Corp. S'holder Litig.*, C.A. No. 6164-VCP, 2011 WL 2028076, at *15 (Del. Ch. May 24, 2011).)

[39] *See, e.g., Barkan v. Amsted Inds., Inc.*, 567 A.2d 1279 (Del. 1989); *Lyondell Chemical Co. v. Ryan*, 970 A.2d 235 (Del. 2009); and C&J Energy Serv., Inc. v. City of Miami Gen. Emps' & Sanitation Emps' Ret. Trust, 107 A.3d 1049, 1067 (Del. 2014).

[40] *Lyondell* 970 A.2d at 242.

[41] *Id.*

Foothold Acquisitions

[158] Where there is or is likely to be a competing bidder for a target, obtaining a foothold position in the target's stock is one strategy that a potential acquirer may use to protect against losing out completely. The price of the target's stock prior to an announcement of an acquisition agreement or hostile bid will likely be lower, potentially reducing the cost of the acquisition. Furthermore, if there is competition and the party with the foothold loses out to another bidder, such party may be able to tender or sell its equity stake to the competing bidder, thereby covering the some of the costs of an unsuccessful bid (and potentially yielding a profit).

[159] Notwithstanding the foregoing, there are numerous limitations with respect to the availability, amount and timing of obtaining significant foothold positions in the target's stock, including:

- an acquiring company must publicly disclose its identity, holdings and intentions on Schedule 13D within 10 days of acquiring more than 5% of a target's stock;
- there may be antitrust filing requirements under the HSR Act (*see* discussion in paragraphs 424–463 below);
- an acquiring company must obtain its foothold position before discussions with the target begin, or risk liability for insider trading;
- obtaining a secret foothold position may make it more difficult to accomplish a negotiated deal with the target's management because it may set a hostile tone that is hard to overcome;
- state anti-takeover statutes may limit the percentage of the foothold that an acquirer can obtain without becoming subject to various restrictions on its ability to vote its acquired shares or effect a business combination with the company (*see, e.g.*, DGCL Section 203); and
- some public companies in the United States have adopted "shareholder rights plans" under which bidders that acquire more than a specified percentage of a company's voting securities (often 10% to 20%) would experience significant dilution in their ownership interest. *See* the discussion set forth below under *Hostile Acquisitions—Understanding the Target's Takeover Defenses—Poison Pills.*

Alternative Proposals

No Shops and Go Shops

[160] A typical "no shop" provision in an acquisition agreement prohibits the target company from actively soliciting alternative bids after such agreement is signed. Although "no shop" provisions are used in some private deals, such provisions are included in most U.S. public company deals because, among other reasons, there is risk in between signing (after the deal is made public) and closing that a third party may become interested in the target company. As described below, however, to ensure that the target's board satisfies its fiduciary duties, these provisions typically allow target boards to consider certain unsolicited offers and terminate the transaction in favor of a better deal.

[161] A variant of a "no shop" provision is a "go shop" provision, which affirmatively permits the target company to actively solicit alternative bids for a specified period of time after the agreement is signed. "Go shop" provisions are typically used in instances where a target company has not conducted an auction or "market check"[42] (or only conducted limited market check), and the target's directors choose to include a go shop provision to help discharge their fiduciary duties under Revlon (for more details above Revlon duties, *see* above). Although not a certainty, Delaware courts have generally found that go shop provisions provide the target's board with strong evidence of the satisfaction of its Revlon duties.[43]

[162] Although the inclusion of a go shop provision essentially permits the target to use the initial bidder as a stalking horse, the initial bidder may be willing to accept such a provision for several reasons. First, it might be difficult for competing bidders to start and complete due diligence in the allotted time. Second, some potential bidders may not want to incur the expense or potential difficulties of trying to overcome a signed deal. Lastly, go shop clauses are typically structured to provide the initial bidder with certain "first-mover" advantages, such as (i) having the right to match any competing bids and (ii) being entitled to a break-up fee if the initial bidder's deal is terminated by the target in order to accept a higher bid.

Fiduciary Outs

[163] When a target's directors have decided to pursue a course of action that will result in the sale of control or the break-up of a company, as described above (*see* discussion above under *Legal Duties of Target's Board in Acquisitions—Revlon Duties*), they are generally under a fiduciary duty to obtain the best deal for shareholders that is reasonably available. As a result, most U.S. merger agreements contain a "fiduciary out" permitting the target's board to terminate the agreement if it receives an unsolicited bid that it determines, upon advice from its lawyers and bankers, constitutes a "superior proposal" so long as the board determines that not accepting such offer would violate the directors' fiduciary duties to shareholders.[44] It usually would be appropriate for the fiduciary out to terminate once the target's shareholders have approved the merger or once the bidder has acquired a majority of the outstanding shares in a tender offer.

[42] A "market check" is an inquiry performed by the target company's board of potential bidders for the target company to see what they would pay to acquire the target. The search is often confined to a subset of possible bidders rather than all of them.

[43] *See, e.g., In re Topps Co. S'holders Litig.*, 926 A.2d 58, 86-87 (Del. Ch. 2007); *see also In re Lear Corp. S'holder Litig.*, 926 A.2d 119-20 (Del. Ch. 2007).

[44] "Fiduciary outs" are so common in U.S. merger agreements that they will typically be included even in strategic, stock-for-stock mergers in which Revlon duties do not apply. Under these circumstances, the target negotiates for a fiduciary out as a business term of the transactions (*i.e.*, to allow the target to terminate to take a better deal) even if not strictly required by the fiduciary duties of the target's directors.

Break-up Fees

[164] Break-up fees are agreed payments to the spurned purchaser in a negotiated acquisition in the event that the target terminates the initial transaction. For a target's directors operating under Revlon duties, break-up fees must be both reasonable and proportionate. A target exercising its fiduciary out is the most common trigger of the break-up fee. If reasonable, break-up fees cover the costs of a losing bid and likely something extra, but they should not be of a size that would be found by a court to be so high so as to effectively preclude a topping bid. Break-up fees have tended to be in the range of 2%–5% of the transaction value.

[165] There is no bright-line test, set percentage or fee amount for the size of a permissible break-up fee.[45] An acquirer will generally want as high of a break-up fee as it is able to negotiate, both to compensate it as much as possible in case its bid is ultimately topped by a competing bidder and to hopefully deter competing bidders (subject to the requirement that the break-up fee cannot be seen as preclusive).

Force the Vote

[166] Force-the-vote provisions are another mechanism that acquirers can use to protect their deal. Such provisions require a target's board to submit a potential acquirer's deal to a shareholder vote, regardless of whether the target's board has changed or withdrawn its support of the deal as a result of a topping bid or otherwise.

[167] Force-the-vote provisions allow shareholders to make the ultimate decision between two competing proposals. Such provisions are beneficial to the initial bidder because forcing a stockholder vote is often a lengthy and time-consuming process and, therefore, serves as a deterrent to other potential bidders. In addition, such delays may incentivize the target's stockholders to vote for the initial bidder's deal, rather than wait for prospective deals to come to fruition.

[168] Although specifically authorized under DGCL, Delaware courts have held that there are limits to force-the-vote provisions (and such provisions are not enforceable in all U.S. jurisdictions). For example, Delaware courts have held that such provisions in conjunction with voting agreements from shareholders to support the deal may be unenforceable if the aggregate effect of the deal protection measures is deemed "preclusive" or "coercive."[46]

[45] *See In re Cogent, Inc. S'holder Litig.*, 7 A.3d 487, 503 (Del. Ch. 2010) (evaluating the reasonableness of the size of a break-up fee and noting that "the reasonableness of such a fee depends on the particular facts surrounding the transaction"). Notably, Delaware courts in recent years have upheld break-up fees ranging from 3.4% to 5.3%. *See In re Smurfit-Stone Container Corp. S'holder Litig.*, 2011 WL 2028076 (Del. Ch. 2011); *In re BioClinica, Inc. S'holder Litig.*, 2013 WL 5631233 (Del. Ch. Oct. 16, 2013).

[46] *See, e.g.*, *Omnicare, Inc. v. NCS Healthcare, Inc.*, 818 A.2d 914 (Del. 2003).

Commitments from Large Shareholders

[169] If there are shareholders with large holdings, one option may be enlist them to commit in advance to support the transaction and, therefore, make the acquisition safer from competition. Shareholder support agreements have as an added advantage that they generally do not require the consent of the target's board.[47]

[170] Despite the advantages of shareholder support agreements, large shareholders are often unwilling to commit themselves contractually upfront. Moreover, as noted above, if the target is a Delaware corporation, shareholder support agreements cannot be used in conjunction with force-the-vote provisions or other deal protection mechanisms to completely preclude competing bids.

[171] If the consideration to be issued in the transaction includes securities that will be registered under the Securities Act, acquirers should review the SEC's interpretations regarding the use of lockups to avoid "gun jumping" issues that may complicate the acquirer's attempt to register its securities.[48]

WHAT IF THE ACQUIRER DOES NOT WANT TO CLOSE THE DEAL?

[172] An acquirer may no longer wish to close a deal following the signing of an acquisition agreement due to a variety of reasons, including: (i) acquirer's remorse, (ii) the inability to obtain acceptable financing or (iii) the deterioration of the target's business. In addition to the closing conditions set forth in the acquisition agreement (*e.g.*, accuracy of representations and warranties, compliance with covenants, and receipt of regulatory approvals), termination rights (and associated reverse break-up fees) and Material Adverse Effect (MAE) concepts may be tools that the acquirer can use to walk away from the deal prior to closing.

"Optionality" and Reverse Break-Up Fees

[173] The concept of "optionality" originated in the private equity context. The governing paradigm was for the private equity sponsor to have a newly formed shell affiliate acting as the acquiring entity and executing the acquisition agreement and limiting the liability of the sponsor (*i.e.*, the only party on the acquirer's side with assets) to a fixed amount, called a reverse break-up fee, that it would promise to directly or indirectly pay to the seller if the conditions to closing were satisfied but the acquirer did not close. This concept in effect granted the private equity sponsor

[47] However, board approval may be necessary to waive provisions in poison pills otherwise applicable to such lockups or to satisfy certain state anti-takeover statutes that may have an adverse impact on persons who acquire an interest in significant blocks of shares without prior board approval.

[48] *See e.g.*, SEC Division of Corporation Finance, Compliance and Disclosure Interpretations, Securities Act Sections, Questions 139.30 (Aug. 11, 2010) and 239.13 (Nov. 26, 2008), *available at* https://www.sec.gov/divisions/corpfin/guidance/sasinterp.htm.

an option to purchase the target company. In contrast, acquisition agreements with strategic acquirers have historically provided the target company with the right to seek specific performance of the agreement and the right to receive full contractual damages (backed by the full assets of the acquirer) if the acquirer breached and walked away from the deal.[49] However, in the evolution of deals the concept of optionality has made its way, in various forms, into strategic deals as well.

[174] In its purest form, the concept of optionality allows the acquirer to walk away from the deal for any reason (including by breaching the agreement) and have no other obligation other than to pay the reverse break-up fee. As noted above, this in effect gives the acquirer an option to purchase the target company. Historically, the amount of the reverse break-up fee mirrored the amount of the break-up fee that the seller paid to the acquirer in the event the target accepted a superior offer (which, as noted above, is typically around 2%–4%). However, while a target company's break-up fee is limited by fiduciary constraints related to deal protection devices, no such limitations apply to an acquirer's reverse break-up fee. Thus, if the acquirer opts to pursue pure optionality in a particular deal, the target will likely attempt to price that option (*i.e.*, fix the size of the reverse break-up fee) without being constrained by the amount of the target's break-up fee. However, more commonly leveraged buyouts provide the target company with limited specific performance rights permitting the target company to exercise equitable remedies to force the buyer to use an agreed-upon level of efforts to satisfy the closing conditions and, if and only if the debt financing is available, draw upon the buyer's equity commitments to close the transaction.

[175] The inclusion (or exclusion) of optionality, in whatever form, is generally a product of many deal-specific conditions, such as the amount of financing relative to the acquirer's size (*i.e.*, is it bet the company size debt), credit and general market conditions, the existence of competing bidders, the seller's eagerness to sell the target company and the purchase price.

Material Adverse Effect Clauses

[176] A material adverse effect (MAE) clause is a mechanism for parties to allocate the risk of adverse changes to the target's business prior to closing. Such clauses typically provide that if the target's business suffers an MAE (the definition of which is typically highly negotiated) prior to closing, the acquirer is not obligated to close the transaction.

[177] The seminal Delaware Chancery Court decision on this topic, *In re IBP Inc. Shareholders Litigation*,[50] and its progeny have established a very high bar for an acquirer to refuse to close on account of the target's business suffering an MAE. *In*

[49] Note, however, that at least one court has held that, unless the merger agreement clearly states otherwise, neither the shareholders of a target company nor the target company itself (on behalf of its shareholders) could collect lost shareholder premium (*i.e.*, what the target shareholders would have received in the merger) as damages for a breach of the merger agreement. *See Consolidated Edison, Inc. v. Northeast Utilities*, 426 F.3d 524 (2d Cir. 2005).

[50] 789 A.2d. 14 (Del. Ch. 2001).

re IBP Shareholders Litigation held that in order for an event to be material, it must "substantially threaten the overall earnings potential of the target" on a long-term basis.[51] Further, one Delaware Chancery Court went so far as to state that the fact that no Delaware court has ever found that an MAE has occurred in the context of an M&A agreement is "not a coincidence."[52] Although it is certainly possible that with the right facts and circumstances a court would allow an acquirer out of a deal on account of a standard MAE clause, it is important for the acquirer to understand the uphill battle it faces in this context. Given the uncertainty surrounding MAEs, if there is a specific event that would make an acquirer reluctant to close the transaction, it may be worth addressing those issues directly elsewhere in the transaction documents. Additionally, an acquirer should include "forward looking" language into an MAE clause which would include prospective damage to the target's future earnings.

[178] Notwithstanding the high bar and considerable uncertainty associated with MAEs, an MAE closing condition remains an important tool for an acquirer to include in an acquisition agreement. Even if the ultimate success of an MAE claim is far from clear, an acquirer's ability to threaten to make an MAE claim remains a powerful negotiating weapon, potentially allowing the acquirer to negotiate a purchase price or other accommodation under certain circumstances.

PUBLIC DISCLOSURES AND PRESS ANNOUNCEMENTS

Court Decisions

[179] In *Basic v. Levinson*,[53] the U.S. Supreme Court made clear that a target's board may be liable for misleading investors about the existence or nonexistence of discussions regarding mergers or other extraordinary corporate events but stopped short of imposing a duty to disclose ongoing merger discussions. There is generally no affirmative duty to disclose merger discussions except when a shareholder has a duty to amend its Schedule 13D or to the extent that the parties believe that there may have been unauthorized "leaks" or to correct false or misleading statements that company representatives may have made to the press or analysts. However, issuers cannot falsely deny that merger negotiations are occurring.

Stock Exchange Rules

[180] The NYSE rules require "a frank and explicit announcement" whenever "rumors or unusual market activity indicate that information on impending developments has leaked out." The American Stock Exchange has a similar rule, and NASDAQ takes a similar position.

---

[51] *Id.* at 68.

[52] Hexion Specialty Chems., Inc. v. Huntsman Corp., 965 A.2d 715, 738 (Del. Ch. 2008).

[53] *Basic Inc. v. Levinson*, 485 U.S. 224 (1988).

HOSTILE ACQUISITIONS

[181] If an acquirer and its target fail to reach agreement on a transaction, several means are available to increase pressure on the target's management and board to consider a bona fide acquisition proposal or, ultimately, to pursue a transaction without the support of the target's management and board. While such "hostile" actions generally will strain relations between an acquirer and its target, the fiduciary duties of the target's management and board will likely preclude it from ignoring entirely a proposal that could increase value for its shareholders.

Understanding the Target's Takeover Defenses

[182] If an acquirer is interested in pursuing a hostile acquisition of a U.S. public company, the first step is understanding the target's takeover defenses. The principal result of these defenses is to strengthen the negotiating position of the target against hostile bidders so that the target's board can obtain the results it believes to be in the best interests of its shareholders. Despite how strong takeover defenses may seem, however, defenses make it more difficult, but not impossible, for an acquirer to acquire its target.

Poison Pills

[183] The strongest, and most famous, takeover defense employed by U.S. public companies is the shareholder rights plan, known as the "poison pill." Under a typical shareholder rights plan, once a bidder acquires, or announces an intention to acquire, more than a specified percentage of the target's stock,[54] all holders other than the bidder may buy additional shares of the target's stock at a substantial discount (a "flip-in plan"). The plans may also provide that, in the event the target is ultimately acquired, the rights become exercisable to buy shares of the acquirer, again at a substantial discount (a "flip-over plan"). A rights plan typically does not require shareholder approval, as the rights plan falls within the board's power to declare a dividend.

[184] A rights plan is highly effective against hostile bids because it substantially dilutes the acquirer and makes the acquisition significantly more expensive.

[185] However, a key limitation of rights plans is the ability of an acquirer to wage a proxy fight to replace the target's incumbent directors in connection with a hostile bid. If the acquirer can wrest control of the board, the poison pill can then be redeemed or amended by the friendly board to exempt the acquirer. This is more difficult to achieve if the target has a staggered board as described below.

[186] The prevalence of poison pills in the U.S. corporate landscape ebbs and flows based on a variety of factors, including the influence of shareholder activists and performance of the U.S. stock markets. Based largely on the growing influence of

[54] A 10% to 15% threshold is common, though stockholders generally favor higher thresholds such as 20%. The lower the threshold, the more aggressive the poison pill.

shareholder activists, in recent times there are fewer U.S. corporations that have poison pills than there have been in the past. However, while the market has been more skeptical of poison pills, there is a general trend favoring poison pills in Delaware case law.[55]

Provisions in Organizational Documents

[187] U.S. public companies may include in their organizational documents certain takeover defenses that make them far less attractive to a would-be acquirer.

Supermajority Voting and Fair Price Provisions

[188] Organizational documents may require a supermajority vote for certain acts, including amending the charter, making the removal of other defensive provisions more difficult. A provision could require that a merger may only be approved by a supermajority, or require such approval to amend certain parts of the charter (including the supermajority provision itself). A common use of supermajority voting is in connection with "fair price" provisions, which require an acquirer to pay at least the same price in the second-step squeeze-out merger as it does in the first-step tender offer, unless the merger was approved by a supermajority. A fair price provision alone won't prevent a hostile takeover by a well-financed acquirer prepared to make a bid for all outstanding shares of the target, but they can help to ensure shareholders won't tender their shares out of fear of receiving a lower price at the squeeze-out. Further, "fair price" provisions do increase cost and uncertainty in a transaction, which can be enough to deter a potential acquirer, especially if the source of financing for the transaction is concerned about being undersecured.

Staggered Boards

[189] Staggered board provisions set multiyear overlapping terms (three years is common) for directors that prevent immediate replacement of a majority of the target's board, thus making it more difficult for an acquirer to obtain board control. Achieving this control is often the only way to achieve certain ends (such as the removal of a poison pill), which makes this provision especially effective when paired with other defenses. Staggered boards are often called classified boards, after the classes that the directors on staggered boards belong to, each having its own time for election.

[190] As with poison pills, there are fewer corporations that have staggered boards today than in the past, though they are still quite common. Other charter provisions that allow for board control of a board are popular as well, such as "blank check" authorization, which allow the board to create a new series of preferred stock that may have special voting, conversation or control rights which would make a takeover more difficult.

[55] *See e.g., Third Point v. Ruprecht*, 2014 WL 1922029 (Del. Ch. May 2, 2014).

No Removal of Directors without Cause

[191] The DGCL provides that directors of a staggered board can be removed by the shareholders only for cause absent a charter providing otherwise. The requirement of cause limits the ability of an insurgent to facilitate a takeover proposal by removing some or all of the directors before their terms are completed. The directors of a Delaware corporation that does not have a staggered board can be removed with or without cause by the majority of its shareholders.[56] Like other charter provisions discussed herein, the rules in this regard vary from state to state.

Exclusive Power of Board of Directors to Fill Vacancy or Newly Created Directorship

[192] While the DGCL establishes a default rule that vacancies and newly created directorships may be filled by a majority of the directors then in office, this can be overridden by contrary text in the charter or bylaws.[57] In order to prevent an insurgent from using a bylaw amendment to increase the size of the board and then filling the newly created board seats[58], many corporate charters provide that only incumbent directors have the power to nominate individuals to fill vacancies created on the board of directors through removal, resignation, an increase in the size of the board or otherwise. A charter provision fixing the number of directors, or giving the board the authority to fix its own size within limits, can also complement this concept.

No Action without Meetings/No Shareholder Right to Call Meetings

[193] The default rule under Delaware law is that unless a corporation's charter provides otherwise, any action that may be taken at a stockholder meeting may also be taken through written consent of the required stockholders without holding a meeting.[59] Delaware law also establishes that special meetings of the stockholders may be called by the board of directors or by any person authorized by the charter or the bylaws.[60] If stockholders have the right to call special meetings or to take action by written consent, an insurgent can engage in proxy contests to gain control of the board of directors at any time of the year, not just at the annual meeting.

---

[56] *See Frechter v. Zier*, 2017 WL 345142, at 4 (Del. Ch. Jan. 24, 2017) holding that a corporation's bylaws requiring a supermajority stockholder vote for the removal of directors were invalid and that Section 141(k) mandates that a majority of stockholders may remove directors with or without cause.

[57] 8 *Del. C.* § 223(a)(1).

[58] *See, e.g., Richman v. DeVal Aerodynamics, Inc.*, 183 A.2d569, 572 (Del. Ch. 1962) (holding that, absent a contrary provision in the charter, stockholders could use an amendment to the bylaws to allow stockholders to create additional directorships and elect directors to fill those positions without first amending the charter).

[59] 8 *Del. C.* § 228.

[60] 8 *Del. C.* § 211(d).

[194] To protect against this threat and force insurgents to act through annual meetings, the corporate charter of a Delaware corporation can eliminate the right of stockholders to act through written consent, and the charter or bylaws can provide that only the board of directors or specified officers have the power to call a special meeting. If provisions of this nature are combined with a staggered board, a proxy fight to gain control of the board could be required to be conducted through two consecutive annual meetings.

State Anti-takeover Laws

[195] State anti-takeover laws vary by state. There are four main types of anti-takeover statutes: (i) business combination statutes, (ii) control share acquisition statutes, (iii) constituency statutes and (iv) fair price statutes. A prominent example of a business combination statute is in Delaware, which prohibits an interested stockholder (*i.e.*, a person who acquires 15% or more of a Delaware corporation's outstanding voting stock without the board's consent) from effecting a business combination with the corporation for three years.[61] The business combination statute in New York establishes a moratorium on business combinations with interested stockholders for five years.[62] Control share acquisition statutes which have been adopted by numerous states including Florida, Massachusetts and Nevada limit the right of an acquirer holding over a stated percentage of the company's stock to vote its shares in the target unless and until the disinterested shareholders ratify the transaction. Several states including New York, Pennsylvania, Connecticut and Ohio have enacted constituency statutes, which permit boards to consider employee, community and long-term corporate interests in deciding whether to pursue a deal or when deciding between two competing deals. Some states, including New York, Pennsylvania, Nevada and Connecticut have adopted fair price statutes, which require that all of the target's stockholders receive the highest cash price paid by the acquirer to any other stockholder. State anti-takeover laws usually permit companies to opt out of or (or in some cases, not opt in) negate the applicability of such laws in their charters.

Pursuing Hostile Acquisition of Control

Foothold Acquisitions/Agreements with Large Shareholders

[196] Two strategies discussed above that can be used to guard (or hedge) against competition from a topping bidder in a friendly deal can also be used by an acquirer in the context of a hostile deal: (i) buying shares of the target in the open market to obtain a foothold ownership interest in the target and (ii) entering into support agreements with large shareholders of the target. Subject to the restrictions, reporting obligations and other considerations discussed above, these may be appropriate strategies for a hostile acquirer to consider in connection with a hostile takeover.

[61] 8 Del. C. § 203(a).
[62] N.Y. Bus. Corp. Law § 912.

Bear Hugs

[197] A bear hug letter is an unsolicited proposal by a potential acquirer to enter into a negotiated transaction with a target. Often bear hug letters request a friendly negotiation, but contain a threat (whether express or implicit) that such potential acquirer will take its offer directly to the target's shareholders (through, for example, a hostile tender offer (*see* below)) if the board does not negotiate. Some bear hug letters are delivered privately to the management and/or the board of directors of the target (which the target may choose to disclose), while other bear hug letters are publicly filed and announced. The target's board of directors, faced with a public announcement of the proposal, may feel pressured to negotiate a deal, or structure an alternative transaction, in anticipation of a hostile bid or shareholder dissatisfaction (or litigation) if the bidder goes away.

Hostile Tender Offers

[198] Another means for an acquirer to seek a hostile acquisition is through a tender offer directly to the target's shareholders. Since such an offer is made directly to the target's shareholders, support of the target's management and board is not required. Generally, the most important advantage of a tender offer is speed (*e.g.*, an all-cash tender offer can be completed in 20 business days). Tender offers can be risky, however, for a number of reasons, including: (i) the acquirer must rely solely on publicly available information about the target, (ii) the target may have certain takeover defenses in place (*e.g.*, if a target company has a poison pill in place, an acquirer would not be able to close the hostile tender offer unless and until the pill is redeemed, either voluntarily or as ordered by a court.), (iii) state anti-takeover statutes may apply, (iv) there may be negative publicity concerns and (v) significant costs associated with unsolicited tender offers.

Proxy Fights

[199] Acquiring control of a target by soliciting shareholder proxies or consents to elect a majority of the board of directors of a target might be an attractive means to accomplish an acquisition. Often, proxy fights are used in conjunction with a firm offer to the shareholders in a hostile takeover contest. In that case, the bidder seeks to replace a majority of the target's board of directors and to dismantle takeover defenses, such as poison pills, by soliciting votes (or proxies) at an annual meeting or special meeting of the shareholder or through action by written consent. Once the board is controlled by bidder-nominated directors and takeover barriers are eliminated, an acquisition can proceed through either a merger, a tender offer or both.

LIKELIHOOD OF LITIGATION

[200] A party considering acquiring a U.S. public company should understand in advance the U.S. litigation climate. Even in the context of friendly deals that offer the target shareholders a substantial premium, it is routine for plaintiffs' lawyers to bring shareholder class action lawsuits against both the target and the acquirer as soon as the deal is announced.[63] Not surprisingly, litigation (initiated by the target and/or the target's shareholders) is even more likely in the context of a hostile deal. Potential acquirers should therefore be prepared for such litigation and understand the associated risks before attempting to acquire public companies in the United States.

SECURITIES OFFERINGS IN THE UNITED STATES BY FOREIGN ISSUERS

[201] The U.S. equity capital markets have been very attractive to foreign issuers for many years. The advent of globally integrated trading markets for equity securities has facilitated capital formation for foreign issuers and underscored the value to foreign issuers of raising equity capital through registered offerings in the U.S. capital market. Despite the burdens associated with registered public offerings, numerous foreign companies have found that the U.S. capital markets offer access to vast new sources of equity capital and opportunities to broaden their shareholder base, open up new trading markets for their securities and enhance the overall valuation of their equity securities. In addition, registered securities of a foreign company can serve as a "currency" for acquiring a U.S. business.

[202] Foreign issuers have also been active participants in the private U.S. capital markets. SEC Rule 144A[64] establishes a nonexclusive "safe harbor" from the registration requirements of the Securities Act of 1933, as amended (the "Securities Act"),[65] for the resale of securities issued in a nonpublic offering. Issuers relying upon Rule 144A may avoid compliance with the relatively burdensome obligations involved in the preparation of a Securities Act registration statement. They may also avoid compliance with SEC requirements concerning disclosure, accounting (including reconciliation of financial statements to U.S. generally accepted accounting principles) and ongoing periodic reporting requirements pursuant to the Securities Exchange

[63] Historically, in Delaware, where more than half of the U.S. publicly traded companies are incorporated, courts regularly approved "disclosure-only" settlements in shareholder class actions challenging public company mergers and acquisitions. In those settlements, the company and director-defendants typically would obtain a global release of all known and unknown claims in exchange for supplemental disclosures (which disclosures were often of questionable and/or minimal value) in the proxy statement prior to the shareholder vote on the transaction. Recently, however, Delaware courts have increasingly scrutinized such disclosure-only settlements, warning that "practitioners should expect that disclosure settlements are likely to be met with continued disfavor in the future unless the supplemental disclosures address a plainly material misrepresentation or omission, and the subject matter of the proposed release is narrowly circumscribed" (*In re Trulia, Inc. S'holder Litig.*, 129 A.3d 884, 898 (Del. Ch. 2016)).

[64] 17 C.F.R. §230.144A.

[65] 15 U.S.C. §77a et seq.

Act of 1934, as amended (the "Exchange Act"),[66] in addition to the disclosure and other requirements of the Sarbanes-Oxley Act of 2002 (collectively with the rules and regulations being adopted under such act, the "Sarbanes-Oxley")[67] and the Dodd-Frank Wall Street Reform and Consumer Protection Act which became law in July 2010 (collectively with the rules and regulations being adopted under such act, the "Dodd-Frank Act").[68]

[203] Issuing securities in the United States by means of a public offering requires a foreign company to comply with a variety of U.S. federal and state securities laws and other regulations. First, a public offering of securities requires the preparation and filing of a registration statement with the SEC. The registration requirements also apply to the issuance of securities in tender offers, mergers, exchange offers or other business combinations in which shareholders are asked to vote or otherwise make an election to receive new securities.[69] Second, companies that have registered securities for public sale in the United States or have securities listed on a U.S. stock exchange (which include NYSE, NYSE MKT (formerly known as NYSE Amex)[70] and NASDAQ) are subject to the ongoing public reporting requirements under the Exchange Act. Third, each U.S. state also regulates the offering of securities. Finally, U.S. stock exchanges impose rules on listed companies that address a broad range of matters relating to, among other things, the issuance of securities, disclosure of corporate developments, corporate governance and the rights of shareholders.

[204] This section summarizes the requirements under U.S. securities laws that a foreign company (other than a Canadian issuer that elects to comply with the SEC's Multi-Jurisdictional Disclosure System) must comply with in making a registered public offering of securities in the United States.

REGISTRATION AND OTHER U.S. LEGAL REQUIREMENTS

Introduction

[205] As a general rule, the Securities Act requires a company to file the appropriate registration statement before the company can publicly offer securities in the United States. Before the securities can be sold, the registration statement must become effective, either by SEC declaration, or automatically for "well-known seasoned issuers."[71] Furthermore, such securities may not be distributed for sale or delivery unless accompanied or preceded by a prospectus that meets the requirements of the Securities Act. Use of the registration statement and prospectus is designed to inform investors of the nature and risks of an investment in the company.

---

[66] 15 U.S.C. §78a et seq.
[67] Pub. L. 107-204, 116 Stat. 745 (2002).
[68] Pub. L. 111-203, 124 Stat. 1376 (2010).
[69] 17 C.F.R. §230.145.
[70] Effective May 2012, NYSE Amex was renamed NYSE MKT. The options market associated with NYSE MKT continues to do business under the name NYSE Amex Options.
[71] As defined in 17 C.F.R. §230.405.

[206] For a variety of reasons, it is often not feasible or advisable for foreign companies to list their securities directly on U.S. stock exchanges. Therefore, foreign companies commonly offer equity securities in the United States through the issuance of ADRs. ADRs are negotiable receipts registered in the name of the holder that evidence underlying shares of non-U.S. equity securities. ADRs are issued by a U.S. depositary, usually a bank, against the deposit of a foreign company's equity securities with a custodian bank, usually located in the foreign company's home country, that acts as an agent for the U.S. depositary bank.

[207] In connection with a public offering of Level III ADRs[72] by a foreign company in the United States, both the company's securities and the ADRs representing those securities must be registered under the Securities Act. As described below, Securities Act registration of the ADRs is effectuated by having the U.S. depositary bank file a Form F-6 with the SEC, and the company will file a Form F-1 (or, in some cases, a Form F-3) with the SEC to register its underlying securities. The company's underlying securities must also be registered under the Exchange Act by filing a Form 8-A or Form 20-F with the SEC.

Registration of the Underlying Securities under the Securities Act

Foreign Private Issuers

[208] Foreign private issuers offering Level III ADRs to the U.S. public must register the shares underlying those ADRs under the Securities Act. A company organized outside of the United States is a "foreign private issuer" unless more than 50% of its outstanding voting stock is directly or indirectly owned of record by residents of the United States and one of the following is true: (i) the majority of its executive officers or directors are U.S. citizens or residents; (ii) more than 50% of its assets are located in the United States; or (iii) its business is administered principally in the United States.[73] In determining the percentage of its stock held by U.S. residents, a foreign company is required to look through brokers, dealers, banks and other nominees located in: (i) the United States; (ii) the issuer's home jurisdiction; and (iii) the jurisdiction that is the primary trading market for the issuer's voting securities, to determine if the owner of the underlying account is a U.S. resident. Foreign companies that do not meet the definition of "foreign private issuer" are subject to the same requirements under U.S. securities laws as U.S. issuers.

[72] ADRs are typically offered pursuant to Level I, II or III programs. Only Level III programs involve a capital raising transaction and a public offering of the ADRs in the United States. While outside the scope of this section, foreign private issuers may also opt to conduct a "restricted" ADR program pursuant to Rule 144A, Regulation S or other available exemption under the Securities Act.

[73] 17 C.F.R. §240.3b-4.

[209] Along with being subject to the disclosure requirements applicable to foreign private issuers, which are less demanding than the requirements applicable to U.S. issuers, foreign private issuers are:

- exempt from the proxy rules applicable to U.S. issuers under section 14 of the Exchange Act;[74]
- not subject to the reporting requirements or the requirement to forfeit short-swing profits when buying or selling securities of the issuer that apply to directors, executive officers and large shareholders of an issuer under section 16 of the Exchange Act;[75] and
- not subject to the requirements of Regulation FD relating to selective disclosure by an issuer of material, nonpublic information relating to the issuer.[76]

Registration Forms: Forms F-1, F-3, and F-4

[210] Form F-1 is the form of registration statement typically required of foreign private issuers raising capital in the U.S. markets for the first time. A foreign private issuer that is subject to the reporting requirements and has timely filed all required reports during the preceding 12 months (or such shorter period as it was required to file reports), and that meets certain other requirements, may respond to certain disclosure requirements of Form F-1 by incorporating by reference from its reports previously filed with the SEC. These issuers may not incorporate by reference to reports to be filed after the effective date of the Form F-1. As a result, these foreign private issuers must file post-effective amendments to update outdated or "stale" information in their registration statements, which the SEC must declare effective.

[211] More seasoned foreign private issuers that have been subject to the reporting requirements of the Exchange Act for at least 12 months and that have timely filed all required reports during the preceding 12 months, subject to certain other requirements, may use Form F-3, a short-form registration statement that allows a foreign private issuer to incorporate much of the required information by reference to its past and future Exchange Act reports, keeping the registration statement current or "evergreen." One of the important requirements for use of Form F-3 in primary offerings of securities for cash (as opposed to secondary offerings by existing shareholders) is that the foreign private issuer must have common equity securities with a market value of at least US$75m[77] outstanding and in the hands of shareholders that are not affiliates[78] of the foreign private issuer. The notion behind this requirement is that information should be sufficiently available to the market regarding issuers with

[74] 15 U.S.C. §78n.
[75] 15 U.S.C. §78p.
[76] 17 C.F.R. §243.100 et seq.
[77] Foreign private issuers that have a market value held by non-affiliates of less than US$75 million may use Form F-3 to register any primary offering, provided that they have a class of equity security listed on a U.S. national securities exchange, are not and have not been shell companies for at least the past 12 months and have not sold a total amount of securities under this exception (including the securities proposed to be sold in this offering) that exceeds one-third (1/3) of their non-affiliate public float during the past 12 months.
[78] An "affiliate" of an issuer is a person or entity controlling, controlled by or under common control with the issuer. Securities Act Rule 405, 17 C.F.R. §230.405.

a substantial public "float" and a history of public reporting with the SEC, without requiring the issuer to reproduce voluminous disclosures in the prospectus.

[212] In cases where a foreign private issuer is offering ADRs directly to target shareholders in an exchange offer or as merger consideration, a registration statement on Form F-4 is required. Form F-4 allows correspondingly greater degrees of incorporation by reference if a foreign private issuer would otherwise be eligible to use Form F-3.[79]

[213] The more significant disclosure requirements generally applicable to registration statements are discussed below in *Disclosure in Registered Public Offerings and Ongoing Reporting Obligations.*

[214] Except as specifically noted below, the discussion that follows describes the issuance of securities in the United States by foreign private issuers that are offering securities in the United States for the first time and do not have listed securities on a U.S. securities exchange.

Exchange Act Registration and Reporting Obligations of Foreign Issuers

Registration

[215] The Exchange Act imposes registration requirements separate from the registration requirements of the Securities Act. Registration of the issuance of securities under the Securities Act does not satisfy the registration requirements of the Exchange Act. A foreign issuer is required to register its entire class of securities under the Exchange Act if: (i) the securities or ADRs representing the issuer's securities will be traded on a U.S. exchange or (ii) the securities are equity securities and are or will be held of record by either 2 000 or more persons worldwide or 500 or more persons who are not accredited investors, as well as more than 300 U.S. resident holders, and the foreign issuer has total assets exceeding US$10m.[80] In addition, if any securities are registered under the Securities Act, the issuer will be subject to the periodic reporting requirements under the Exchange Act at least through the end of the calendar year in which the registration occurs.[81]

[79] An issuer that does not qualify as a foreign private issuer would have to use Form S-1, S-3, or S-4 which, as a general matter, have similar eligibility requirements to their Form F-1, F-3, and F-4 counterparts. A discussion of the requirements of these forms is beyond the scope of this section.

[80] A foreign private issuer that has 300 or more U.S. resident holders of the securities of such class may be exempt from such registration by Exchange Act Rule 12g3-2(b) if the class of securities is not listed on a U.S. securities exchange, the issuer maintains a listing on a foreign exchange that constitutes its "primary trading market" and the issuer has published, in English, on its website, information that it is required to make public under the laws of its home country or under the requirements of its foreign exchange, which is discussed in "– Rule 12g3-2(b) Exemption."

[81] Section 15(d) of the Exchange Act, 15 U.S.C. §78o(d). In order for a foreign private issuer to terminate its reporting obligations, it must meet the following tests: (i) the class of securities (a) has an average daily trading volume in the United States for a recent 12-month period of no greater than 5% of the average daily trading volume of the securities on a worldwide basis for the same period or (b) is held of record by less than either 300 persons worldwide or 300 persons in the United States; (ii) the foreign private issuer must have been a reporting company for at least 12 months, have filed

[216] If a foreign private issuer is already subject to the reporting requirements of the Exchange Act and is seeking to register a new class of securities under the Exchange Act, or is concurrently filing a registration statement under the Securities Act, the issuer is eligible to use a Form 8-A registration statement. Form 8-A is a short-form document that incorporates by reference certain information from the issuer's Securities Act document. If a foreign private issuer is not eligible to use Form 8-A, it must prepare a registration statement under the Exchange Act on Form 20-F, which requires substantial disclosure and may require several months to complete as a result of SEC review. Form 20-F is also the form used by foreign private issuers to file annual reports with the SEC. The disclosure requirements for Form 20-F are discussed in greater detail later in paragraphs 276–292.

[217] In the case of a listing on the NYSE, NYSE MKT or NASDAQ, the Exchange Act registration statement will become effective upon: (i) the later of receipt by the SEC of certification from the exchange or the filing of the Form 8-A with the SEC (if the securities are not concurrently being registered under the Securities Act), or (ii) the latest of receipt by the SEC of certification from the exchange, the filing of the Form 8-A with the SEC or the effectiveness of the Securities Act registration (if the securities are concurrently being registered under the Securities Act).

Periodic Reporting

Form 20-F

[218] If a company has a class of securities registered under the Exchange Act, it is required to file periodic reports with the SEC. Form 20-F is the annual report form used by foreign private issuers. It must be filed not later than 120 days after the end of the issuer's fiscal year. Typically, the comprehensive information contained in the registration statement used in connection with a public offering (or set forth in the Form 20-F filed in connection with the company's initial registration under the Exchange Act) is revised and updated to produce the Form 20-F annual report.

[219] An issuer's Chief Executive Officer ("CEO") and Chief Financial Officer ("CFO") are required to certify each time the issuer files an Exchange Act report, including, in the case of foreign private issuers, the issuer's Form 20-F, that they have read the report and that, to their knowledge, (i) the financial statements accurately reflect the issuer's financial position, and (ii) the report does not contain any material misstatements or omissions. They also certify that they:

---

all of its required reports and have filed at least one annual report under the Exchange Act; (iii) the foreign private issuer must not have sold securities in the United States, with certain exceptions, during the previous 12 months in an offering registered under the Securities Act; (iv) the foreign private issuer must, for at least 12 months prior to termination, have maintained a listing of the class of securities being terminated on one or more non-U.S. securities exchanges that, singly or in the aggregate, constitute the "primary trading market" for those securities; and (v) the foreign private issuer must comply with certain specified procedural requirements. *See* Exchange Act Rule 12h-6, 17 C.F.R. §240.12h-6.

(a) are responsible for establishing and maintaining the issuer's disclosure controls and procedures and internal control over financial reporting;
(b) have evaluated the effectiveness of those controls and procedures;
(c) have disclosed in the report any change in the issuer's internal control over financial reporting that has materially affected, or is reasonably likely to materially affect, the issuer's internal control over financial reporting; and
(d) have disclosed to the issuer's auditors and the audit committee of the issuer's board of directors:
- all significant deficiencies and material weaknesses in the design or operation of the issuer's internal control over financial reporting; and
- any fraud, whether or not material, that involves management or other employees who have a significant role in the issuer's internal control over financial reporting.

Form 6-K

[220] A foreign private issuer is not required to file quarterly or other interim reports with the SEC. However, it will be obliged to furnish to the SEC under cover of Form 6-K any significant information: (i) required to be disclosed publicly in the jurisdiction of its domicile, incorporation or organization, (ii) filed with and made public by a stock exchange on which the foreign private issuer's securities are traded, or (iii) distributed by the foreign private issuer to its security holders (either directly or by means of a press release). Information in the foregoing categories must be furnished to the SEC promptly after being made public. Reports on Form 6-K need not be certified by the foreign private issuer's CEO or CFO.

[221] Not all information made public must be furnished to the SEC under cover of Form 6-K. Essentially, all that the SEC requires is that information a foreign private issuer deems of material importance to its security holders, such as information relating to the acquisition of assets, the results of a resolution put to the vote of shareholders, a change in management or control, material legal proceedings, or material increases or decreases in outstanding securities or indebtedness be furnished to the SEC under cover of Form 6-K.

XBRL

[222] The SEC has adopted rules requiring companies to provide financial statement information in an interactive data format.[82] The interactive financial data must be filed with the SEC and posted on the issuer's corporate website. The interactive financial data rules apply to foreign private issuers that prepare their financial statements in accordance with U.S. generally accepted accounting principles ("U.S. GAAP") and to foreign private issuers that prepare their financial statements using International Financial Reporting Standards ("IFRS") as issued by the International Accounting Standards Board ("IASB").[83]

[82] *See* SEC Release Nos. 33-9002; 34-59324 (Jan. 30, 2009).
[83] *See* SEC Release Nos. 33-10320; 34-80128 (March 1, 2017).

Rule 12g3-2(b) Exemption

[223] Rule 12g3-2(b) permits a foreign private issuer to claim an exemption from Exchange Act reporting requirements in relation to any particular issuance of equity securities without the need for an application or notification to the SEC if:

- the issuer, at the time of issuance of the securities, maintains a listing of the subject class of securities on one or more non-U.S. exchanges that constitute the primary trading market for those securities;
- the issuer is not required to file or furnish reports under section 13(a) or 15(d) of the Exchange Act; and
- the issuer publishes, in English, on its Internet website (or through an electronic information delivery system generally available to the public in its primary trading market) specified non-US disclosure documents that are required to be made public from the first day of its most recently completed fiscal year, unless the issuer is claiming the exemption upon or following its recent Exchange Act deregistration.

[224] This exemption is automatic for foreign private issuers that meet the conditions specified above. In order to maintain the exemption, the issuer must publish its non-U.S. disclosure documents on an ongoing basis and for each subsequent fiscal year, in English, on its Internet website or through an electronic information delivery system generally available to the public in its primary trading market. The issuer must maintain a non-U.S. listing of the subject class of securities and not register a class of securities under section 12 of the Exchange Act or incur reporting obligations under 15(d) of the Exchange Act.

[225] Once obtained, the Rule 12g3-2(b) exemption will remain in effect until the foreign private issuer either:

- no longer electronically publishes, in English, the required non-U.S. disclosure documents;
- no longer maintains a listing for the subject class of securities on one or more exchanges in a primary trading market; or
- registers a class of securities under section 12 of the Exchange Act or incurs reporting obligations under section 15(d) of the Exchange Act.

[226] Although complying with Rule 12g3-2(b) is only one way to satisfy the information availability requirement of Rule 144A, it is the most frequent way for a non-SEC reporting foreign company issuing ADRs pursuant to Rule 144A to satisfy that requirement.

Termination of Registration

[227] Rule 12h-6 under the Exchange Act permits a foreign private issuer of equity securities to terminate its Exchange Act reporting obligations if its average daily trading volume in the United States is less than 5% of its worldwide trading volume in a recent 12-month period. The issuer may include off-market transactions, including transactions in alternate trading systems, for the purpose of making this calculation.

In certain circumstances the issuer must wait 12 months before terminating its Exchange Act reporting obligations. Foreign private issuers may also terminate their reporting obligations if they have less than 300 holders on any date within 120 days before filing for deregistration. Foreign private issuers must have filed Exchange Act reports for 12 months before they can terminate their registration obligations.

Beneficial Ownership Reports

[228] Section 13(d) of the Exchange Act[84] requires that any person who acquires, directly or indirectly, beneficial ownership[85] of more than 5% of any class of equity securities that is registered under the Exchange Act report such beneficial ownership to the issuer, the exchange (if any) on which the security is listed and the SEC. This rule also applies to any person whose ownership of equity securities exceeds the 5% level at the time the issuer registers under the Exchange Act. Regulation 13D-G of the Exchange Act sets out the form of schedule required to be filed. The applicable schedule usually must be filed within 10 days after an cquisition of securities that brings the owner above the 5% level and must be amended promptly after any material change in the information disclosed in the filing. The Dodd-Frank Act permits the SEC to shorten the 10-day period. An increase or decrease in percentage ownership of 1% or more is deemed material for this purpose.

The Sarbanes-Oxley Act

[229] Foreign companies whose equity securities or ADRs are registered with the SEC pursuant to the Exchange Act are required to comply with the Sarbanes-Oxley Act, which imposes additional disclosure, corporate governance and certification obligations upon companies and their management. *Annex A* to this section contains a summary of the Sarbanes-Oxley Act and its applicable requirements, which should be reviewed carefully when contemplating a registered offering.

Foreign Corrupt Practices Act

[230] The U.S. securities laws subject all issuers who publicly offer securities or choose to list an existing class of securities on a national securities exchange to the provisions of the Foreign Corrupt Practices Act (the "FCPA"). The FCPA prohibits such issuers and all officers, directors, employees and shareholders acting on behalf of such issuers from offering bribes to any foreign official, foreign political party, party official or candidate for political office for the purpose of influencing any act or decision in order to obtain business. The FCPA also prohibits payments to any person to serve as an agent in an effort to influence the persons listed in the previous sentence. Foreign private issuers found to have violated the anti-bribery provisions

[84] 15 U.S.C. §78m(d).

[85] 17 C.F.R. §240.13d-3 defines "beneficial owner" to include any person who, directly or indirectly, has the power to invest or vote the securities.

of the FCPA are subject to a fine of up to US$2m, and officers, directors, employees, agents and shareholders who are convicted of willful violations of the FCPA are subject to a fine of up to US$100 000 and imprisonment for up to five years.

[231] The FCPA also imposes accounting and recordkeeping standards, requiring those who are subject to its provisions:

(i) to make and keep books, records and accounts that accurately reflect transactions and dispositions of assets of the company; and
(ii) to devise and maintain a system of internal accounting controls sufficient to provide reasonable assurance that:
  - transactions are executed in accordance with management's authorization;
  - transactions are properly recorded as to permit preparation of financial statements and to maintain accountability for assets;
  - access to assets is permitted only with management's authorization; and
  - comparisons between recorded accountability of assets with actual assets are made at reasonable intervals and appropriate action is taken with respect to any differences discovered.

[232] Regulations adopted under the FCPA prohibit any falsification of records that must be kept and also prohibit a company's officers and directors from making any false or misleading statements or omissions in connection with audits or documents to be filed with the SEC. Willful violations of the recordkeeping and accounting controls provisions of the FCPA may lead to criminal liability.

JOBS Act

[233] The Jumpstart Our Business Startups Act of 2012 and the rules and regulations that implement that Act (collectively, the "JOBS Act") was enacted in an effort to create additional jobs in the United States through the growth of small companies and startups. To achieve that goal, the JOBS Act aimed to ease certain regulatory burdens on smaller companies and to expand and facilitate capital formation in the United States by, among other things, making changes to certain federal securities laws and rules governing the U.S. capital formation process. Although many of the granular details of the JOBS Act are beyond the scope of this chapter, some of the more substantial measures through which the JOBS Act aimed to expand and facilitate U.S. capital formation include:

- Exempting "emerging growth companies"[86] from certain disclosure, internal control certification and other requirements in connection with initial public offerings.

[86] The JOBS Act defines an "emerging growth company" as a company with annual gross revenues of less than US$1 070 000 000 (initially US$1bn, but adjusted for inflation by the SEC in 2017) during its most recent fiscal year, and a company will remain an "emerging growth company" until the earlier of (i) the end of the fiscal year in which its revenues exceed US$1 070 000 000, (ii) the end of the fiscal year following the fifth anniversary of its initial public offering, (iii) the date on which it has issued, publicly or privately, more than US$1bn in nonconvertible debt over a three-year period and (iv) the date on which it becomes a "large accelerated filer" under U.S. federal securities laws.

- Lifting the ban on general solicitation and general advertising in certain private placements of securities.
- Creating an exemption under the Securities Act for certain "crowdfunding" offerings whereby eligible companies may conduct small securities offerings (*i.e.*, an issuer is permitted to raise a maximum aggregate amount of US$1 070 000 in a 12-month period) through the use of Internet "funding portals" registered with the SEC.
- Amending the Securities Act to permit companies to conduct offerings to raise up to US$50m through a "mini-registration" process similar to Regulation A (sometimes referred to as Regulation A+) (*see* paragraph 318 below).
- Implementing higher triggering thresholds for SEC reporting obligations under the Exchange Act (*e.g.*, the holders of record threshold for triggering Section 12(g) registration for issuers (other than banks and bank holding companies) was raised from 500 or more persons to either (i) 2 000 or more persons or (ii) 500 or more persons who are "not accredited investors" (*see* the discussion of this concept below)).

State Regulation

[234] While each of the states within the United States also has securities laws, known as "blue sky" laws, which require the registration of securities publicly offered within the state's borders, state registration can be avoided in most public offerings and private placements. Section 18 of the Securities Act[87] provides that, among other things, offerings of securities that are listed or authorized for listing on the NYSE, NYSE MKT or NASDAQ are exempt from registration under state blue sky laws. Private placements that are exempt from Securities Act registration pursuant to SEC rules or regulation issued under section 4(a)(2)[88] of the Securities Act (*i.e.*, Rule 506 of Regulation D) are also exempt from registration under state blue sky laws, but a state can still require that issuers make a notice filing with the state and pay a fee. Private placements are discussed in greater detail later in paragraphs 301–372.

THE REGISTRATION PROCESS

Documentation in Public Offerings

[235] In connection with a registered public offering of securities or ADRs, two main documents must be prepared: the prospectus and the underwriting agreement.

[87] 15 U.S.C. §77r.
[88] 15 U.S.C. §77d(2).

Prospectus

[236] As discussed in detail below under *Disclosure in Registered Public Offerings and Ongoing Reporting Obligations*, a prospectus is the offering document that is delivered to prospective purchasers of SEC-registered securities and conforms to the requirements of the SEC registration form on which the securities have been registered.

Underwriting Agreement

[237] The underwriting agreement is the contract pursuant to which the underwriters agree to purchase the securities from the issuer. While the form of the underwriting agreement will depend on who the managing underwriter is, the substance of the underwriting agreement is fairly standard. Discussed below are a number of issues that customarily are the subject of close consideration by issuers.

Representations and Indemnities for Material Misstatements or Omissions

[238] The underwriting agreement contains representations and warranties made by the issuer concerning the issuer's due organization, compliance with laws, the veracity of the disclosure in the prospectus and numerous other matters. One issue that is typically the subject of much discussion is the representation of the selling shareholders (if any shareholders are selling shares in the offering) with respect to the absence of material misstatements in, or omissions from, the registration statement. The underwriters will typically require selling shareholders to represent that there are no material misstatements in or omissions from the registration statement. The selling shareholders may resist such a provision if they are not familiar with the details of the issuer's business (*i.e.*, where the selling shareholders are "silent" investors), have not participated in the preparation of the registration statement, and/or are not participating significantly in the offering (*i.e.*, the number of shares being offered by them is small in comparison to the aggregate number of shares being offered). A related issue is the extent to which the selling shareholders will indemnify the underwriters for liabilities arising out of material misstatements or omissions. If the selling shareholders are required to indemnify the underwriters for liabilities arising out of material misstatements or omissions, they may seek to have their exposure limited (*e.g.*, to the proceeds of the offering that they receive).

"Blackout Period"

[239] The underwriting agreement will typically contain a number of agreements by the issuer. One of these agreements is commonly referred to as the "blackout" provision, pursuant to which the issuer agrees for a specified period of time not to offer, sell, contract to sell or otherwise dispose of any securities of the issuer that are similar to the securities that are the subject of the underwriting agreement or of any securities convertible into similar securities of the issuer. The parties may exclude from this provision issuances pursuant to outstanding options, to the conversion of outstanding convertible securities, or to employee compensation plans. The "blackout" period is typically 90 to 180 days in the case of an initial public offering of equity securities, but may be longer or shorter.

Payment of Expenses

[240] In the underwriting agreement, the issuer generally agrees to pay certain expenses of the offering. Typically the issuer will agree to pay the fees and expenses of its own counsel and accountants, of the depositary, of the transfer agent and the registrar, the filing fees in connection with the Securities Act and various state securities or "blue sky" registrations and review of the offering by the Financial Industry Regulatory Authority ("FINRA") (the successor to The National Association of Securities Dealers, Inc.), and the printing expenses. The underwriters typically pay the fees and expenses of their own counsel in connection with a registered public offering, although this arrangement may be viewed as negotiable by the underwriters.

"Market-Out Provisions"

[241] Customarily included among the conditions to closing is a provision commonly referred to as a "market-out provision." This provision will allow the underwriters to choose not to close, or alternatively to terminate, their obligations under the underwriting agreement if any one of a number of events occurs. Among these events are: (i) a suspension or limitation in trading in securities generally on the NYSE or the issuer's home exchange; (ii) a general moratorium on banking activities in New York or the financial center of the issuer's home country; (iii) the outbreak or escalation of hostilities involving the United States or the issuer's home country; (iv) any other change in the securities markets in general or in political, financial or economic conditions; or (v) any material adverse change involving the issuer or its business which, in the judgment of the managing underwriter, makes it inadvisable or impracticable to proceed with the offering on the terms contemplated in the underwriting agreement. The effect of this is to place on the issuer and the selling shareholders the risk of an independent and unforeseen event which adversely affects the underwriters' ability to market the securities. While this provision is often the subject of much discussion, there are few instances in which an underwriter has invoked such a clause to terminate an underwriting commitment.

Indemnification/Contribution

[242] Underwriting agreements include a provision in which the issuer agrees to indemnify the underwriters for losses and costs that the underwriters suffer or incur resulting from material misstatements in, or omissions of material information from, the registration statement. Typically, the issuer does not indemnify for information provided by the underwriters specifically for use in the registration statement—which is usually quite limited. In return, the underwriters agree to indemnify the issuer for any losses that the issuer suffers or costs that it incurs resulting from material misstatements in, or omissions from, the information provided by the underwriters specifically for use in the registration statement.

[243] It is the SEC's view that indemnification provisions are unenforceable because they are against public policy and prohibited by the Securities Act and the Exchange Act. Several U.S. courts have found such provisions unenforceable.

[244] For this reason, underwriting agreements also contain a provision providing for contribution by the issuer and the underwriters for losses suffered and costs incurred in relation to the relative benefits received by each party if the indemnification provision is found to be inapplicable or unenforceable.

Due Diligence

[245] In order to understand better the business of the issuer and to be able to assist in drafting an accurate and meaningful prospectus, the managing underwriter, its counsel and the issuer's counsel will simultaneously conduct an extensive review of the properties and material agreements of the issuer, including all loan agreements and debt instruments to which the issuer is party, and all material contracts and governmental authorizations. In addition, such parties will also conduct a series of discussions with the issuer's senior management, its financial staff and its outside accountants.

[246] This review also serves to establish a record that the underwriters have made a reasonable investigation upon which their "due diligence" defense against liability can be based. As discussed below, every person, other than the issuer, against whom liability may be asserted under the Securities Act may avoid such liability by showing that he or she had, after reasonable investigation, reasonable grounds to believe and did believe, that there were no material misstatements in or omissions from the registration statement.

[247] In addition to this managing underwriter's review, the underwriters seek to strengthen their "due diligence" defense by requiring delivery to them of opinions and letters from the issuer's counsel and accountants with respect to matters covered by the registration statement. The underwriting agreement will require that the issuer's counsel deliver an opinion as to the issuer's proper formation and authorization to do business, as to the valid issuance of the offered securities, and as to certain other legal matters, including the absence of material litigation, specified in the underwriting agreement.

[248] Because the Sarbanes-Oxley Act has imposed requirements on reporting companies regarding such things as corporate governance, audit committees and disclosure, underwriters will seek to limit liability by obtaining information from issuers relevant to the reporting obligations of that Act. For example, this may include inquiries into the existence of any financial arrangements between the issuer and its senior management. The underwriting agreement will also require that the issuer's counsel deliver an opinion regarding the adequacy of disclosure in the registration statement. Finally, the issuer will be asked to supply a "comfort letter"—a letter from its independent public accountants verifying various financial data contained in the registration statement.

Preparing the Registration Statement

[249] The issuer, its counsel and independent auditors typically have primary responsibility for preparing the first draft of the registration statement, which is then carefully reviewed and commented upon by the managing underwriter and its counsel. In the case of a prospectus relating to stock to be issued in a merger or an exchange offer, the acquirer and the target will work together to prepare the joint proxy statement/prospectus to be mailed to the shareholders of the target.[89] When the registration statement, including all relevant exhibits, is completed and assembled, it is filed with the SEC and, where required, with the various state securities commissioners and FINRA.[90,91]

[250] After filing, the SEC registration process can be expected to take approximately 45 to 90 days. Registration statements of first-time registrants are typically reviewed. While it is the SEC's policy to provide comments to the registrant within 30 days of the filing of the original registration statement and within 10 days of the filing of an amendment, the review process can take longer depending upon the complexity of the registrant's business and the SEC's workload. The SEC's policy is to issue a letter commenting upon areas of the disclosure in the registration statement deemed insufficient and asking clarifying questions where the SEC staff believes it requires more information. The issuer and its attorneys and accountants then prepare responses and, in rare instances, hold conferences with the SEC staff to discuss any unresolved issues. One or more amendments to the registration statement are usually required and additional comment letters from the SEC are common.

[251] The SEC's Office of International Corporate Finance makes a particular effort to be helpful and flexible when dealing with non-U.S. issuers. Although it will not do so for domestic issuers, the SEC staff has, in the past, shown a willingness to review registration statements of foreign issuers on an expedited basis under some circumstances. Also, it is the staff's policy that first-time foreign private issuers can submit registration statements for an initial public offering on a confidential basis before the document is actually filed and made publicly available. SEC staff members frequently make themselves available by telephone to foreign issuers and their advisors prior to the filing of the registration statement to discuss particular disclosure problems and will consider making accommodations for compelling reasons. On the other hand, foreign private issuers taking advantage of accommodation

[89] If a shareholder vote of the target is being solicited in connection with a merger and the target is subject to the Exchange Act proxy rules, then the prospectus included in the registration statement must also include certain information specified by those proxy rules. *See* General Instruction E. to Form F-4.

[90] Filing with FINRA, where applicable, is an obligation of the underwriters.

[91] Under the JOBS Act, if they have not previously filed a registration statement with the SEC, foreign private issuers and foreign government issuers may submit confidential draft registration statements to the SEC for its review. Additionally, any foreign private issuer that comes within the definition of an "emerging growth company" under the JOBS Act can use the confidential submission procedure to the same extent as a domestic "emerging growth company." However, foreign private issuers, whether submitting draft registration statements pursuant the SEC's nonpublic submission policy for non-U.S. issuers or as an "emerging growth company" under the JOBS Act, will be required to publicly file all previously submitted draft registration statements at or around the time they publicly file their registration statements.

for "emerging growth companies" under the JOBS Act can submit registration statements for an initial public offering on a confidential basis as long as they satisfy the requirements thereunder.

[252] Like U.S. issuers, foreign private issuers are required to file, among other things, Securities Act registration statements and Exchange Act reports electronically through the SEC's Electronic Data Gathering, Analysis and Retrieval, or EDGAR, system. Submissions made to the SEC on a confidential basis, such as a registration statement for a foreign private issuer's initial registered offering, will continue to be made in paper form.

[253] During the period after the registration statement is filed with the SEC, and prior to the registration statement being declared effective (the "pre-effective period"), the preliminary prospectus included in the registration statement is circulated by the underwriters to prospective investors. During this pre-effective period, offers to purchase can be solicited, but not accepted, as legally binding commitments. Also during this period, the managing underwriter will arrange for a series of presentations, commonly referred to as the "roadshow," by the issuer's executive officers to selected institutional investors in various cities. The basic financial terms (other than the public offering price and the price to the underwriters) of the underwriting agreement between the issuer and the managing underwriter, acting on behalf of the underwriting syndicate, are also negotiated in the pre-effective period.

Effectiveness of the Registration Statement and Pricing the Securities

[254] After the SEC has reviewed the final amendment to the registration statement and all outstanding comments have been resolved, the SEC will declare the registration statement effective.

[255] SEC rules require that the issuer disclose in the registration statement filed with the SEC a good faith estimate of the range of the maximum offering price and maximum number of ADRs to be offered. The negotiation of the financial terms between the issuer and the underwriters (including the determination of the public offering price) will be completed either immediately before or shortly after the registration statement is declared effective. If these negotiations are completed before the registration statement is declared effective, the underwriting agreement will be executed, a final "pricing" amendment to the registration statement will be filed with the SEC, and, immediately after the registration statement is declared effective, the underwriters will complete sales of shares to investors identified during the pre-effective period. If the offering is successful, all sales will be confirmed within hours, or even minutes, of SEC effectiveness.

[256] Rule 430A under the Securities Act[92] permits registration statements to be declared effective that do not include pricing information, so long as the

[92] 17 C.F.R. §230.430A.

registration statement is otherwise complete in all respects. If Rule 430A is being relied upon, the negotiation of the public offering price and underwriting discount will be completed shortly after the registration statement is declared effective. The underwriting agreement will then be executed and sales confirmed immediately thereafter. When the parties are relying upon Rule 430A, a copy of the final prospectus, reflecting the agreed-upon offering price and underwriting discount, must be filed with the SEC within two business days after the date of determination of the offering price.

Restrictions during Registration

[257] During the period from the time the issuer reaches an understanding with the underwriters or makes a decision to undertake an offering until the registration statement is declared effective and the prospectus delivery obligations have expired (the "registration period"), U.S. securities laws place certain restrictions on the release of information and on other market activities by the issuer and persons associated with, or acting on behalf of, the issuer. These restrictions apply whether such information is communicated within or outside of the United States. Communications in violation of U.S. securities laws and SEC rules is referred to as "gun jumping."

[258] The severity of the restrictions applicable to an issuer depends upon the size and length of reporting history of the issuer. Those that are "well-known seasoned issuers" may make offers before a registration statement is filed with the SEC. Prior to the filing of a registration statement, it is unlawful for all other issuers to offer to sell or to solicit an offer to buy any security. The term "offer" has been broadly construed by the SEC to include not just express offers by an issuer, but other publicity efforts, which "although not couched in terms of an express offer, may in fact contribute to conditioning the public mind or arousing public interest in the issuer or the securities of the issuer."[93]

[259] It is also unlawful to deliver a prospectus during the registration period relating to any security for which a registration statement has been filed unless the prospectus meets the technical and detailed disclosure requirements prescribed by the Securities Act. "Prospectus" is broadly defined under the Securities Act, and has been interpreted by the SEC to include written communications, including e-mails and other electronic documents, that could arguably encourage the sale of a security during the registration period as part of a selling effort. A quote from an executive of the issuer that appears in a newspaper story or on a radio or television interview can also constitute a "prospectus" in violation of this prohibition. Securities Act rules permit issuers and underwriters to use certain types of written offering materials not meeting the requirements of a prospectus, called "free writing prospectuses," so long as certain conditions are met, including that the information in the free writing prospectus not conflict with information contained in the registration statement, that in some cases the free writing prospectus be accompanied or preceded by a

[93] SEC Release No. 33-5180 (Aug. 16, 1971).

preliminary prospectus or a final prospectus, and that in some cases the free writing prospectus be filed with the SEC.

[260] The U.S. securities laws do not require a "news blackout" prior to the completion of the offering. However, communications during the registration period to the press, public or shareholders concerning the offering or other nonfactual information concerning the business or future prospects of the issuer should be carefully considered, generally discouraged and, in any case, held to a minimum. Such communications may be construed as part of a selling effort to "condition the market" and may result in delays in the offering schedule, and may potentially result in serious civil and criminal liability. Securities Act Rule 163A[94] provides that communications made more than 30 days prior to the filing of a registration statement will generally not be considered an offer of a security so long as the communication does not reference a securities offering, provided that reasonable steps are taken to prevent further distribution or publication of such communication during the 30 days immediately preceding the date of filing of the registration statement.

[261] Securities Act Rule 134,[95] which applies to communications made after a registration statement has been filed, and Rule 135,[96] which applies to all communications made during the registration period, set forth specific information notices regarding an offering that may be publicly disseminated without running afoul of the U.S. securities laws. The information permitted to be disclosed under these rules is quite limited. Also, Securities Act Rule 135e[97] provides a safe harbor for offshore press activities conducted in connection with an offering by a foreign private issuer or foreign government issuer, provided the offering is not being, or to be, conducted solely in the United States. Under this safe harbor, a foreign private issuer or foreign government issuer may provide foreign and U.S. journalists with access to offshore press conferences, offshore meetings with representatives of the issuer or press-related materials released offshore without engaging in gun jumping, provided that the conditions of the rule are satisfied. However, any press conference, meeting or press-related materials relating to the offering in any way should be reviewed by counsel.

[262] Issuers must also regulate communications made via the Internet or through their websites. During the registration period, issuers should limit both direct and hyperlinked information on their websites to prospectuses meeting the requirements of section 10 of the Securities Act and permissible communications under available safe harbors.[98] The posting of regularly released factual information, such as financial information, is generally permitted. Issuers undertaking an initial public offering should not establish a website contemporaneously with such initial public offering,

---

[94] 17 C.F.R. §230.163A.
[95] 17 C.F.R. §230.134.
[96] 17 C.F.R. §230.135.
[97] 17 C.F.R. §230.135e.
[98] SEC Release Nos 33-7856, 34-42728 (May 4, 2000).

as the content could be viewed as conditioning the market, without any "ordinary course of business" practice having been established.[99]

[263] In addition, subject to certain exceptions, issuers, underwriters and persons on behalf of whom securities are being distributed are also broadly prohibited, by Regulation M under the Exchange Act,[100] from bidding for or purchasing, or inducing others to bid for or purchase, certain securities until the subject distribution has been completed. The SEC's trading practices rules, including Regulation M, impose a number of restrictions particularly relevant to the activities of underwriters and their affiliates, such as "stabilization," "passive market-making" and the publication of analysts' research reports. A detailed discussion of these regulations is outside the scope of this section.

Liability under the U.S. Federal Securities Laws

Section 11 of the Securities Act

[264] The Securities Act can subject an issuer and its directors and officers and other parties involved in an offering to substantial liability. Section 11 of the Securities Act[101] provides that if any part of a registration statement, when such part became effective under the Securities Act, contained an untrue statement of a material fact or omitted to state a material fact necessary in order to make the statements therein not misleading, any person acquiring such a security can sue: (i) the issuer; (ii) every person who signed the registration statement; (iii) every person who was a director of the issuer at the time of the filing of that part of the registration statement, even if the person did not sign the registration statement;[102] (iv) every expert who, with his consent, has been named in the registration statement as having prepared or certified any portion of the registration statement; and (v) every underwriter. Section 11 contains no requirement that any such person have acted with fraudulent intent or that any such misstatement or omission have been relied upon in connection with its purchase.[103] In addition, civil penalties are provided for under section 11 and criminal penalties are provided for under section 24 of the Securities Act.[104]

---

[99] *Id.*

[100] 17 C.F.R. §242.100 et seq.

[101] 15 U.S.C. §77k.

[102] The Securities Act requires that the registration statement be signed by the issuer, its principal executive officer, its principal financial officer, its comptroller or principal accounting officer, a majority of the members of its board of directors and, in the case of a foreign issuer, by its duly authorized representative in the United States. *See* s. 6(a) of the Securities Act, 15 U.S.C. §77f(a).

[103] If the purchaser bought securities after the issuer made available an earnings statement covering at least the 12-month period after the registration statement's effective date, the purchaser must prove that it actually relied on the misstatements or omissions in the registration statement. *See* s. 11(a) of the Securities Act, 15 U.S.C. §77k(a).

[104] 15 U.S.C. §77x.

[265] Liability under section 11 is absolute against the issuer. However, all other identified persons may be able to avoid liability for any part of the registration statement not purporting to be made on the authority of any expert if such person had, after reasonable investigation, reasonable grounds to believe, and did believe, at the time such part of the registration statement became effective under the Securities Act, that the registration statement contained no material misstatements or omissions.[105] This is referred to as the "due diligence" defense, discussed above in "The Registration Process—Due Diligence."

Section 12(a)(2) of the Securities Act

[266] Section 12(a)(2) of the Securities Act[106] also serves as a basis for liability for participants in a registered public offering of securities.[107] Under section 12(a)(2), "any person who . . . offers or sells a security . . . by means of a prospectus or oral communication, which includes an untrue statement of material fact or omits to state a material fact necessary in order to make the statements, in the light of the circumstances under which they were made, not misleading . . ." is liable for any investment loss suffered by any purchaser of the security. Liability is determined for section 12(a)(2) purposes as of the "time of sale," which is at the time the investor agrees to purchase the securities being offered (and before delivery of the final prospectus), not the settlement date.

[267] Section 12(a)(2) has been applied to issuers, underwriters, directors, officers and principal shareholders. However, the U.S. Supreme Court has ruled that Section 12(a)(2) does not apply to unregistered offerings or secondary market transactions. Section 12(a)(2) does not require fraudulent intent on the part of the seller, nor must a purchaser prove that it relied on the misstatement or omission, though the purchaser cannot have knowledge of the misstatement or omission at the time of the purchase.

[268] Like section 11, section 12(a)(2) provides a defendant with a due diligence defense to a lawsuit, although the standard to establish the defense under section 12(a)(2) differs from the section 11 standard. Section 12(a)(2) provides that a defendant shall not be liable under that section "if he did not know, and in the exercise of reasonable care, could not have known, of such untruth or omission."

Section 10(b) of the Exchange Act

[269] Section 10(b) of the Exchange Act and Exchange Act Rule 10b-5 also subject issuers of securities and other participants in a securities offering to liability. Under Exchange Act Rule 10b-5, it is unlawful: "(a) to employ any device, scheme, or artifice to defraud, (b) to make any untrue statement of a material fact or to omit to state

[105] Section 11(b)(3) of the Securities Act, 15 U.S.C. §77k(b)(3).

[106] 15 U.S.C. §77l(a)(2).

[107] *Gustafson v. Alloyd Co.*, 613 U.S. 561 (1995), The Court held that Sections 12(a)(2) does not apply to private offerings of securities or secondary market transactions.

a material fact necessary in order to make the statements made, in the light of the circumstances under which they were made, not misleading, or (c) to engage in any act, practice or course of business that operates or would operate as a fraud or deceit upon any person, in connection with the purchase or sale of any security."

[270] Private litigants are entitled to bring actions under Rule 10b-5 against any person alleged to have engaged in the unlawful conduct specified in that rule. In addition to the unlawful conduct, the plaintiff must establish that the defendant acted with "scienter," or an intent to defraud, deceive or manipulate. Generally, courts have found recklessness to satisfy the scienter requirement, but not simple negligence or even inexcusable negligence.[108] In a private action alleging a violation of Rule 10b-5, the plaintiff must also prove that it relied on the wrongful conduct and that such wrongful conduct caused the plaintiff's loss. However, a plaintiff need not prove that he or she directly relied on the wrongful conduct to the plaintiff's detriment. Rather, proof of reliance can also be established indirectly pursuant to the "fraud-on-the-market theory."[109] Under the fraud-on-the-market theory, courts recognize that the wrongful conduct served to inflate the price of the stock artificially, and a plaintiff is permitted to prove reliance indirectly by virtue of his or her dependence on the market to set the stock price. Because the misrepresentation affected the stock price, and the plaintiff bought the stock based on the affected price, the plaintiff indirectly relied on the wrongful conduct that misled the market as a whole.

[271] Section 17 of the Securities Act[110] contains a broad anti-fraud provision, which mirrors closely the language of Rule 10b-5. Unlike Rule 10b-5, however, actions under section 17 do not require proof of fraudulent intent or recklessness, but may be brought in respect of a person's negligence. Most U.S. courts have held that there is no private right of action under section 17—actions may only be brought by the SEC. The persons liable and the remedies available under section 17 are broadly similar to those under Rule 10b-5.

[272] Because of the scienter, reliance and causation elements, an action under Rule 10b-5 is more difficult to sustain than an action under section 11 or 12(a)(2) under the Securities Act. However, section 10(b) and Rule 10b-5 have far broader application than section 11, which applies only to misstatements or omissions in Securities Act registration statements at the time of effectiveness, and section 12(a)(2), which applies only to prospectuses and oral statements used in a registered public offering of securities. Rule 10b-5 can apply to any purchase or sale of a security, including a private placement of securities, or secondary market transactions, including actions or omissions of the issuer, its officers and directors in violation of that rule that cause a decline in the price of the issuer's stock.

[108] *See, e.g., DSAM Global Value Fund v. Altris Software, Inc.*, 288 F.3d 385, 388-89 (9th Cir. 2002).
[109] *See Basic v. Levinson*, 485 U.S. 224 (1988).
[110] 15 U.S.C. §77q.

DISCLOSURE IN REGISTERED PUBLIC OFFERINGS AND ONGOING REPORTING OBLIGATIONS

[273] It is important for foreign private issuers to consider the initial and ongoing disclosure requirements of the Securities Act, the Exchange Act and other U.S. federal securities laws at the time they are considering accessing the U.S. capital markets. This section discusses the general disclosure requirements under U.S. federal securities laws for foreign private issuers and outlines various considerations relating to disclosure, including events that trigger an affirmative duty to disclose information.

Registration Statements and Annual Reports

[274] The SEC has adopted an integrated disclosure system. This means that one set of disclosure rules applies for both registered public offerings under the Securities Act and ongoing reporting obligations under the Exchange Act. As discussed in detail above in paragraphs 205–234, Form F-1 is the form of registration statement typically required of foreign private issuers raising capital in the U.S. markets for the first time and Form 20-F is the annual report form used by foreign private issuers for ongoing reporting obligations. As a result of the integrated disclosure system, most of the information that a foreign private issuer is required to include in its Form F-1 (and the prospectus forming a part thereof) is based on the information that the issuer is required to disclose in its Form 20-F.

[275] Following is a discussion of the more significant disclosure requirements of Form 20-F. Form 20-F has a number of disclosure requirements in addition to those discussed below and also contains instructions to assist in responding to many of these items. Foreign private issuers should obtain a copy of, and read closely, the Form 20-F before attempting to respond to the form's disclosure requirements.

Information Concerning the Registrant

[276] Item 3 of Form 20-F, "Key Information," requires the disclosure of selected financial information for the registrant's five most recent fiscal years[111], a statement of the registrant's capitalization and indebtedness and risk factors that would make an investment in the registrant speculative or of high risk. The risk factors section is one of the most important elements of a registrant's disclosure for liability purposes, and fulsome and tailored disclosure should be made regarding, among other things, (i) risks relating to the registrant's business and operations, such as dependence on key executives, dependence on key suppliers or customers, leverage and material litigation, (ii) risks relating to the industry in which the registrant operates and (iii) risks relating to the registrant's organizational structure and governing documents.

[111] Notwithstanding this requirement, a foreign private issuer that qualifies as an "emerging growth company" under the JOBS Act is not required to provide selected financial information for any period prior to the earliest audited period presented in its IPO registration statement. 15 U.S.C. §77g(a).

[277] Item 4 of Form 20-F, "Information on the Company," requires disclosure of significant events in the history and development of the registrant, as well as an overview of the registrant's business, including descriptions of principal products and services, principal competitive markets, seasonality of the business, sources and availability of raw materials, marketing channels, dependence on patents, licenses and contractual arrangements, material effects of governmental regulations and material properties.

Operational and Financial Review and Prospects

[278] Item 5 of Form 20-F, "Operating and Financial Review and Prospects" (referred to by U.S. issuers as "Management's Discussion and Analysis of Financial Condition and Results of Operations," or "MD&A") requires a wide-ranging discussion by management of the registrant's:

- results of operations, including reasons for year-to-year changes in line items over a three-year period, plus any interim periods for which financial statements are required, and a description of unusual or infrequent events that affected income and known trends or uncertainties, the impact of inflation and foreign currency fluctuation and any information regarding any governmental, economic, fiscal, monetary or political factors;
- short-term and long-term liquidity and capital resources, including internal and external sources of liquidity, sources and amounts of cash flow (including any legal or economic restrictions on the ability of subsidiaries to transfer funds to the registrant), level of borrowings at the end of the period under review, material capital expenditure commitments and information concerning the registrant's financial instruments, debt maturity profile and currency and interest rate structure;
- research and development policies for the last three years, including the amount spent on research and development activities sponsored by the registrant during the last three fiscal years;
- significant recent trends in production, sales and inventory, the state of the order book and selling prices and known trends that are reasonably likely to materially impact the registrant's revenue, income from continuing operations, profitability, liquidity or that would cause reported financial information not to be indicative of future operating results or financial condition;
- off-balance sheet arrangements that have or are reasonably likely to have a current or future effect on the registrant's financial condition, changes in financial condition, revenues or expenses, results of operations, liquidity, capital expenditures or capital resources that is material to investors; and
- known contractual obligations as of the latest fiscal year balance sheet in tabular format showing payments due within one year, from one to three years, from three to five years, in more than five years and in total.

[279] In addition, the SEC has noted that MD&A requires disclosure "where a trend, demand, commitment, event or uncertainty is both presently known to management and reasonably likely to have material effects on the registrant's financial condition or results of operation."[112]

[280] The SEC has emphasized that the purpose of MD&A is to provide a narrative explanation of a company's financial statements that enable investors to see the company through the eyes of management and provide a context within which the registrant's financial information should be analyzed.[113] The MD&A should not simply be a mechanical recitation of financial statements in narrative form (such as descriptions of the dollar amounts and percentage changes in income or other financial statement line items) or a series of technical responses to MD&A disclosure requirements (such as identifying an accounting principle used without discussing potential uncertainties in applying the accounting principle or in making material estimates that the accounting principle requires). In essence, MD&A should tell the story behind the results and share with investors management's thoughts about the future.

Compensation

[281] Item 6.B of Form 20-F, "Compensation," requires disclosure of the amount of compensation paid, and benefits in kind granted, to all directors and members of administrative, supervisory or management bodies during the registrant's last full fiscal year. Disclosure of compensation is required on an individual basis unless individual disclosure is not required in the registrant's home country and is not otherwise publicly disclosed by the registrant, which is often the case. If such compensation was paid pursuant to a bonus or profit-sharing plan, the registrant must describe the plan and the basis upon which the individual participates. If the compensation is paid in the form of stock options, the title, amount exercise price, purchase price (if applicable) and expiration date must be disclosed. In addition, the registrant must disclose the total amount set aside or accrued to provide pension, retirement or similar benefits to such individuals.

Officers, Directors and Employees

[282] Item 6 of Form 20-F requires the registrant to disclose information about its directors, senior management and key employees, including business experience,

---

[112] SEC Release No. 33-6835 (May 18, 1989).

[113] *See Interpretation: Commission Statement about Management's Discussion and Analysis of Financial Condition and Results of Operations*, SEC Release Nos. 33-8056; 34-45321; FR-61 (Jan. 22, 2002), *Interpretation: Commission Guidance Regarding Management's Discussion and Analysis of Financial Condition and Results of Operations*, SEC Release Nos. 33-8350; 34-48960 (Dec. 19, 2003), *Commission Guidance on Presentation of Liquidity and Capital Resources Disclosures in Management's Discussion and Analysis*, SEC Release Nos. 33-9144; 34-62934 (Sep. 17, 2010).

business activities performed outside the registrant, age, any arrangement pursuant to which such person was selected as a director or member of senior management and any family relationships among such persons. The registrant must also describe the composition of the its audit committee and remuneration committee and the charter or terms of reference under which such committees operate.

[283] The registrant must also disclose, with respect to each director or member of an administrative, supervisory or management body, the date of expiration of such person's current term of office, details of such person's service contract that provide benefits payable upon termination (or an appropriate negative statement) and information concerning such person's share and stock option ownership in the registrant.

[284] With respect to employees, disclosure is required regarding the number of persons employed by the registrant, the relationship between management and labor unions, and arrangements involving the granting of shares or stock options to employees.

Major Shareholders

[285] Item 7.A of Form 20-F, "Major Shareholders," requires disclosure of the beneficial owners of more than 5% of the registrant's voting securities (unless home country disclosure requires a lower percentage, in which case the lower percentage applies), any significant changes in percentage ownership of the major shareholders during the past three years and whether the registrant's major shareholders have different voting rights, as well as the portion of the registrant's securities held in its home country and any known arrangements that may result in a change in control in the registrant.

Other Disclosures

[286] In addition to the detailed information set forth above, Form 20-F requires annual disclosure of, among other things, (i) certain legal, arbitration and government proceedings, (ii) certain transactions between the registrant and related parties, (iii) changes in, and disagreements with, the registrant's certifying accountant and (iv) significant differences in the corporate governance practices of listed foreign private issuers compared to the corporate governance practices applicable to domestic companies under the relevant exchange's listing standards.

[287] Although the regulations and forms under the U.S. federal securities laws include many specific disclosure requirements, those specific disclosure requirements are not exhaustive and, even where they do apply, are not always dispositive of disclosure issues.[114] Both Securities Act Rule 408[115] and Exchange Act Rule 12b-20[116] expressly require the inclusion of any additional material information necessary to make the statements required to be made in filings under those Acts, in the light of the circumstances under which they were made, not misleading. Therefore, it is necessary to evaluate the materiality of any particular matter on a case-by-case basis and from a qualitative as well as a quantitative point of view. For example, the SEC has applied Rule 408 to foreign private issuers in order to elicit discussion of economic, political and legal factors particular to the foreign private issuer's domicile, including such matters as tax policy, expropriation risks, currency fluctuation and devaluation risks, and problems relating to energy, unemployment and inflation.

Financial Information

[288] Items 8 and 18 of Form 20-F generally require that the registrant provide three years of audited financial statements.[117] These financial statements are comprised of a balance sheet, income statement, statement of stockholders' equity and statement of cash flows, as well as notes to the financial statements. The SEC's Regulation S-X[118] and Staff Accounting Bulletins govern the precise form and content of financial statements required to be filed under the Securities Act and the Exchange Act.

[289] The financial statements must be reported on by independent certified public accountants meeting the U.S. standards for auditor independence set forth in Regulation S-X. The accountant's report must include a statement to the effect that the audit was conducted in accordance with U.S. generally accepted auditing standards.

[290] Ordinarily, Regulation S-X requires that a registrant prepare its financial statements in accordance with U.S. GAAP. However, a foreign private issuer may instead prepare its financial statements in accordance with the accounting principles (including IFRS) accepted in the foreign private issuer's home country, so long as those financial statements are reconciled to U.S. GAAP. However, a foreign private issuer that prepares its financial statements in accordance with IFRS as issued by the IASB need not reconcile its financial statements to U.S. GAAP. If financial statements are not prepared in accordance with IFRS as issued by the IASB, Items 17 and 18 of

[114] For example, Instruction 1 to Item 101 of Regulation S-K, 17 C.F.R. §229.101, explains that registrants should take into consideration both quantitative and qualitative factors and cautions that information that may not appear significant in quantitative terms nevertheless might be material and should be disclosed. In addition, some courts have interpreted the specific requirements of the regulations and forms as merely setting minimum disclosure standards, and have found material omissions to exist even where the specific disclosure requirements have been satisfied. *Bertoglio v. Texas Int'l Co.*, 488 F. Supp. 630, 661 (D. Del. 1980).

[115] 17 C.F.R. §230.408.

[116] 17 C.F.R. §240.12b-20.

[117] A foreign private issuer that qualifies as an "emerging growth company" under the JOBS Act need only provide two years of audited financial statements in its IPO registration statement. 15 U.S.C. §77g(a). In addition, Instruction 1 to Item 8.A.2 provides that registrants need not provide a balance sheet for the earliest of the three-year periods if that balance sheet is not required by a jurisdiction outside the United States.

[118] 17 C.F.R. §229.10 et seq.

Form 20-F provide the rules pursuant to which a foreign private issuer must reconcile financial statements prepared under foreign accounting principles to U.S. GAAP. Reconciliation of a foreign private issuer's financial statements typically involves a considerable amount of effort.

[291] In view of the complexity of the SEC's rules and regulations regarding financial statements, a foreign private issuer contemplating a registered public offering in the United States should consult with an accounting firm experienced in complying with U.S. federal securities laws as early in the process as is practicable.

Exhibits

[292] A foreign private issuer is required to file with the SEC a number of exhibits to its registration statement. Such exhibits generally include, among other things, the registrant's organizational documents (*e.g.*, articles of association), indentures and material loan agreements, voting trust agreements, material contracts, a list of significant subsidiaries and consents of experts and counsel. Exhibits are required to be filed even if they contain sensitive commercial or other information. However, the SEC will consider requests to keep limited portions of such exhibits confidential.

Periodic Reports on Form 6-K

[293] Foreign private issuers are required to furnish to the SEC under cover of Form 6-K any significant information (i) required to be disclosed publicly in the jurisdiction of its domicile, incorporation or organization, (ii) filed with and made public by a stock exchange on which the foreign private issuer's securities are traded or (iii) distributed by the foreign private issuer to its security holders (either directly or by means of a press release). In addition, foreign private issuers must also submit, on a semi-annual basis, an interim balance sheet as of the end of the second fiscal quarter and an income statement that covers the first two fiscal quarters. Interim financial statements need not be reconciled to U.S. GAAP.[119]

Stock Exchange Requirements

[294] As discussed in further detail below under *Listing on a National Securities Exchange*, foreign private issuers making a registered offering of shares or ADRs in the United States frequently list those securities on one of three national securities exchanges in the United States: the NYSE, NYSE American or NASDAQ. Stock exchange rules also provide a source of disclosure obligations, and the requirements of the NYSE, NYSE American and NASDAQ are similar. For example, the NYSE Listed Company Manual provides that a listed company is "expected to release quickly to the public any news or information which might reasonably be expected to materially affect the

[119] NYSE Listed Company Manual §203.03 and NASDAQ Listing Rule §5250(c)(2).

market for its securities."[120] The Manual goes on to state that a listed company should "act promptly to dispel unfounded rumors which result in unusual market activity or price variations." The NYSE also has an immediate release policy for certain types of material of events and developments, including annual and quarterly earnings, dividend announcements, mergers, acquisitions, tender offers, stock splits, major management changes, and any substantive items of unusual or nonrecurrent nature.[121]

Other Disclosure Requirements

[295] The Dodd-Frank Act requires disclosure by foreign private issuers regarding the use of "conflict minerals," which include cassiterite (used to make tin), columbite-tantalite (used to make tantalum), gold, wolframite (used to make tungsten), certain derivatives, and any other minerals specified by the U.S. Secretary of State originating in the Democratic Republic of Congo or one of its nine bordering nations ("Covered Countries"). The rules, which are applicable to many, if not most, issuers engaged in manufacturing, require issuers to determine whether any conflict minerals are "necessary to the functionality or production" of a product that it manufactures or contracts to manufacture. If an issuer concludes that conflict minerals are necessary to the functionality or production of a product it manufactures or has contracted to manufacture, then the rules require it to file a Form SD with the SEC containing certain prescribed disclosures.

[296] The Iran Threat Reduction and Syria Human Rights Act of 2012 requires disclosure by foreign private issuers regarding a wide range of proscribed activities, including:

- violations of the Iran Sanctions Acts of 1996 or the Comprehensive Iran Sanctions, Accountability and Divestment Act of 2010;
- transactions with persons or entities listed on the U.S. Department of the Treasury's Office of Foreign Assets Control's Specially Designated Nationals and Blocked Persons; and
- transactions with the government of Iran or any entity that is owned or controlled, directly or indirectly, by the government of Iran.

LISTING ON A NATIONAL SECURITIES EXCHANGE

[297] Foreign private issuers making a registered offering of shares or ADRs in the United States frequently list those securities on one of three national securities exchanges in the United States: the NYSE, NYSE American (formerly known as the NYSE MKT or the NYSE Amex) or NASDAQ. The NYSE is known for listing large, established companies, while the NYSE American targets small to medium-sized companies. NASDAQ, which is divided into several markets with differing listing requirements, attracts technology and start-up businesses and may be especially

[120] NYSE Listed Company Manual §202.05.
[121] NYSE Listed Company Manual §202.06.

significant for smaller foreign private issuers that do not have the seasoned business experience and financial resources necessary for listing on the NYSE or NYSE American.

[298] Each of the exchanges has listing requirements designed primarily for foreign private issuers, in addition to the regular listing requirements for U.S. companies that foreign private issuers can also rely upon. The listing requirements include quantitative initial listing requirements, which an issuer must satisfy in order to gain listing on the exchange, and continuing quantitative listing requirements, which an issuer must satisfy in order to maintain its listing. The website for the NYSE and NYSE American, located at http://www.nyse.com, and NASDAQ, located at http://www.nasdaq.com, detail the requirements, which include a minimum number of security holders and a minimum number of publicly held securities, as well as specified financial standards. In addition, to list securities on an exchange, the class of securities must be registered under the Exchange Act, as discussed above in paragraphs 215–234.

[299] An issuer meeting the requirements for listing its shares on a national securities exchange will also have to comply with the separate reporting requirements and corporate governance obligations of that exchange, sometimes referred to as the qualitative listing requirements. While each exchange has a unique set of rules, there are substantial similarities among these rules from exchange to exchange, including requirements that the issuer have a board of directors the majority of which is comprised of "independent" directors, an audit committee that has at least three members, satisfies the independence requirements of Rule 10A-3 under the Exchange Act, and consists solely of "independent" directors who have the requisite financial experience and expertise, and a code of business conduct and ethics for directors, officers and employees. As a general matter, the NYSE, NYSE American and NASDAQ permit a foreign private issuer to follow its home country practice in lieu of the requirements of the exchange, subject to the compliance with certain disclosure and notification requirements, but in all cases issuers must comply with Rule 10A-3 under the Exchange Act relating to audit committees and their independence.[122]

[300] The process for listing on an exchange is relatively straightforward, and usually begins with a telephone call with a listing representative at the applicable exchange. Following the initial call, a listing application is prepared, usually in draft form, and submitted with the necessary supporting materials, such as resolutions of the board of directors and legal opinions regarding the validity and nonassessability of the securities, to the applicable exchange. Following a determination by the exchange that the issuer qualifies to have its securities listed on the exchange, the listing application and supporting materials are finalized and submitted to the exchange. An initial fee is due at the time of listing, and each exchange also imposes an annual listing fee and fees for listing additional securities of a class of previously listed securities.

---

[122] NYSE Listed Company Manual §303A.00 and NASDAQ Listing Rule §5615(a)(3).

EXEMPTIONS FROM U.S. SECURITIES LAWS

[301] It is possible to offer and sell securities in the United States without registration under the Securities Act by conducting a private placement in reliance upon certain exemptions from the Securities Act's registration requirements. It is also possible to offer securities outside the United States in transactions that are not subject to registration under the Securities Act.

Private Placements

Section 4(a)(2) Statutory Exemption

[302] Section 4(a)(2) of the Securities Act (formerly section 4(2) but re-designated section 4(a)(2) by the JOBS Act) provides the statutory foundation for the private placement market in the United States, by exempting "transactions by an issuer not involving any public offering" from registration under the Securities Act. Whether or not a "public offering" is involved depends principally on the types of persons to whom the securities are offered and the manner in which the offer is made. Generally, to qualify for this exemption, the offer must be made to persons who are sufficiently sophisticated so as not to need the protections afforded by the Securities Act. Securities that are offered pursuant to the section 4(a)(2) exemption generally carry significant restrictions on resale. While section 4(a)(2) does not define a "private placement," a combination of SEC regulatory practice, case law and standardized procedures and documentation have provided issuers and practitioners with a high level of comfort that a properly structured transaction will qualify for the section 4(a)(2) exemption.

SEC—Established Safe Harbors under Regulation D

[303] Regulation D[123] sets out rules that provide issuers with limited "safe harbors" from the registration requirements of the Securities Act for private placements. The safe harbors provided for by Regulation D are set forth in Rules 504 and 506. A previous safe harbor was set forth in seldom-used Rule 505, which was repealed in May 2017. Rule 506 is a safe harbor under section 4(a)(2) of the Securities Act while Rule 504 is under an exemption for small offerings set out in section 3(b) of the Securities Act.[124] An issuer, however, must also meet certain of the safe harbors' general requirements set forth in Rules 501, 502, 503, 507 and 508.

[304] An offering which does not meet the safe harbor provisions of Regulation D may still qualify for an exemption from registration under either section 4(a)(2) or section 3(b) of the Securities Act. A preliminary note to Regulation D states that an issuer's failure to satisfy all of the terms and conditions any rule in Regulation D

[123] 17 C.F.R. §2;230.500-508.
[124] 15 U.S.C. §77c(b).

shall not raise any presumption that the exemption provided by section 4(a)(2) of the Securities Act is not available.[125]

Rule 504

[305] Rule 504[126] exempts from the registration requirements of the Securities Act offers and sales of securities by issuers that are not:

- subject to the reporting requirements of section 13 or 15(d) of the Exchange Act;
- investment companies;
- development stage companies that either have no specific business plan or purpose or have indicated that their business plans are to engage in a merger or acquisition with an unidentified company or companies; and
- disqualified under Rule 504's "bad actor" disqualification provisions.

[306] The maximum aggregate offering price of securities under Rule 504 may not exceed US$5m, less the aggregate offering price of all securities sold within the 12 months before the start of and during the offering of securities in reliance on Rule 504 or in violation of section 5(a) of the Securities Act. The offering must meet certain general terms and conditions set forth in Rule 501 and comply with the integration requirements set forth in Rule 502(a) discussed below. In general, the offering must also comply with Rule 502(c), which prohibits the issuer and anyone acting on its behalf from offering and selling securities by means of a general solicitation or advertising, and Rule 502(d), which provides that any securities sold pursuant to Rule 504 will be "restricted" securities and subject to the limitations on resale discussed below.

Rule 506

[307] Offers and sales in any aggregate offering amount meeting the following requirements will be exempt from registration under Rule 506[127]

- if a purchaser is not an "accredited investor" (*see* the discussion of this concept below), the issuer must have a reasonable belief that the offeree, either alone or with his purchaser representative(s), has sufficient knowledge and experience in financial and business matters in order to evaluate the value, merits and risks of the investment in question;
- the securities may be purchased by an unlimited number of accredited investors plus no more than 35 persons who are not accredited investors; and
- the offering must meet certain general terms and conditions set forth in Rule 501 and comply with the integration and information requirements set forth in Rule 502.

[308] Under Rule 506(c), issuers can offer securities through means of general solicitation if (i) the purchasers in the offering are all accredited investors and (ii) the issuer has taken reasonable steps to verify that its investors are accredited investors.

[125] 17 C.F.R. §2;230.500(c).
[126] 17 C.F.R. §230.504.
[127] 17 C.F.R. §230.506.

Rule 506(c) sets forth a principles-based method of verification which requires an objective determination by the issuer as to whether the steps taken are reasonable in the context of the particular facts and circumstances of each purchaser and transaction. Any securities sold pursuant to Rule 506 will be "restricted" securities and subject to the limitations on resale discussed below.

Form D Filing with SEC

[309] An issuer offering or selling securities in reliance on Regulation D must file a notice of sales on Form D with the SEC within 15 calendar days of the first sale of securities in the offering. Issuers are required to amend a previously filed Form D in circumstances described in Rule 503. The Form D and any amendments must be filed electronically via the SEC's EDGAR system.[128]

Integration

[310] Any offering made pursuant to Regulation D must be integrated for the purposes of the safe harbors with certain offerings of similar securities made at the same time or within six months prior to or following the current Regulation D offering.[129] The integration provisions of Regulation D are intended to prevent an issuer from avoiding the registration provisions of the Securities Act by splitting one larger offering into two or more smaller offerings. The determination of whether separate sales of securities are part of the same offering depends on the particular facts and circumstances. The following factors should be considered in determining whether offers and sales should be integrated for purposes of Regulation D:

- whether the sales are part of a single plan of financing;
- whether the sales involve issuance of the same class of securities;
- whether the sales have been made at or about the same time;
- whether the same type of consideration is received; and
- whether the sales are made for the same general purpose.

[311] The integration provisions of Regulation D are quite complex, but, in general, an issuer following the requirements of the regulation should be able to avoid integration problems. In particular, an offering complying with the requirements of Regulation D in the United States and an unregistered offering outside of the United States pursuant to Regulation S, the safe harbor exemption for offshore offerings (*see* discussion below), will not be integrated for purposes of determining the validity of the Regulation D offering.

Accredited Investors

[312] "Accredited investors" include banks, registered broker-dealers, insurance companies, investment companies, most employee benefit plans, certain 501(c)(3) organizations, individuals with a net worth of over US$1m (or earned income in the amounts and for the period specified), directors, executive officers or general partners of the issuer or entities in which all owners are accredited investors. The definition

---

[128] 17 C.F.R. §230.503.
[129] 17 C.F.R. §230.502(a).

of "accredited investor" included any persons that the issuer reasonably believed met the "accredited investor" the criteria at the time the securities were sold.[130] Therefore, an issuer that reasonably believed that the investor was an accredited investor at the time of the Regulation D offering will not lose the benefit of the safe harbor provided by Rule 506 if the issuer later discovers that the purchaser was not accredited and, therefore, sold securities to more than 35 persons who are not accredited investors.

Disclosure

[313] There are no specific disclosure requirements under Rule 504. The disclosure requirements under Rule 506 require that purchasers, other than accredited investors, have access to the same type of information which typically is found in Part I of a registration statement filed under the Securities Act. However, there are no specific disclosure requirements if an offer is being made only to accredited investors. Where an offer is being made to both accredited and nonaccredited investors, the accredited investors should receive the same information as the nonaccredited investors.[131]

Procedures

[314] Over the years, practitioners have developed a set of procedures intended to meet the requirements of section 4(a)(2) and Regulation D. One procedure is for the issuer to receive a written acknowledgment and agreement from each purchaser that (i) it is a sophisticated investor and has received all information that it has requested regarding the investment (and, if the purchaser is an accredited investor, confirmation of that status), (ii) it is not purchasing the securities with a view to distribution, and (iii) the securities have not been registered under the Securities Act and, absent registration of any resale under the Securities Act or the availability of an exemption from such registration (which may require the delivery of a legal opinion to that effect), resales will not be permitted. In addition, certificates evidencing the securities often contain restrictive legends indicating the applicable transfer restrictions or, in the case of uncertificated securities, sometimes called dematerialized securities, that the securities can be subject to stop transfer instructions to prevent unauthorized resales.

Resales of Privately Placed Securities

[315] Securities purchased in a private placement are deemed to be "restricted" by the SEC and may not be immediately resold in the U.S. public markets.

[316] Rule 144 under the Securities Act[132] provides a nonexclusive safe harbor for resales in the United States of "restricted securities." Rule 144 permits holders of restricted securities to begin reselling these securities after a six-month holding period if the issuer has been a reporting company in the United States for at least 90 days (one year if not). At the end of this six-month holding period, persons who are not affiliates of the issuer, and have not been affiliates during the preceding three months, may freely resell their restricted securities provided that certain public information requirements are met. At the end of a one-year holding period, such persons may

[130] 17 C.F.R. §230.501(a).
[131] 17 C.F.R. §230.502(b).
[132] 17 C.F.R. §230.144.

freely resell their restricted securities. At the end of a six-month holding period, affiliates may begin to sell restricted securities in limited amounts, provided, among other things, that certain public information requirements are met. Affiliates are subject to certain additional limitations, including the amount of securities which may be sold and the manner of sale, and must file notice of sale with the SEC on Form 144 in circumstances described in Rule 144.

[317] Rule 144 is not available when a purchaser of "restricted securities" sells such securities prior to the expiration of the applicable holding period. However, market participants have developed procedures that permit resales by one purchaser in a private placement to another. These procedures essentially require the new purchaser to be bound by and comply with the same restriction on resale as the original purchaser. Typically, these resale limitations include certain procedural requirements (such as the delivery of a legal opinion) designed to ensure compliance with these legal restrictions.

SEC—Established Safe Harbors under Regulation A

[318] Additional section 3(b) safe harbors are available under Regulation A.[133] Regulation A (sometimes referred to as "Regulation A+") was amended in May 2015 to implement Title IV of the JOBS Act, which created a new category of exempt publicly offered securities under section 3(b) of the Securities Act for up to US$50m of securities offered and sold in any twelve-month period. Regulation A is limited to offerings of equity securities, including warrants, debt securities and debt securities convertible into or exchangeable into equity interests, including any guarantees of such securities. Asset-backed securities do not qualify for Regulation A. Securities sold in Regulation A offerings are not considered restricted securities and are freely transferable.

[319] Regulation A allows companies to raise money under two different tiers, Tier 1 and Tier 2, which have different disclosure requirements. More disclosure is required for Tier 2 offerings, including audited financial statements. Issuers are required to indicate the tier the offering is being made under on the cover of the offering document. The new rules modernize the existing framework under Regulation A by, among other things, requiring that disclosure documents be filed on EDGAR, allowing an issuer to make a confidential submission with the SEC, permitting certain "testing the waters" communications, and disqualifying bad actors.

[320] *Tier 1.*[134] Tier 1 exempts smaller offerings raising up to US$20m in any twelve-month period with no more than US$6m or 30% annually sold by selling securities holders. Tier 1 offerings are subject to both SEC and state blue sky pre-sale review.

[321] *Tier 2.*[135] Tier 2 exempts offerings raising up to US$50m in any twelve-month period with no more than US$15m or 30% annually sold by selling securities holders. Tier 2 offerings are subject to SEC, but not state blue sky, pre-sale review. Investors in

[133] 17 C.F.R. §230.251 *et seq.*
[134] 17 C.F.R. §230.251(a)(1).
[135] 17 C.F.R. §230.251(a)(2).

a Tier 2 offering will be subject to investment limits (except when securities are sold to accredited investors or are listed on a national securities exchange), and Tier 2 issuers will be required to comply with periodic reporting and filing requirements, including current reports, semi-annual reports and annual reports. Regulation A provides a means for an issuer in a Tier 2 offering to concurrently list a class of securities on a national exchange.

[322] Regulation A is available only to U.S. and Canadian companies that are not required to file reports under the Exchange Act. In addition, the safe harbor is not available to blank-check companies, investment companies (including business development companies) registered or required to be registered under the 1940 Act and entities issuing fractional undivided interests in oil or gas rights, or similar interests in other mineral rights. Regulation A is not available for use by issuers that have not filed with the SEC the ongoing reports required by Regulation A during the two years immediately preceding the filing of a new offering statement, issuers that have had their registration revoked pursuant to an Exchange Act section 12(j) order in the last five years and certain bad actors.

[323] A Regulation A offering is not subject to integration with any <u>prior</u> offers or sales of securities or with the following categories of <u>subsequent</u> offers or sales:

- Securities Act-registered offerings, except in the case of a prior abandoned Regulation A offering that was offered to investors other than qualified institutional buyers or institutional accredited investors;
- employee benefit plan transactions;
- Regulation S transactions;
- Securities Act section 4(a)(6) crowdfunded offerings; and
- offers and sales made more than six months after the completion of the Regulation A offering.

Rule 144A Placements

Rule 144A

[324] Rule 144A, adopted by the SEC in April 1990, provides a nonexclusive safe harbor from registration for resales of certain securities to "qualified institutional buyers" ("QIBs") by persons other than the issuer. So long as during the initial sale the issuer exercises "reasonable care" that subsequent sales will be made only in compliance with applicable securities laws, it need not police subsequent resales to ensure such compliance. The SEC adopted Rule 144A to increase the liquidity of privately placed securities by allowing unrestricted resales among QIBs and to increase access to the U.S. capital markets by foreign issuers. In connection with the adoption of Rule 144A, a predecessor to FINRA created the PORTAL (Private Offerings, Resales and Trading through Automated Linkages) trading system (discussed below) for Rule 144A eligible securities, with the intent of further increasing the liquidity of privately placed securities.

[325] In a "Rule 144A" placement, an issuer will sell, in reliance upon section 4(a)(2) or another exemption from registration, its securities to one or more investment banking firms which will then resell, in reliance upon Rule 144A, the securities to a larger number of QIBs. From an issuer's standpoint, Rule 144A placements are very similar to traditional underwritten public offerings.

Rule 144A Criteria

[326] A sale in compliance with Rule 144A must meet four basic criteria: (a) the securities must be sold only to QIBs; (b) the securities must not, when issued, be of the same class as securities listed on a U.S. securities exchange or quoted in a U.S. automated interdealer quotation system; (c) the seller and the prospective purchaser must have the right to obtain certain information about the issuer if such information is not publicly available; and (d) the seller must ensure that the prospective purchaser knows that the seller may rely on Rule 144A.[136] General solicitation is permitted under Rule 144A, as long as the purchasers are limited to QIBs or to purchasers that the seller and any person acting on behalf of the seller reasonably believe are QIBs.

QIBs

[327] A QIB generally is defined as an institution (such as an insurance company, registered investment company or pension or employee benefit plan) acting for its own account or for the account of other QIBs, that in the aggregate owns and invests on a discretionary basis at least US$100m (US$10m in the case of registered dealers) in securities of unaffiliated companies (including securities issued or guaranteed by the U.S. government). QIBs also include U.S. banks, savings and loan associations, and registered broker-dealers. QIBs may not buy for managed or other fiduciary accounts that are not themselves QIBs.

Eligible Securities

[328] Both debt and equity securities may be sold under Rule 144A, provided that when such securities were issued (as opposed to at the time of the resale), they were not of the same class as securities listed on a national securities exchange or quoted through an interdealer quotation system. This limitation prevents trading in side-by-side public and private markets for essentially the same securities. Securities which are traded in the over-the-counter market (*i.e.*, traded in the "pink sheets"), but not quoted through an interdealer quotation system, are not considered publicly traded securities ineligible for Rule 144A resales.

[329] Securities that are convertible into or exchangeable for securities so listed or quoted are eligible for resale under Rule 144A if, at the time of issuance, the effective conversion premium for such convertible or exchangeable securities is 10% or more. Warrants to purchase securities so listed or quoted are eligible for resale under Rule 144A if they are not exercisable for at least three years or if, at the time of issuance, their effective exercise premium is 10% or more.

[136] 17 C.F.R. §230.144A.

Information

[330] The availability of Rule 144A is conditioned upon sellers and prospective purchasers of Rule 144A securities having the right to obtain certain information about the issuer. The right to obtain the information will generally be contained in a covenant in the terms of the security or the purchase agreement. If the issuer is neither subject to the reporting requirements of the Exchange Act nor exempt from reporting pursuant to Rule 12g3-2(b) under the Exchange Act, it must make available, upon request, to the holders of any privately placed securities and any prospective purchasers the following information (which must be reasonably current in relation to the date of resale): (i) a very brief statement of the nature of the business of the issuer and the products and services it offers; and (ii) the issuer's most recent balance sheet and profit and loss and retained earnings statement and similar financial statements for such part of the two preceding fiscal years as the issuer has been in operation (the financial statements should be audited, to the extent reasonably available).

Buyer's Awareness of Seller's Reliance upon Rule 144A

[331] A seller of privately placed securities must take reasonable care to ensure that the buyer is aware that the seller may rely on the exemption from registration afforded by Rule 144A. This requirement may be fulfilled by the use of a special confirmation notice specifying the seller's potential reliance on that rule's exemption.

144A Documentation

[332] In the case of a private placement of securities under Rule 144A, an offering memorandum and a purchase agreement are prepared, which are similar in many respects to the prospectus and underwriting agreement used in registered public offerings.

Offering Memorandum

[333] The offering memorandum is a disclosure document that provides information similar to a prospectus in a general public offering, but the offering memorandum is not subject to the detailed requirements of U.S. securities laws. Despite being exempt from registration, the offering and the offering memorandum will be subject to the anti-fraud provisions under U.S. securities laws.

[334] Not being subject to the detailed requirements of the U.S. securities laws has a number of advantages. For instance, where an offering is made in multiple jurisdictions, one offering document may be used for both the Rule 144A and the foreign tranche, if appropriate.

Purchase Agreement

[335] The purchase agreement is the contract between the issuer and the initial purchaser setting forth the terms of the issuer's sale and the initial purchaser's purchase of the securities. Rule 144A permits private placements to be structured like traditional public offerings where a group of initial purchasers, though likely small in number, will commit to purchase all of the offered securities and will offer them for resale, in this case under Rule 144A, to their customers. Liquidity will be enhanced through the ability to resell, under Rule 144A, to a large group of QIBs, or in the issuer's home market as well as through the PORTAL system.

[336] In most respects, the purchase agreement will be identical to the underwriting agreement prepared in connection with a public offering of securities. There will be representations, warranties and agreements to be made by the issuer, and there will be legal opinion and accountant's comfort letter delivery requirements. The issuer will also provide indemnification to the initial purchasers for any liability arising from a material misstatement in, or omission from, the offering memorandum.

Secondary Trading System (PORTAL)

[337] In connection with approving Rule 144A, the SEC also approved the establishment of PORTAL, a screen-based computer and communications system designed to facilitate the secondary trading of securities that qualify for Rule 144A. PORTAL may be used to disseminate quotations and transaction information; it also provides for clearance and settlement through the PORTAL system or permits participants to make other arrangements for clearance and settlement. Only institutional investors that qualify as QIBs are permitted to trade through PORTAL.

The Advantages of a Registered Public Offering versus a Rule 144A Placement

Public Offering Advantages

[338] The most significant advantage for a foreign issuer selling its securities through a registered public offering is the liquidity of the trading market. Securities sold in a registered public offering may be freely resold, other than by affiliates of the issuer. This provides two important advantages over Rule 144A placements. First, the securities may be sold initially, and may be resold, to individuals, expanding the potential market. Second, registered securities are eligible for trading on a national securities exchange and for quotation in an interdealer quotation system. A listing on a U.S. exchange may enhance the trading and liquidity of the issue.

[339] In addition to the advantages of liquidity, listing on a national securities exchange brings with it other advantages. Chief among these advantages is the coverage the stock may receive from securities analysts in the United States. Typically, the securities analysts of the lead managers will follow the company's performance and will issue periodic reports on the issuer's prospects. Favorable reports may help increase the price of the issuer's stock. Another advantage is the greater ability to use shares of the company's stock in connection with acquisitions. If a foreign issuer's stock is publicly traded in the United States, a potential seller may be more willing to accept the stock as payment because of the enhanced ability to resell the stock and because the value of the stock will have been set by a large and liquid market.

Rule 144A Placement Advantages

Disclosure and Ongoing Reporting Requirements

[340] The most significant advantages of a Rule 144A placement consist of the ability to avoid the SEC's detailed disclosure requirements applicable to offering documents and the ongoing periodic reporting requirements of the Exchange Act and the disclosure, corporate governance and auditing requirements of the Sarbanes-Oxley Act. All of these obligations are avoided by an issuer relying upon Rule 144A in the distribution of its securities. While investor expectations and market practice in Rule 144A placements have resulted in disclosure that closely approximates the level of disclosure in a registered public offering, foreign private issuers are not required to comply with the comprehensive disclosure requirements of Form 20-F in preparing their offering memoranda. Issuers may disclose certain information which SEC rules and regulations do not permit to be disclosed, including non-GAAP compliant financial information. Likewise, certain information which may be regarded as sensitive (*e.g.*, executive officer compensation) need not be disclosed. Furthermore, because a Rule 144A offering memorandum is distributed to a fairly discrete group of institutional investors, there is a greater chance of protecting the confidentiality of the information disclosed than there is in connection with a public offering.

Timing

[341] Rule 144A placements, as compared with registered public offerings, provide an issuer more control over the timing of the offering, as well as quicker access to the capital markets.

[342] In a public offering, a registration statement meeting the formal requirements of the regulations under the Securities Act must be prepared and submitted to the SEC for review. First-time foreign issuers should allow a minimum of 45 to 90 days from the filing of the initial registration statement to the date the SEC declares the registration statement effective and offers and sales can be made. A detailed discussion of the timing of a public offering is contained above under "The Registration Process—Preparing the Registration Statement."

[343] By comparison, a less detailed offering memorandum may be prepared in connection with a Rule 144A placement in limited cases. Even if a detailed offering memorandum is required, potential purchasers in a Rule 144A placement may be confirmed almost immediately after distribution of the offering memorandum, thus saving the substantial time which must be allowed for SEC review.

Expenses

[344] The expenses in connection with a Rule 144A placement are usually lower than the expenses in connection with a registered public offering. The SEC charges a filing fee, based on the proposed maximum aggregate offering price, with the fee rate adjusted annually. There are also filing fees in connection with review by FINRA and the NYSE, NYSE Amex or NASDAQ, if applicable, which will not be necessary in a Rule 144A placement. If, in a public offering, the securities are to be listed on the NYSE or NYSE Amex, the listing fees can be substantial. The fees involved in listing on NASDAQ are less burdensome. By contrast, in connection with a Rule 144A placement, there are no exchange listing fees. In either case, there will be accounting and legal fees as well as printing expenses.

Resales of Restricted Securities: The Section "4(a)(1½)" Exemption

[345] The so-called Section "4(1½)" resale procedure (or Section "4(a)(1½)" exemption as it is also referred to) (the "Section "4(1½)" Exemption") is not formally established by any written SEC rule or regulation. Rather it has been relied on and used by securities professionals and has developed through case law and judicial interpretation and has been recognized by the SEC for years.

[346] The exemption was developed as a basis to allow for resales of restricted securities among sophisticated investors that could buy securities from an issuer without needing the protection of the Securities Act registration and prospectus delivery requirements.

[347] It is generally considered that for a resale to be private for the purposes of the Section "4(a)(1½)" Exemption,

- the resale should be to a limited number of purchasers (approximately less than 25) who are sophisticated enough to be able to evaluate the risks of the investment (especially if the seller is affiliated with the issuer);
- there should be no public advertising or general solicitation with respect to the securities;
- information about the issuer which is available to the seller should be provided to the purchaser;
- the seller must not have purchased the securities with a view to resale (although no specific holding period is required, generally a holding period of six months or more will evidence the seller's original investment intent); and
- the purchaser should represent that it is acquiring the securities for investment, and not for resale.

[348] In practice, the Section "4(1½)" resale procedure is used in resales of unregistered securities in the following circumstances:

- private resales of restricted securities;
- offerings where an issuer sells unregistered securities in a private placement under Section 4(a)(2) to initial purchasers and the initial purchasers subsequently resell to QIBs under "Rule 144A only" offerings and to institutional accredited investors under the Section "4(a)(1½)" resale procedure (*see* paragraphs 302 and 324);
- secondary offerings of securities that are not Rule 144A eligible;
- secondary offerings of securities where the issuer is unable or unwilling to comply with the Rule 144A(d)(4) information requirements; and
- primary offerings of shares (or rights) of foreign private issuers where the shares (or shares underlying rights) are of the same class as shares (or share underlying ADRs) already listed on the NYSE or NASDAQ.

Section 4(a)(7) Exemption

[349] On December 4, 2015, the Fixing America's Surface Transportation Act (the "FAST Act") was signed into law by President Barack Obama. Although the primary purpose of the FAST Act is to provide funding certainty for surface transportation, it also made several changes to federal securities laws, including the introduction of a nonexclusive safe harbor for private resales under Section 4(a)(7) of the Securities Act (the "Section 4(a)(7) Exemption"). The Section 4(a)(7) Exemption codifies certain aspects of the Section "4(1½)" Exemption, but also differs in certain key respects, for example a holding period is not required under the Section 4(a)(7) Exemption. The FAST Act makes clear that the Section 4(a)(7) Exemption does not replace the Section "4(1½)" Exemption which may still be relied upon by sellers whom are either unwilling or unable to comply with the requirements of the new Section 4(a)(7). The aim of the Section 4(a)(7) Exemption is to provide holders of restricted securities with improved liquidity and greater predictability.

[350] A resale of securities is exempt under Section 4(a)(7) if the following conditions are met:

- the purchaser is an "accredited investor" within the meaning of Regulation D;
- there is no general solicitation or advertising;
- the seller is not the issuer or a subsidiary of the issuer;
- neither the seller nor any person who has been or will be paid for its participation in the transaction is qualified as a "bad actor" under Regulation D;
- the issuer is engaged in business, not in the organizational stage or in bankruptcy or receivership, and is not a blank check, blind pool, or shell company that has no specific business plan or purpose and has not indicated that its primary business plan is to engage in a merger with an unidentified person;
- the transaction does not relate to an unsold allotment to, or a subscription or participation by, a broker or dealer as an underwriter of the securities;
- the securities have been authorized and outstanding for at least 90 days; and
- for securities of issuers not subject to periodic reporting under the Securities Exchange Act, a variety of specified information including financial information about the issuer has been delivered to the purchaser.

Regulation S

[351] U.S. securities laws may be implicated even when raising capital outside of the United States in connection with a U.S. acquisition. While the registration requirements under the Securities Act apply to offers and sales involving "interstate commerce" or use of the U.S. mails, section 2(a)(7) of the Securities Act[137] defines that term as meaning "trade or commerce in securities between any foreign country and any state." As a result, the Securities Act has the potential to be applied to offshore offerings even where there is only a modest nexus to the United States. In 1990, the

[137] 15 U.S.C. §77b(7).

SEC adopted Regulation S to provide a safe harbor from registration for offerings that have only incidental U.S. jurisdictional contacts.[138]

[352] Under Regulation S, any offer or sale that occurs "outside the United States" generally is not subject to the Securities Act. Regulation S contains two safe harbors applicable to primary offerings and secondary resales that establish conditions that, if satisfied, will mean that the transaction will be deemed to be "outside the United States." Both safe harbors require that the offer and sale be made in an "offshore transaction" and that there be no "directed selling efforts" in the United States.

[353] Under Securities Act Rule 902(h),[139] any offer or sale of securities is made in an "offshore transaction"[140] if no offers are made to persons in the United States and:

- the buyer is (or the seller reasonably believes that the buyer is) offshore at the time the buy order is originated;
- in connection with primary offerings, the transaction is executed in, on or through a physical trading floor of an established securities exchange located outside the United States; or
- in connection with secondary sales, the transaction is executed in, on or through the facilities of a designated offshore securities market and the transaction is not prearranged with a buyer in the United States.

[354] "Directed selling efforts" consist of any activity undertaken for the purpose of, or that could reasonably be expected to result in, conditioning the market in the United States for the securities being offered in reliance on Regulation S.[141] The placement of an advertisement in a publication "with a general circulation in the United States"[142] that refers to the Regulation S offering could be deemed to constitute directed selling efforts if it could reasonably be expected to condition the market in the United States. There are, however, exceptions to the limitation on advertising, including the placement of certain tombstone advertisements, the dissemination of routine information of a character normally published by a company and unrelated to an effort to sell the securities and legitimate selling activities carried on in the United States in connection with registered or exempt offerings, including Rule 144A offerings. The publication or distribution of a research report in accordance with Rule 138(c)[143] or Rule 139(b)[144] by a broker or dealer at or around the time of an offering in reliance on Regulation S will not cause the transaction to fail to be an offshore transaction nor will it be considered "directed selling efforts."

[138] 17 C.F.R. §230.901 et seq.
[139] 17 C.F.R. §230.902(h).
[140] The definition specifically excludes offers and sales of securities targeted to identifiable groups of U.S. citizens living abroad, such as members of U.S. armed forces serving overseas.
[141] 17 C.F.R. §230.902(c)(1).
[142] Any publication that is printed primarily for distribution in the United States or has had, during the preceding 12 months, an average circulation in the United States of 15 000 or more copies per issue. 17 C.F.R. §230.902(c)(2).
[143] 17 C.F.R. §230.138(c).
[144] 17 C.F.R. §230.139(b).

[355] Securities Act Rule 135e[145] provides a safe harbor for offshore press activities conducted in connection with an offering by a foreign private issuer or foreign government issuer. Under this safe harbor, a foreign private issuer or foreign government issuer may provide foreign and U.S. journalists with access to offshore press conferences, offshore meetings with representatives of the issuer or press-related materials released offshore without such activities being deemed to be "directed selling efforts" within the meaning of Regulation S, provided that the conditions of Rule 1353 are met.

[356] In a combined offering that includes both a Regulation S offering outside the United States and a Rule 144A offering in the United States, it is necessary to observe the restrictions on directed selling efforts. The posting of offering or solicitation materials (such as a prospectus) on an Internet website could be considered an activity taking place in the United States. The SEC has indicated, however, that an Internet offer would not require registration under the Securities Act where the offerors implement adequate measures to prevent investors in the United States from participating.[146] Other information available on the Internet (including by hyperlink to or from the websites of offering participants) should also be controlled to ensure that it does not constitute improper publicity.

[357] The SEC has an active monitoring program and may launch an inquiry if any publicity concerning an offering appears in the United States, particularly if statements are attributed to an offering participant. The SEC may delay or postpone an offering to allow a "cooling-off" period for the effects of improper publicity to dissipate. The SEC also may demand that underwriters associated with dissemination of improper publicity be removed from the selling syndicate. Improper publicity can result in an offering losing its exemptions under Regulation S, thereby making it an illegal unregistered offering in the United States. A purchaser may bring a lawsuit to rescind the purchase of the securities (recovering the consideration paid plus interest, minus the amount of any income received therefrom) or to recover damages if the securities are no longer owned. Additional liability may arise if publicity relating to the offering is shown to contain a material misstatement or omission, or otherwise to violate the anti-fraud provisions of the U.S. securities laws.

Offering Categories

[358] There are three categories of securities offerings under the primary offering provisions of Rule 903 of Regulation S. Each category and its corresponding restrictions vary, based on the type of securities offered, whether the issuer is a U.S. or foreign entity, its registration status under the Exchange Act and, if the issuer is a foreign entity, whether the United States is the principal trading market for its securities. The rules applicable to each category of securities offering and the related conditions and defined terms are detailed and should be reviewed carefully and complied with fully in order to ensure compliance with Regulation S. Set forth below is a summary

[145] 17 C.F.R. §230.135e.
[146] SEC Release Nos. 33-7516; 34-39,779 (Mar. 23, 1998).

of the categories of securities offerings and references to the specific rules that apply and which merit detailed review and consideration.

Category 1

[359] Provided that securities are offered and sold in offshore transactions with no directed selling efforts, offerings meeting one of the following four additional conditions listed in Rule 903(b)(1)[147] need not comply with any additional conditions to be exempt from Securities Act registration requirements:

- the offering is of securities of a foreign private issuer for which there is no "substantial U.S. market interest";
- the securities are offered and sold in "overseas directed offerings";
- the securities are backed by the full faith and credit of a foreign government; or
- the securities are issued pursuant to certain employee benefit plans.

[360] *Substantial U.S. Market Interest.* Rule 902(j) of Regulation S[148] contains separate definitions of "substantial U.S. market interest" for equity and debt securities.

[361] *Overseas Directed Offering.* Rule 903(b)(ii) of Regulation S[149] defines "overseas directed offering" to include two types of offerings - an offering of a foreign issuer's securities or a domestic issuer's nonconvertible debt securities, in each case that is directed into a single foreign country to the residents thereof if such offering is conducted in accordance with local laws and practices and which otherwise fits within the condition of Rule 903(b)(ii).

Category 2

[362] Securities in Category 2 include those that are not eligible for Category 1 and that are equity securities of a foreign issuer that is a reporting issuer under the Exchange Act, and debt securities of a reporting issuer and a nonreporting foreign issuer. An offering of securities encompassed by Category 2, in addition to being offered in offshore transactions with no directed selling efforts, must also comply with the offering restrictions and transactional restrictions described in Rule 903(b)(2) of Regulation S.[150]

[363] The requisite "offering restrictions" are set forth in the definition of that term in Rule 902(g). Rule 903(b)(2) requires that any offer or sale of securities, if made prior to the expiration of a 40-day "distribution compliance period," may not be made to a "U.S. person" or for the account of a U.S. person, other than a distributor. Rule 903(b)(2) also requires that distributors selling securities to a distributor, dealer or other similar person prior to the expiration of the 40-day distribution compliance period provide a notice to such purchaser that the purchaser is subject to the same distribution restrictions on offers and sales. Rule 902(f) defines "distribution compliance period" and Rule 902(k) defines "U.S. person."

[147] 17 C.F.R. §230.903(b)(1).
[148] 17 C.F.R. §230.902(j).
[149] 17 C.F.R. §230.903(b)(ii).
[150] 17 C.F.R. §230.903(b)(2).

Category 3

[364] Securities that are not eligible for Categories 1 and 2 are covered by Category 3. These would include debt securities of nonreporting U.S. issuers, equity securities of reporting and nonreporting domestic issuers and equity securities of nonreporting foreign issuers with substantial U.S. market interest. An offering of securities encompassed by Category 3, in addition to being offered in offshore transactions with no directed selling efforts, must also comply with the offering restrictions requirement applicable to Category 2 offerings and with the transactional restrictions of Rule 903(b)(3) for Category 3 offerings of debt securities or equity securities.[151]

Rule 904: Secondary Sales

General

[365] Rule 904 of Regulation S[152] provides a safe harbor for secondary transactions by persons other than issuers and distributors. As with primary offerings under Rule 903, sales made under Rule 904 must be made in offshore transactions with no directed selling efforts. Depending on the persons selling the securities, additional restrictions apply.

Persons Not Involved in the Distribution

[366] Persons other than (i) dealers and others receiving compensation or a fee with respect to the securities offered and (ii) affiliates of the issuer or a distributor may rely on the resale safe harbor with no additional conditions.

Affiliates of Issuers and Distributors

[367] Resales of securities by officers and directors who are deemed to be affiliates of the issuer or distributor solely because of such position may be made in reliance on the resale safe harbor, provided that no special selling compensation is provided in connection with such offer and sale of securities, other than a customary broker's commission. As a general rule, normal sales transactions executed through the facilities of a designated offshore securities market will satisfy Rule 904.

Rule 905

[368] Under Rule 905 of Regulation S,[153] an offshore resale under Rule 901 (which provides that for purposes only of Section 5 of the Securities Act, the terms offer, offer to sell, sell, sale, and offer to buy shall be deemed not to include offers and sales that occur outside the U.S.) or Rule 904 of equity securities that are "restricted securities" within the meaning of Rule 144 will not affect the restricted status of such securities.

[151] 17 C.F.R. §230.903(b)(3).
[152] 17 C.F.R. §230.904.
[153] 17 C.F.R. §230.905.

Cross-Border Rights Offerings, Exchange Offers and Business Combinations

Rights Offerings

[369] Securities Act Rule 801[154] provides an exemption from registration for offers and sales of securities in a rights offerings by a foreign private issuer if U.S. resident holders hold no more than 10% of the outstanding class of securities that is the subject of the rights offering. To avail itself of this exemption, the issuer must allow U.S. holders to participate in the rights offering on terms at least as favorable as those offered to other holders of securities that are the subject of the offer. An issuer is not, however, required to extend the rights offering to security holders in those states or jurisdictions that require registration or qualification. The securities offered in the rights offering must be equity securities of the same class held by the offerees in the United States. Rights issued to U.S. holders may not be transferred except in accordance with Regulation S. Any informational documents published or disseminated in the rights offering must be furnished to the SEC in English on Form CB by the first business day after publication or dissemination. The information documents must also contain a legend stating that the offering document is subject to disclosure requirements different from those applicable to U.S. issuers and highlighting the difficulty that a U.S. holder may encounter in obtaining and enforcing court judgments against the foreign private issuer.

Exchange Offers or Business Combinations

[370] Securities Act Rule 802[155] provides an exemption from registration for offers and sales of securities issued in an exchange offer or as consideration in an exchange offer or business combination where the target company is a foreign private issuer and U.S. resident holders do not hold more than 10% of the securities that are the subject of the exchange offer or business combination. If the securities are to be issued by a successor registrant (*e.g.*, in a merger or amalgamation transaction where a new holding company's securities are issued to both companies in the business combination), U.S. resident holders may not hold more than 10% of such class of securities of the successor registrant, measured immediately after the completion of the business combination.

[371] To avail itself of this exemption, the foreign private issuer must allow U.S. holders to participate in the exchange offer or business combination on terms at least as favorable as those offered to other holders of securities that are the subject of the offer. An issuer is not, however, required to extend the exchange offer to security holders in those states or jurisdictions that require registration or qualification. Any informational documents published or disseminated in connection with the exchange offer or business combination must be furnished to the SEC in English on Form

[154] 17 C.F.R. §230.801.
[155] 17 C.F.R. §230.802.

CB by the first business day after publication or dissemination. Any informational document must contain the legend prescribed by Rule 802(b).[156]

[372] Acquirers of foreign companies also have available to them certain exemptions from the tender offer rules of the U.S. securities laws. These exemptions are discussed in greater detail in paragraphs 301–371 above.

Annex A
Sarbanes-Oxley Act of 2002

The Sarbanes-Oxley Act, which was adopted by Congress in 2002 in response to the collapse of several prominent U.S. companies as a result of financial fraud, applies to both domestic and foreign companies whose securities (including debt securities) are registered with the SEC, and represents a broad expansion of U.S. securities laws in the areas of corporate governance, accounting matters, disclosure, enforcement and other topics. Following adoption of the Sarbanes-Oxley Act, the SEC released a number of regulations implementing the provisions of that Act.

A number of the provisions of the Sarbanes-Oxley Act conflict with regulations or customary practices in the home jurisdictions of some foreign issuers. In many such instances, the SEC has been flexible in applying some of these provisions and has stated that it is willing to consider case-by-case exemptions in others. However, careful compliance with the certification and disclosure requirements is an important consideration for any foreign company contemplating a public offering in the United States. The following summarizes the more significant provisions created by the Sarbanes-Oxley Act.

The Sarbanes-Oxley Act applies to U.S. and foreign private issuers: (i) with ordinary shares or securities that are represented by Level II or Level III ADRs that are publicly traded on the NYSE, NYSE Amex or NASDAQ; (ii) that file reports with the SEC under Section 15(d) of the Exchange Act (including Form 20-F); or (iii) that have filed a registration statement under the Securities Act that has not yet become effective and that has not been withdrawn. The Sarbanes-Oxley Act does not apply, however, to non-U.S. issuers that submit information to the SEC pursuant to Exchange Act Rule 12g3-2(b), such as issuers whose securities are represented by Level I ADRs.

A. Corporate Governance Standards for Directors and Executive Officers

1. *CEO/CFO Certification of Reports*

The Sarbanes-Oxley Act contains two certification provisions, one subject to civil penalties and one subject to criminal penalties, that require an issuer's Chief Executive Officer and Chief Financial Officer (or their equivalents, whether or not they hold those titles) to certify, among other things, the accuracy and completeness of the issuer's periodic reports filed with the SEC, as well as the adequacy of the issuer's internal control over

[156] 17 C.F.R. §230.802(b).

financial reporting and disclosure controls and procedures.[157] For purposes of this certification, "periodic reports" include each annual Form 20-F, but do not include reports on Form 6-K, even if they contain quarterly financial information.

2. Senior Management Code of Ethics

Issuers are required to disclose in their periodic reports whether they have adopted a code of ethics applicable to their principal executive officer, principal financial officer and principal accounting officer or comptroller.[158] If an issuer has not adopted an appropriate code of ethics, the issuer must disclose the reasons for not doing so. The code of ethics must include standards reasonably necessary to promote: (i) honest and ethical conduct, including the handling of actual or apparent conflicts of interest between personal and professional relationships; (ii) full, fair, accurate, timely and understandable disclosure in SEC reports and other public communications; (iii) compliance with applicable governmental rules; (iv) prompt internal reporting of violations of the code; and (v) accountability for adherence to the code. A foreign issuer must disclose in its Form 20-F any changes to or waivers, including implicit waivers, of its code of ethics during the year covered by the report. Foreign issuers are strongly encouraged (but are not required) to make more prompt disclosure of changes and waivers on a Form 6-K or on their websites.

Foreign issuers will need to consider, among other things, whether to produce a code of ethics that meets Sarbanes-Oxley Act requirements and, if so, whether to produce a standalone code or to incorporate it within a pre-existing internal code of conduct (noting, however, that it is not a requirement of the Combined Code for companies listed on the London Stock Exchange to adopt codes of conduct).

In addition, foreign private issuers with a secondary listing on the NYSE or NASDAQ will need to take into account that the SEC has approved additional corporate governance rules for the NYSE and NASDAQ. The NYSE and NASDAQ rules provide for independent governance, audit and nominating committees, but many of these provisions are not mandatory for companies with a primary listing outside the United States. Instead, the NYSE and NASDAQ rules require foreign private issuers to disclose, on their websites or in their annual reports filed with the SEC, the ways in which their corporate governance practices differ from those requirements under NYSE or NASDAQ rules. These rules are discussed in greater detail in Annex C, "Corporate Governance Listing Standards."

3. Prohibition on Extending or Arranging Personal Loans to Directors and Executive Officers

With limited exceptions for some types of loans made in the ordinary course of business by certain types of issuers, such as FDIC-insured banks and brokerage firms, foreign private issuers are prohibited from, directly or indirectly, extending, maintaining or arranging for the extension of personal loans or guaranteeing such loans to their

[157] Sarbanes-Oxley Act ss. 302 and 906. 17 C.F.R. §240.13a-14 and 17 C.F.R. §240.15d-14.
[158] Sarbanes-Oxley Act s. 406. SEC Regulation S-K, Item 406. Form 20-F, Item 16B.

directors or executive officers.[159] Personal loans that were in existence on July 30, 2002 are permitted to continue in effect, provided there is no material modification to any term or any renewal of the loan.

Loans are widely defined so that certain other emoluments may also be caught. Although common corporate practices, such as cashless options, cash advances for business expenses and tax gross-ups for expatriates, could be caught by the broad wording of the statute, many U.S. law firms have taken the view that these types of credit extensions are not personal loans.

Compare the equivalent regime in the United Kingdom, where the restriction on loans applies only to directors (and their connected persons), not non-board executives, and where, unlike under the Sarbanes-Oxley Act provisions, certain exceptions are allowed including where small sums are provided to meet expenditures incurred for business purposes.

4. *Forfeiture by CEO and CFO of Certain Bonuses and Profits*

If, as a result of misconduct, an issuer must prepare an accounting restatement due to the material non-compliance by the issuer with any financial reporting requirement under the U.S. securities laws, the CEO and CFO are required to reimburse the issuer for: (i) any bonus or other incentive-based or equity-based compensation he or she received from the issuer during the 12-month period following the first public issuance or filing with the SEC of the financial document that did not comply with such financial reporting requirement; and (ii) any profits he or she realized from the sale of securities of the issuer during that same 12-month period.[160] The Sarbanes-Oxley Act creates a private right of action for a company's shareholders to recover the bonuses and profits on behalf of the company.

5. *Prohibition of Improper Influence on Audits*

The Sarbanes-Oxley Act provides that no action may be taken by any director or officer of an issuer (or other person acting under the direction of any of them) to fraudulently influence, coerce, manipulate or mislead any independent auditor of the issuer's financial statements for the purpose of rendering the financial statements materially misleading.[161]

6. *Prohibition of Service as a Director or Officer*

An individual can be barred by court order, at the request of the SEC, from serving as an officer or director of a public company if he or she has violated the general anti-fraud provisions of the U.S. securities laws and his or her activities are found by the court to show him or her to be "unfit."[162] In addition, the SEC, in an administrative cease and desist proceeding, may bar an individual from serving as a director or an officer of a public company if, after notice and hearing, it has found that the individual

[159] Sarbanes-Oxley Act s. 402.
[160] Sarbanes-Oxley Act s. 304.
[161] Sarbanes-Oxley Act s. 303. 17 C.F.R. §240.13b2-2.
[162] Sarbanes-Oxley Act ss. 305 and 1105.

has violated the general anti-fraud provisions of the U.S. securities laws and that the individual's conduct demonstrates unfitness to serve as an officer or director.

7. Pension Fund Blackout Periods

The purchase, sale or other acquisition or transfer of any equity security of an issuer by a director or executive officer is prohibited during a blackout period with respect to defined pension funds if the equity security was acquired or would be acquired in connection with his or her service or employment as a director or executive officer.[163] A blackout period means any period of more than three consecutive days during which the ability of not fewer than 50% of the participants or beneficiaries under all individual account plans maintained by the issuer to purchase, sell or otherwise acquire or transfer an interest in any equity security of the issuer held in such plan is temporarily suspended by the issuer or by a fiduciary of the plan. For foreign issuers, the number of U.S. participants affected must represent more than 15% of the issuer's total worldwide workforce on a consolidated basis or 50 000 persons.

B. Requirements for Audit Committees and Audit Services and Restrictions on Non-Audit Services from Auditors

1. Audit Committee Provisions

a. Independence. Each member of the audit committee of a listed company must (i) be unaffiliated with the issuer and its subsidiaries of a listed company and (ii) not accept any compensation, directly or indirectly, from the issuer or any subsidiary thereof (including consulting, advisory or other compensatory fees) other than for service as a member of the board of directors or on any board committee.[164] If an issuer does not have an audit committee, the Sarbanes-Oxley Act imposes these requirements on the entire board of directors. The NYSE, NYSE Amex and NASDAQ prohibit the listing of any company that is not in compliance with these audit committee requirements. In addition, there is a general exemption for foreign issuers that have a board of auditors or statutory auditors established pursuant to home country laws or listing requirements, which in turn meet various requirements.

SEC Rule 10A-3 provides exemptions from the independence requirements for foreign private issuers to allow, among other things:

- audit committee members of a dual holding company (two separate holding companies that are foreign private issuers organized in different national jurisdictions) to serve on the audit committees of both issuers or serve on a joint audit committee without being considered affiliates of the listed issuer;
- nonmanagement employee directors to serve on the audit committee, so long as the employees are not executive officers of the issuer within the meaning of the Exchange Act;

[163] Sarbanes-Oxley Act s. 306. SEC Regulation BTR.
[164] Sarbanes-Oxley Act s. 301. 17 C.F.R. §240.10A-3.

- a foreign private issuer to use a supervisory or nonmanagement board as the audit committee, so long as all of the members meet the independence requirement;
- a representative of a more than 50% stockholder to serve on the audit committee (so long as the no-compensation prong of the independence test is satisfied and the representative is not an executive officer of the issuer, within the meaning of the Exchange Act) as an observer and not a voting member or chair of the audit committee; and
- to permit a foreign government representative to serve on the audit committee, subject to certain conditions.[165]

The NYSE and NASDAQ rules relating to audit committees are discussed in Annex C, "Corporate Governance Listing Standards."

b. Financial Expert. Issuers are required to disclose in their annual report filed with the SEC whether or not their audit committee includes at least one member who is a "financial expert" (and, if not, the reasons), but are not required to have a financial expert on their audit committees.[166] Issuers must also disclose in their annual report whether or not any financial expert is "independent" as defined by their current applicable listing standards, or if the issuer is not a listed issuer, under another SEC approved definition. The SEC has defined "financial expert" to mean a person who has:

- an understanding of generally accepted accounting principles ("GAAP") and financial statements;
- an ability to assess the general application of such principles in connection with accounting for estimates, accruals and reserves;
- experience in preparing, auditing, analyzing or evaluating financial statements that present a breadth and level of complexity of accounting issues that are generally comparable to the breadth and complexity of issues that can be reasonably expected to be raised by the issuer's financial statements, or experience actively supervising one or more persons engaged in such activities;
- an understanding of internal controls and procedures for financial reporting; and
- an understanding of audit committee functions.

c. Responsibilities. Audit committees of listed issuers are responsible for the appointment, compensation, retention and oversight of the work of the issuer's independent auditor for the purposes of preparing or issuing any audit report (and any related work).[167] In addition, the independent auditor must report directly to the audit committee. In particular, audit committees of listed issuers must be responsible for the following:

[165] 17 C.F.R. §240.10A-3.
[166] Sarbanes-Oxley Act s. 407. SEC Regulation S-K, Item 407(d)(5). Form 20-F, Item 16A.
[167] Sarbanes-Oxley Act s. 301. 17 C.F.R. §240.10A-3.

- **Selecting and Overseeing Independent Auditors.** Audit committees must be directly responsible for the appointment, compensation, retention and oversight of the issuer's auditor, including the resolution of disagreements between management and the issuer's auditor regarding financial reporting;
- **Establishing Complaint Procedures.** The audit committee must establish procedures for the receipt, retention and treatment of complaints that the issuer receives regarding accounting, internal accounting controls or auditing matters, and procedures for the confidential, anonymous submission of concerns regarding questionable accounting or auditing matters;
- **Engaging Advisors.** The audit committee must have the authority to engage independent counsel and other advisors, as it determines necessary to carry out its duties; and
- **Providing Adequate Funding.** The company must provide appropriate funding, as determined by the Audit Committee, to pay compensation to the independent auditor and any outside advisors so engaged.

In addition, audit committees are required to:

- preapprove the provision of all audit and non-audit services by the independent auditor (subject to a *de minimis* exception);
- consider reports from the independent auditor on (i) the issuer's critical accounting policies and practices, (ii) all alternative treatments of financial information permitted within GAAP that have been discussed with management, the ramifications of the use of such treatments and the treatment preferred by the auditor, and (iii) all other material written communications between the accountants and management;
- resolve disagreements between the independent auditor and management regarding the issuer's financial reporting; and
- become involved in analyzing any deficiencies in internal controls and any management or employee fraud identified in the CEO/CFO certifications described above.[168]

Foreign private issuers will need to consider the extent to which the requirements of the Sarbanes-Oxley Act conflict with similar home rules.

d. Home Country Provisions. To the extent the foreign issuer's home jurisdiction requires or permits shareholders ultimately to vote on, approve or ratify such requirements, if the foreign issuer provides a recommendation or nomination to shareholders, then the audit committee must be responsible for making the recommendation or nomination.

e. Procedures for Handling Accounting Complaints; Protection of "Whistleblowers." As noted above, the audit committee of listed companies must establish procedures for the receipt, retention and treatment of complaints received by the issuer regarding accounting, internal accounting controls or auditing matters and for the

[168] 17 C.F.R. §240.10A-3.

confidential, anonymous submission of concerns regarding questionable accounting or auditing matters. The NYSE, NYSE Amex and NASDAQ prohibit the listing of any company that is not in compliance with this requirement. In addition, issuers and their officers, directors and agents are prohibited from discharging, demoting or otherwise discriminating against any employee who lawfully provides information regarding any conduct the employee reasonably believes constitutes a violation of the U.S. securities laws or financial fraud statutes to any governmental authority, by testimony or otherwise, in any proceeding pending or about to be commenced concerning such a violation or to any person with supervisory authority over the employee or authorized by the issuer to investigate such conduct (which includes the audit committee and auditors and counsel engaged by the audit committee), *i.e.*, so-called whistleblowers.

2. Regulation of Audit Services

The Sarbanes-Oxley Act imposes restrictions on an issuer's relationship with its auditor in connection with providing audit services.

a. Employment of Former Personnel of Issuer's Auditor. An accounting firm is prohibited from providing any audit service to an issuer if the lead partner responsible for the audit of the issuer, the audit partner responsible for reviewing the audit or other member of the audit engagement team accepts a position with the issuer in a financial reporting oversight role during the one-year period preceding the date of the initiation of the audit for the year in which the audit professional became employed by the issuer.

b. Rotation of Audit Partners. The lead audit partner responsible for the audit of an issuer and the audit partner responsible for reviewing the audit must change every five years and are subject to a five-year time-out before they can again be involved with providing audit services to the issuer. All other partners involved with the audit engagement of the issuer must change every seven years and are subject to a two-year time-out before they can again be involved with providing audit services to the issuer.

3. Restrictions on Non-Audit Services

The Sarbanes-Oxley Act places significant restrictions on audit firms providing non-audit services to their clients.

a. Restricted Non-Audit Services. An auditor providing any of the following services to a client would not be considered "independent" with regard to that client:

- management functions or human resources;
- broker or dealer, investment adviser or investment banking services; or
- legal services and expert services unrelated to the audit.

In addition, providing any of the following services will also impair an auditor's independence, unless it is reasonable to conclude that the results of the services will not be subject to audit procedures during an audit of the client's financial statements:

- bookkeeping or other services related to the accounting records or financial statements of the issuer;
- financial information systems design and implementation;
- appraisal or valuation services, fairness opinions or contribution-in-kind reports;
- actuarial services; or
- internal audit outsourcing services.

In addition, an auditor's independence will be impaired by providing any other services that the Public Company Accounting Oversight Board (the "PCAOB") determines, by regulation, is impermissible. To date, the PCAOB has determined that an auditor's independence is impaired if the auditor, or any affiliate of the auditor, receives a contingent fee from the issuer for any service or product or if the auditor is involved in marketing or otherwise opining in favor of aggressive tax shelter schemes or in selling personal tax services to individuals who play a direct role in preparing the financial statements of the issuer.

b. Preapproval Requirements; Non-Audit Services. All audit, review and attest services (including providing comfort letters in underwritings) and any permissible non-audit services, such as permissible tax services, may only be provided to an issuer if approved in advance by the audit committee of the issuer or provided pursuant to preapproval policies and procedures adopted by the audit committee of the issuer. Consideration and approval of such services may be delegated to an independent director of the audit committee. Any such approvals by delegation must be presented to the audit committee at its next meeting. The percentage of services that are approved pursuant to delegation must be disclosed in the next Form 20-F filed with the SEC. Services other than audit, review and attest services do not need prior approval if the amount paid for such services meets a *de minimis* standard, the services were not recognized at the time of engagement to be non-audit services and the provision of the services was promptly brought to the attention of the audit committee and were approved prior to the completion of the audit by the audit committee or one or more members of the committee with authority to grant such approvals.

4. Public Company Accounting Oversight Board

To address the perceived deficiencies in the regulation of the accounting profession, the Sarbanes-Oxley Act created the PCAOB for accounting firms that audit public companies. Accounting firms (including non-U.S. firms) that prepare audit reports for foreign private issuers or that play a substantial role in the preparation or furnishing of an audit report are required to register with the PCAOB.

In registering, accounting firms must consent to comply with any request of the PCAOB or the SEC for testimony or production of documents, including audit work papers. If a registered accounting firm relies on an opinion or material services of a non-U.S. accounting firm in issuing all or part of its audit report or opinion, the registered accounting will be deemed to have secured the agreement of the non-U.S. accounting firm to such production as a condition of its reliance on the opinion of that non-U.S. accounting firm, and the non-U.S. public accounting firm will be deemed to have given these consents.

The PCAOB's functions include:

- establishing rules governing auditing, quality control, ethics, independence and other standards relating to the preparation of audit reports of issuers;
- conducting inspections of registered accounting firms (annually for firms that audit more than 100 issuers that are required to file reports with the SEC and at least once every three years for all other firms); and
- conducting investigations and disciplinary proceedings (including imposing appropriate sanctions) concerning registered accounting firms and their associated persons.

C. Expanded Company Disclosures

1. Accuracy of Financial Reports: Material Correcting Adjustments by the Independent Auditor

Each financial report filed with the SEC that contains financial statements that are required to be prepared in accordance with, or reconciled to, GAAP must reflect all "material correcting adjustments" that have been identified by the issuer's independent auditor in accordance with GAAP and SEC rules.[169]

2. Restrictions on Use of Pro Forma Financial Information

Pro forma financial information (*i.e.*, figures that are not prepared in accordance with GAAP, such as "pro forma earnings," "core earnings" or "EBITDA") must be presented in a manner that does not contain an untrue statement of a material fact or omit to state a material fact necessary to render the information not misleading. The presentation of non-GAAP financial measures must include a reconciliation of the pro forma disclosure to the issuer's financial condition and results of operations as prepared in accordance with GAAP. The rules apply to all non-GAAP financial measures regardless of whether the information is contained in an SEC filing, in any press release or in some other public disclosure.

A more complete discussion of the disclosure requirements with respect to non-GAAP financial measures contained in a registration statement or Form 20-F is set forth above under the caption *Disclosure in Registered Public Offerings and Ongoing Reporting Obligations—Registration Statements and Exchange Act Reports—Non-GAAP Financial Measures.* However, in connection with disclosures of non-GAAP financial measures contained in press releases and other public disclosures, the rules do not apply to foreign issuers, provided that the foreign issuer is listed on an exchange outside of the United States, the information was released outside of the United States (even if it was simultaneously released in the United States) and the non-GAAP financial measure is not derived from a number prepared in accordance with, or derived from, a measure prepared in accordance with U.S. GAAP.

[169] Sarbanes-Oxley Act s. 401.

3. Off-Balance Sheet Transactions

In each annual report filed with the SEC, foreign private issuers must disclose all material off-balance sheet transactions, arrangements, obligations (including contingent obligations) and other relationships with unconsolidated entities or persons that may have a material current or future effect on the issuer's financial condition, results of operations, liquidity, capital expenditures, capital resources or significant components of revenues or expenses, in accordance with regulations to be adopted by the SEC.[170]

4. Management Assessment of Internal Controls and Auditor's Attestation

A foreign issuer's annual report filed with the SEC must contain an "internal control report" stating that management is responsible for establishing and maintaining an adequate internal control structure and procedures for financial reporting, and assessing the effectiveness of the internal control structure and procedures for financial reporting.[171]

Management is also required to disclose any material weakness in the company's internal control over financial reporting and may not conclude that the internal control structure and procedures for financial reporting are effective if there are one or more material weaknesses in the internal control structure. A "material weakness" is a deficiency in the design or operation of internal controls that could adversely affect a company's ability to record, process, summarize and report financial data. A "material weakness" represents a greater deficiency than a "significant deficiency" (which has the same meaning as the term "reportable condition" used in accounting literature), but multiple significant deficiencies may in the aggregate constitute a material weakness.

A company's independent auditors must have some involvement in the internal control process because the independent auditors must attest to the internal control report. The SEC has reminded companies and their auditors that independent auditors are prohibited from engaging in certain non-audit services. Observing that coordination between companies and their auditors is necessary, the SEC emphasized the importance of management's active involvement in the internal controls process. While independent auditors may assist a company in documenting internal controls, management may not delegate its responsibility to assess internal controls to the company's independent auditors. For example, management may not simply accept responsibility for the documentation and testing performed by the independent auditor.

Foreign private issuers are subject to the same requirements regarding the management report on internal control over financial reporting as are domestic issuers. However, foreign private issuers do not have to disclose material changes to internal control over financial reporting on a quarterly basis since they do not file quarterly reports; instead, changes must be discussed in the annual internal control report. In addition, foreign private issuers may use an internal control framework developed in their home country, although they will have to include a management evaluation

[170] Sarbanes-Oxley Act s. 401. SEC Regulation S-K, Item 303(a)(4). Form 20-F, Item 5.E.
[171] Sarbanes-Oxley Act s. 404. SEC Regulation S-K, Item 308(a). Form 20-F, Item 15.

as to the effectiveness of internal controls, even if such an evaluation is not part of the internal control framework in use in their country.

The Dodd-Frank Act exempted companies that are neither large accelerated filers nor accelerated filers from the requirement of providing audit reports on internal control over financial reporting.[172]

D. Increased Enforcement and Penalties

1. *Criminalization of Misconduct*

The Sarbanes-Oxley Act imposes criminal penalties for the following acts of misconduct (some of which were already subject to criminal provisions of U.S. federal securities and other laws):

- knowingly or willfully filing a false CEO/CFO certification under Section 906 of the Sarbanes-Oxley Act;[173]
- knowingly or willfully destroying any audit work papers;[174]
- destroying, altering or falsifying records done with the intent to impede, obstruct or influence any governmental investigation or the administration of any federal governmental function or any bankruptcy proceeding;[175]
- discriminating in the terms and conditions of employment with respect to employees who provide information or who assist in investigations of U.S. securities law violations by U.S. federal regulatory or law enforcement agencies, the U.S. Congress or with respect to company personnel with supervisory or investigatory authority or those who file, testify, participate in or otherwise assist in proceedings filed or about to be filed involving alleged violations of the U.S. securities laws or SEC regulations or securities fraud;[176] and
- knowingly executing or attempting to execute a scheme or artifice to defraud any person in connection with any security of a public company or obtaining by means of false or fraudulent pretenses, representations or promises any money or property in connection with the purchase or sale of any security of a public company.[177]

2. *Increased Penalties and Other Remedies*

The Sarbanes-Oxley Act establishes new fines and criminal penalties for securities fraud violations involving accounting irregularities and financial fraud, including sanctions applicable to directors, officers and professionals that have committed, conspired with or "aided and abetted" the commission of violations.[178] Liabilities for

[172] *See Internal Control Over Financial Reporting in Exchange Act Periodic Reports on Non-Accelerated Filers*, Release 33-9142, 34-62914 (Sep. 15, 2010).
[173] Sarbanes-Oxley Act s. 906.
[174] Sarbanes-Oxley Act s. 802.
[175] Sarbanes-Oxley Act s. 802.
[176] Sarbanes-Oxley Act ss. 806 and 1106.
[177] Sarbanes-Oxley Act s. 807.
[178] Sarbanes-Oxley Act ss. 902, 903, 904 and 1106.

judgments or settlements for violating U.S. securities laws or committing securities fraud will be non-dischargeable in bankruptcy.[179]

3. Statute of Limitations

The Sarbanes-Oxley Act extends the applicable statute of limitations for private rights of action for securities fraud to the earlier of (i) two years (from the existing one-year period) after discovery of the facts constituting the violation and (ii) five years (from the existing three-year period) after such violation.[180] This extension may resurrect securities fraud cases that were previously cut off by the old statute of limitations but are now within the new statute of limitations.

4. Responsibilities of Counsel

Attorneys appearing before the SEC in the representation of issuers are required to report "evidence of" a material violation of U.S. securities law or breach of fiduciary duty or similar violation by the issuer or any agent thereof to the issuer's chief legal officer and chief executive officer. If the report is not properly responded to through adopting appropriate remedial measures or sanctions for the violations, attorneys must report the evidence to the audit committee (or another committee comprised solely of non-employees of the issuer, sometimes referred to as a "qualified legal compliance committee") or to the full board. The rules apply to all attorneys who are appearing and practicing before the SEC whether or not they are U.S. citizens and they also apply to supervisory and subordinate in-house attorneys, although there is an exception for foreign attorneys appearing before the SEC only in consultation with counsel admitted or licensed to practice in a state or other U.S. jurisdiction who is appearing and practicing before the SEC.

Annex B
Listing on a National Securities Exchange

An issuer meeting the requirements for listing its shares on a national securities exchange, such as the NYSE, NYSE Amex or NASDAQ will also have to comply with the separate reporting requirements and corporate governance obligations of that organization. Exchanges require that an issuer agree to make prompt public disclosure of any information that might reasonably be expected to affect the market price for its listed securities and to act promptly to dispel any unfounded rumors that cause unusual market activity in such securities. Issuers are also required to make available to their shareholders annually, in advance of their annual meetings, their financial statements for the most recent fiscal year, in consolidated form.

[179] Sarbanes-Oxley Act s. 803.
[180] Sarbanes-Oxley Act s. 804.

I. NYSE Listing Requirements

Set forth below is a summary of the listing requirements for foreign private issuers for the NYSE:[181]

Distribution

Round Lot Shareholders	5 000 worldwide
Publicly Held Shares	2.5m worldwide
Aggregate Market Value of Publicly Held Shares	US$100m worldwide

Financial Standards

Pre-Tax Income	US$100m cumulative in latest three fiscal years with US$25m minimum in each of the most recent two years
OR	
Valuation/Revenue (Rules Differ for Affiliated Companies)	US$500m global market capitalization, US$100m in revenue (most recent 12-month period) and US$100m aggregate cash flow for last 3 years with US$25m in each of previous 2 years; or US$750m global market capitalization and US$75m in revenue (most recent fiscal year)

In addition to the numerical standards, it should be noted that the NYSE will not list ADRs of foreign private issuers subject to foreign exchange or other restrictions against the free exchange into U.S. dollars of dividends or other distributions to shareholders or of the proceeds of sales in the foreign market.

A company must have a closing price, or an offering price if listing in connection with an initial public offering, of at least US$4 per share at the time of listing.

II. NYSE Amex Listing Requirements

The NYSE Amex standards for original listing are as follows[182]:

[181] NYSE Rule 103.01 as it appears in the NYSE Listed Company Manual on August 15, 2013. Foreign private issuers may elect to qualify instead under the NYSE's domestic listing criteria.

[182] <https://www.nyse.com/publicdocs/nyse/listing/NYSE_American_Initial_Listing_Standards.pdf> (as posted on October 28, 2017).

Quantitative Standards

Criteria	Listing Standards			
	Standard 1	Standard 2	Standard 3	Standard 4
Pre-tax income[1]	US$750 000	N/A	N/A	N/A
Market capitalization	N/A	N/A	US$50m	US$75m **OR** At least US$75m in total assets and US$75m in revenues
Market value of public float	US$3m	US$15m	US$15m	US$20m
Minimum price	US$3	US$3	US$2	US$3
Operating history	N/A	2 years	N/A	N/A
Shareholders' equity	US$4m	US$4m	US$4m	N/A
Public shareholders/ Public float (shares)[2]	Option 1: 800/500 000 Option 2: 400/1 000 000 Option 3: 400/500 000[3]			

[1] Required in the latest fiscal year, or two of the three most recent fiscal years.
[2] Public shareholders and public float do not include shareholders or shares held directly or indirectly by any officer, director, controlling shareholder or other concentrated (*i.e.*, 10% or greater), affiliated or family holdings.
[3] Option 3 requires a daily trading volume of 2 000 shares during the six months prior to listing.

Non-U.S. companies who do not meet the above-referenced distribution guidelines may qualify for NYSE Amex with 800 round lot public shareholders worldwide, 1m publicly held shares worldwide and a US$3m market value of public float worldwide.

NASDAQ Listing Requirements

The NASDAQ is divided into three markets: The NASDAQ Global Select Market, The NASDAQ Global Market and The NASDAQ Capital Market. More substantial NASDAQ issuers may qualify for inclusion in The NASDAQ Global Select Market or the NASDAQ Global Market.

Following are general summaries of the qualification standards for initial listing on each of NASDAQ's three markets. The summaries are based on a listing of common stock or ordinary shares (or ADRs evidencing such shares), and the rules may vary for other classes or types of securities (such as preferred stock or warrants). Also, special rules may apply in the case of an issuer that is a non-Canadian foreign private issuer. In addition, in the case of non-Canadian foreign private issuers with listed ADRs, it is the underlying shares evidenced by the ADRs that will be considered in determining the qualification for initial inclusion of the ADRs on NASDAQ.

NASDAQ Global Select Market.

The NASDAQ Global Select Market has the most stringent listing requirements of NASDAQ's three markets. To qualify for initial listing on the NASDAQ Global Select Market, an issuer must meet both the Financial Requirements and the Liquidity Requirements described below:

Financial and Qualitative Requirements. To qualify for inclusion in the NASDAQ Global Select Market, an issuer (other than a closed-end management investment company) must meet all of the criteria under one of the three financial standards:[183]

NASDAQ Global Select Market Initial Listing Requirements[1]

Requirements	Standard 1 Listing Rules 5315(e) and 5315(f)(3)(A)	Standard 2 Listing Rules 5315(e) and 5315(f)(3)(B)	Standard 3 Listing Rules 5315(e) and 5315(f)(3)(C)	Standard 4 Listing Rules 5315(e) and 5315(f)(3)(D)
Pre-tax earnings[2] (income from continuing operations before income taxes)	Aggregate in prior three fiscal years ≥ US$11m and Each of the two most recent fiscal years ≥ US$2.2m and each of the prior three fiscal years ≥ US$0	N/A	N/A	N/A

[183] NASDAQ, *Initial Listing Guide*, <https://listingcenter.nasdaq.com/assets/initialguide.pdf> (as posted on October 28, 2017).

NASDAQ Global Select Market Initial Listing Requirements (Cont'd)

Requirements	**Standard 1 Listing Rules 5315(e) and 5315(f)(3)(A)**	**Standard 2 Listing Rules 5315(e) and 5315(f)(3)(B)**	**Standard 3 Listing Rules 5315(e) and 5315(f)(3)(C)**	**Standard 4 Listing Rules 5315(e) and 5315(f)(3)(D)**
Cash flows[3]	N/A	Aggregate in prior three fiscal years ≥ US$27.5m and Each of the prior three fiscal years ≥ US$0	N/A	N/A
Market capitalization[4]	N/A	Average ≥ US$550m over prior 12 months	Average ≥ US$850m over prior 12 months	US$160m
Revenue	N/A	Previous fiscal year ≥ US$110m	Previous fiscal year ≥ US$90m	N/A
Total assets	N/A	N/A	N/A	US$80m in the most recently completed fiscal year
Stockholders' equity	N/A	N/A	N/A	US$55m
Bid price[5]	US$4	US$4	US$4	US$4
Market makers[6]	3 or 4	3 or 4	3 or 4	3 or 4
Corporate governance[7]	Yes	Yes	Yes	Yes

[1] These requirements apply to all companies, other than closed-end management investment companies. A closed-end management investment company, including a business development company, is not required to meet the financial requirements of Rule 5315(f)(3). If the common stock of a company is included in The NASDAQ Global Select Market, any other security of that same company, such as other classes of common or preferred stock, which qualifies for listing on The NASDAQ Global Market shall also be included in The NASDAQ Global Select Market. A company whose business plan is to complete an initial public offering and engage in a merger or acquisition with one or more unidentified companies within a specific period of time, as described in IM-5101-2, is not eligible to list on The NASDAQ Global Select Market.

[2] In calculating income from continuing operations before income taxes for purposes of Rule 5315(f)(3)(A), NASDAQ will rely on a company's annual financial information as filed with the Securities and Exchange Commission (SEC) in the company's most recent periodic report and/or registration statement. If a company does not have three years of publicly reported financial data, it may qualify under Rule 5315(f)(3)(A) if it has: (i) reported aggregate income from continuing operations before income taxes of at least US$11m and (ii) positive income from continuing operations before income taxes in each of the reported fiscal years. A period of less than three months shall not be considered a fiscal year, even if reported as a sub period in the company's publicly reported financial statements.

[3] In calculating cash flows for purposes of Rule 5315(f)(3)(B), NASDAQ will rely on the net cash provided by operating activities reported in the statements of cash flows, as filed with the SEC in the company's most recent periodic report and/or registration statement, excluding changes in working capital or in operating assets and liabilities. A period of less than three months shall not be considered a fiscal year, even if reported as a stub period in the company's publicly reported financial statements.

[4] In the case of a company listing in connection with its initial public offering, compliance with the market capitalization requirements of Rules 5315(f)(3)(B) and 5315(f)(3)(C) will be based on the company's market capitalization at the time of listing.

[5] The bid price requirement is not applicable to a company listed on The NASDAQ Global Market that transfers its listing to The NASDAQ Global Select Market.

[6] A company that also satisfies the requirements of Rule 5405(b)(1) or 5405(b)(2) is required to have three market makers. Otherwise, the company is required to have four market makers. An electronic communications network (ECN) is not considered a market maker for the purpose of these rules.

[7] In addition to the above quantitative requirements, companies must comply with all corporate governance requirements as set forth in the Rule 5600 Series.

Liquidity Requirements. In addition to meeting one of the standards specified above, issuers (other than closed-end management investment companies) must meet all liquidity criteria in their specific category for initial inclusion on the NASDAQ Global Select Market.[184]

[184] NASDAQ, *Initial Listing Guide*, < https://listingcenter.nasdaq.com/assets/initialguide.pdf > (as posted on October 28, 2017).

NASDAQ Global Select Market Initial Listing Requirements

New Company Listings

Requirements	**Initial Public Offerings and Spin-Off Companies**	**Seasoned Companies: Currently Trading Common Stock or Equivalents**	**Affiliated Companies[1]**	**Listing Rules**
Round lot shareholders **or** Total shareholders **or** Total shareholders and Average monthly trading volume over past twelve months[2]	450 **or** 2 200	450 **or** 2 200 **or** 550 and 1.1m	450 **or** 2 200 **or** 550 and 1.1m	5315(f)(1)
Publicly held shares[3]	1 250 000	1 250 000	1 250 000	5315(e)(2)
Market value of publicly held shares **or** Market value of publicly held shares and Stockholders' equity	US$45m	US$110m **or** US$100m and US$110m	US$45m	5315(f)(2)

[1] Companies affiliated with another company listed on The NASDAQ Global Select Market. For purposes of Rule 5315, a company is affiliated with another company if that other company, directly or indirectly though one or more intermediaries, controls, is controlled by, or is under common control of the company. For purposes of these rules, control means having the ability to exercise significant influence. Ability to exercise significant influence will be

presumed to exist where the parent or affiliated company directly or indirectly owns 20% or more of the other company's voting securities, and also can be indicated by representation on the board of directors, participation in policy making processes, material intercompany transactions, interchange of managerial personnel, or technological dependency.

[2] Round lot and total shareholders include both beneficial holders and holders of record.

[3] Publicly held shares is defined as total shares outstanding, less any shares held directly or indirectly by officers, directors or any person who is the beneficial owner of more than 10% of the total shares outstanding of the company.

NASDAQ Global Market.

The NASDAQ Global Market (formerly known as the NASDAQ National Market) is NASDAQ's middle tier market. Its listing standards are not as stringent as those for The NASDAQ Global Select Market, but are more stringent that the listing standards for The NASDAQ Capital Market.

Issuers that choose to list their securities on The NASDAQ Global Market must meet minimum initial inclusion financial requirements. An issuer must meet all of the requirements under at least one of the four listing standards for initial listing:[185]

NASDAQ Global Market Initial Listing Requirements[1]

Requirements	**Income Standard Listing Rules 5405(a) and 5405(b)(1)**	**Equity Standard Listing Rules 5405(a) and 5405(b)(2)**	**Market Value Standard Listing Rules 5405(a) and 5405(b)(3)**[2]	**Total Assets/ Total Revenue Standard Listing Rules 5405(a) and 5405(b)(4)**
Income from continuing operations before income taxes (in latest fiscal year **or** in two of last three fiscal years)	US$1m	N/A	N/A	N/A
Stockholders' equity	US$15m	US$30m	N/A	N/A

[185] NASDAQ, *Initial Listing Guide*, < https://listingcenter.nasdaq.com/assets/initialguide.pdf > (as posted on October 28, 2017).

NASDAQ Global Market Initial Listing Requirements (Cont'd)

Requirements	Income Standard Listing Rules 5405(a) and 5405(b)(1)	Equity Standard Listing Rules 5405(a) and 5405(b)(2)	Market Value Standard Listing Rules 5405(a) and 5405(b)(3)[2]	Total Assets/ Total Revenue Standard Listing Rules 5405(a) and 5405(b)(4)
Market value of listed securities[3]	N/A	N/A	US$75m	N/A
Total assets and Total revenue (in latest fiscal year **or** in two of last three fiscal years)	N/A	N/A	N/A	US$75m and US$75m
Publicly held shares[4]	1.1m	1.1m	1.1m	1.1m
Market value of publicly held shares	US$8m	US$18m	US$20m	US$20m
Bid price	US$4	US$4	US$42	US$4
Shareholders (round lot holders)[5]	400	400	400	400
Market makers[6]	3	3	4	4
Operating history	N/A	2 years	N/A	N/A
Corporate governance[7]	Yes	Yes	Yes	Yes

[1] Companies must meet the bid price, publicly held shares, and round lot holders requirements as set forth in Rule 5405(a) and at least one of the Standards in Rule 5405(b).

[2] Seasoned companies (those companies already listed or quoted on another marketplace) qualifying only under the Market Value Standard must meet the market value of listed securities and the bid price requirements for 90 consecutive trading days prior to applying for listing.

[3] The term, "listed securities," is defined as "securities listed on NASDAQ or another national securities exchange."

[4] Publicly held shares is defined as total shares outstanding, less any shares held directly or indirectly by officers, directors or any person who is the beneficial owner of more than 10% of the total shares outstanding of the company.

[5] Round lot holders are shareholders of 100 shares or more. The number of beneficial holders is considered in addition to holders of record.
[6] An electronic communications network (ECN) is not considered a market maker for the purpose of these rules.
[7] In addition to the above quantitative requirements, companies must comply with all corporate governance requirements as set forth in the Rule 5600 Series.

NASDAQ Capital Market. The NASDAQ Capital Market (formerly the SmallCap Market) is the last of NASDAQ's three markets and has the least onerous initial listing financial requirements.[186]

NASDAQ Capital Market Initial Listing Requirements[1]

Requirements	Equity Standard Listing Rules 5505(a) and 5505(b)(1)	Market Value of Listed Securities Standard Listing Rules 5505(a) and 5505(b)(2)[2]	Net Income Standard Listing Rules 5505(a) and 5505(b)(3)
Stockholders' equity	US$5m	US$4m	US$4m
Market value of publicly held shares	US$15m	US$15m	US$5m
Operating history	2 years	N/A	N/A
Market value of listed securities[3]	N/A	US$50m	N/A
Net income from continuing operations (in the latest fiscal year or in two of the last three fiscal years)	N/A	N/A	US$750 000
Bid price	US$4	US$4	US$4
Publicly held shares[4]	1m	1m	1m
Shareholders (round lot holders)[5]	300	300	300
Market makers[6]	3	3	3
Corporate governance[7]	Yes	Yes	Yes

[1] Companies must meet the bid price, publicly held shares, round lot holders, and market makers requirements as set forth in Rule 5505(a) and at least one of the Standards in Rule 5505(b).

[186] NASDAQ, *Initial Listing Guide,* < https://listingcenter.nasdaq.com/assets/initialguide.pdf > (as posted on October 28, 2017).

[2] Seasoned companies (those companies already listed or quoted on another marketplace) qualifying only under the Market Value of Listed Securities Standard must meet the market value of listed securities and the bid price requirements for 90 consecutive trading days prior to applying for listing.

[3] The term, "listed securities," is defined as "securities listed on NASDAQ or another national securities exchange."

[4] Publicly held shares is defined as total shares outstanding, less any shares held directly or indirectly by officers, directors or any person who is the beneficial owner of more than 10% of the total shares outstanding of the company. In the case of ADRs, at least 400 000 shall be issued.

[5] Round lot holders are shareholders of 100 shares or more. The number of beneficial holders is considered in addition to holders of record.

[6] An electronic communications network (ECN) is not considered a market maker for the purpose of these rules.

[7] In addition to the above quantitative requirements, companies must comply with all corporate governance requirements as set forth in the Rule 5600 Series.

Annex C
Corporate Governance Listing Standards

NYSE

NYSE listed companies must adhere to at least the minimum standards of corporate governance specified by the NYSE's rules. Pursuant to the NYSE's corporate governance requirements, foreign private issuers are generally permitted to follow home country practice in lieu of these corporate governance standards except that foreign private issuers must comply with Rule 10A-3 under the Exchange Act relating to audit committees, the CEO must notify the NYSE in writing promptly after any executive officer becomes aware of any non-compliance with any applicable provisions of the listing requirements and the listed company must submit an executed Written Affirmation annually to the NYSE and each time a change occurs to the board of directors or any of the board committees subject to the NYSE listing standards. Foreign private issuers must generally disclose any significant ways in which their corporate governance practices differ from those followed by domestic companies under NYSE listing standards.[187] A foreign private issuer that is required to file an annual report on Form 20-F with the SEC must include the statement of significant differences in that annual report. All other foreign private issuers may either include the statement of significant differences in an annual report filed with the SEC or on or through their website. The NYSE has stated that only a brief, general summary of the significant differences is required. The following discussion is applicable to U.S. listed companies, but to the extent that a foreign private issuer's practices differ from these requirements, those differences must be described as set forth in the preceding sentence.

[187] NYSE Rule 303A.11 and NYSE Rules 303A.06 and 303A.12(b).

Under the listing standards, a majority of the directors of a listed company must consist of independent directors. No director qualifies as independent unless the board of directors affirmatively determines that the director has no material relationship with the listed company (either directly or as a partner, shareholder or officer of an organization that has a relationship with the company).[188]

When assessing the materiality of a director's relationship with the listed company, the board of directors should consider the issue not merely from the standpoint of the director, but also from that of persons or organizations with which the director has an affiliation. For this purpose, material relationships may include commercial, industrial, banking, consulting, legal, accounting, charitable and familial relationships, among others. However, ownership of a significant amount of stock, by itself, is not a bar to a finding of independence.

The basis for the board of director's determination that a relationship is not material must be disclosed in the listed company's annual meeting proxy statement (or, if none, its annual report filed with the SEC).

In addition, the NYSE has adopted certain categories of relationships that would preclude a determination of independence.

Executive Sessions of the Board of Directors

Non-management directors of each NYSE listed company must meet at regularly scheduled executive sessions, without management present, to promote open discussion. Directors who are not independent, but who are not officers of the listed company, may participate in these executive sessions, but, at least once a year, the board of directors should schedule an executive session that includes only independent directors. Alternatively, the independent directors, as opposed to the non-management directors, may meet in regular executive sessions.[189]

If one director is chosen to preside at all of the executive sessions, his or her name must be disclosed in the annual meeting proxy statement or, if none, the annual report filed with the SEC, or by making the applicable disclosure on the company's website. Alternatively, the listed company may disclose the procedure by which a presiding director is selected for each executive session. Also, listed companies must disclose a method for interested parties to communicate directly with the presiding director or with non-management or independent directors as a group.

Nominating/Corporate Governance Committee

Each listed company must have a nominating/corporate governance committee composed entirely of independent directors.[190] The nominating/corporate governance committee must have a written charter that addresses:

- the committee's purpose and responsibilities, which, at a minimum, must be to identify individuals qualified to become board members, consistent with criteria approved by the board of directors, and to select, or to recommend that the board of directors select, the director nominees for the next annual meeting of shareholders; develop and recommend to the board of directors

[188] NYSE Rules 303A.01 and 303A.02.
[189] NYSE Rule 303A.03.
[190] NYSE Rule 303A.04.

a set of corporate governance principles applicable to the listed company; and oversee the evaluation of the board of directors and management; and
- an annual performance evaluation of the nominating/corporate governance committee.

In addition, the written charter should address the following items: committee member qualifications; committee member appointment and removal; committee structure and operations; and committee reporting to the board. Finally, the written charter should give the committee sole authority to retain and terminate any search firm to be used to identify director candidates and the sole authority to approve the search firm's fees and other retention terms.

If the listed company is legally required by contract or otherwise to provide third parties with the ability to nominate directors (e.g., through the terms of preferred stock or a shareholders agreement), the selection and nomination of those directors need not be subject to the nominating committee process.

Compensation Committee

Each listed company must also have a compensation committee composed entirely of independent directors.[191] The compensation committee must have a written charter that addresses:

- the committee's purpose and responsibilities, which, at a minimum, must be to have direct responsibility to: (i) review and approve corporate goals and objectives relevant to CEO compensation, evaluate the CEO's performance in light of those goals and objectives, and, either as a committee or together with the other independent directors (as directed by the board of directors), determine and approve the CEO's compensation level based on this evaluation; (ii) if not delegated to the compensation committee, make recommendations to the board of directors with respect to non-CEO compensation, incentive-compensation plans and equity-based plans; and (iii) produce a compensation committee report on executive compensation as required by the SEC to be included in the listed company's annual meeting proxy statement or annual report filed with the SEC; and
- an annual performance evaluation of the compensation committee.

In addition, the written charter should address the following items: committee member qualifications; committee member appointment and removal; committee structure and operations; and committee reporting to the board. Finally, if a compensation consultant is to assist in the evaluation of director, CEO or executive officer compensation, the written charter should give the committee sole authority to retain and terminate the consulting firm and the sole authority to approve the search firm's fees and other retention terms.

In determining the long-term incentive component of CEO compensation, the compensation committee should consider the listed company's performance and relative shareholder return, the value of similar incentive awards to CEOs at comparable companies and the awards given to the listed company's CEO in past years.

[191] NYSE Rule 303A.05.

Audit Committee

In addition to meeting the general independence standards established by the NYSE described below, in accordance with Rule 10A-3 of the Exchange Act, no member of the audit committee may, other than in his or her capacity as a member of the audit committee, the board of directors or any other board committee:

- accept, directly or indirectly, any consulting, advisory or other compensatory fee from the issuer or any subsidiary;[192] or
- be an affiliated person of the listed company or any subsidiary thereof.

Each listed company must have an audit committee composed of at least three directors, all of whom must be independent.[193] Each member of the audit committee must be financially literate (as that qualification is interpreted by the listed company's board of directors in its business judgment), or must become financially literate within a reasonable period of time after his or her appointment to the audit committee. In addition, at least one member of the audit committee must have accounting or related financial management expertise (as the listed company's board of directors interprets that qualification in its business judgment). If a director qualifies as an audit committee financial expert, the board of directors may presume that he or she has accounting or related financial management experience.

If an audit committee member simultaneously serves on the audit committee of more than three public companies, the board of directors must determine that the simultaneous service does not impair the ability of the member to effectively serve on the listed company's audit committee and disclose this determination either on or through the listed company's website or in its annual meeting proxy statement or, if none, its annual report filed with the SEC.

The audit committee must have a written charter that addresses:

- the committee's purpose, which, at a minimum, must be to: (i) assist the board of directors' oversight of the integrity of the listed company's financial statements, the listed company's compliance with legal and regulatory requirements, the independent auditors' qualifications and independence, and the performance of the listed company's internal audit function and independent auditors; and (ii) prepare the audit committee report required by the SEC to be included in the listed company's annual meeting proxy statement, or if none, its annual report;
- an annual performance evaluation of the audit committee; and
- the duties and responsibilities of the audit committee, which, at a minimum, must include:
  - being directly responsible, subject to limited exceptions, for the appointment, compensation, retention and oversight of the work of any independent auditor engaged (including resolution of disagreements between management and the independent auditor regarding financial reporting)

[192] Compensatory fees do not include the receipt of fixed amounts of compensation under a retirement plan for prior service with the listed company provided that such compensation is not contingent in any way on the continued service.

[193] NYSE Rule 303A.07.

for the purpose of preparing or issuing an audit report or performing other audit, review or attest services for the listed company, and each such independent auditor must report directly to the audit committee;
- the establishment of procedures for the receipt, retention and treatment of complaints received by the listed company regarding accounting, internal accounting controls or auditing matters; and the confidential, anonymous submission by employees of the listed company of concerns regarding questionable accounting or auditing matters;
- the authority to engage independent counsel and other advisers as the committee determines necessary to carry out its duties;
- the ability to receive adequate funding, as determined by the audit committee, in its capacity as a committee of the board of directors, for payment of the compensation to any independent auditor engaged for the purpose of preparing or issuing an audit report or performing other audit, review or attest services for the listed company, compensation to any advisers employed by the audit committee and ordinary administrative expenses of the audit committee that are necessary or appropriate in carrying out its duties;
- at least annually, obtain and review a report by the independent auditor describing: the firm's internal quality-control procedures; any material issues raised by the most recent internal quality-control review or peer review of the firm or by any inquiry or investigation by governmental or professional authorities, within the preceding five years, respecting one or more independent audits carried out by the firm and any steps taken to deal with any such issues; and to assess the auditor's independence, all relationships between the independent auditor and the listed company (after reviewing this report, the audit committee will be in a position to evaluate the auditor's qualifications, performance and independence, to consider whether there should be regular rotation of the audit firm and to report its conclusions to the full board of directors);
- discuss the listed company's annual audited financial statements and quarterly financial statements with management and the independent auditor, including the listed company's disclosures under its MD&A;
- discuss the listed company's earnings press releases, as well as financial information and earnings guidance provided to analysts and rating agencies, which may be done generally and need not be done in advance of each release or discussion;
- discuss policies with respect to risk assessment and risk management to govern the process by which it is handled;
- meet separately, periodically, with management, with internal auditors (or persons performing that function) and with independent auditors;
- review with the independent auditor any audit problems or difficulties and management's responses thereto, including any accounting adjustments that were noted or proposed by the auditor but were "passed" (as immaterial or otherwise), any communications between the audit team and the audit firm's national office respecting auditing or accounting issues presented by the engagement, any management or internal control letters issued, or

proposed to be issued, by the independent auditors, and the responsibilities, budget and staffing of the listed company's internal audit function;
  - set clear hiring policies for employees or former employees of the independent auditors; and
- report regularly to the board of directors, in particular regarding any issues that arise with respect to the quality or integrity of the listed company's financial statements, the listed company's compliance with legal or regulatory requirements, the performance and independence of the listed company's independent auditors or the performance of the internal audit function.

The audit committee must also review: (i) major issues regarding accounting principles and financial statement presentations, including any significant changes in the listed company's selection or application of accounting principles, and major issues as to the adequacy of the listed company's internal controls; (ii) analyses prepared by management and/or the independent auditor setting forth significant financial reporting issues and judgments made in connection with the preparation of the financial statements; (iii) the effect of regulatory and accounting initiatives, as well as off-balance sheet structures, on the financial statements of the listed company; and (iv) the type and presentation of information to be included in earnings press releases, paying particular attention to any use of pro forma or adjusted non-GAAP information, as well as review any financial information and earnings guidance provided to analysts and rating agencies.

Finally, each listed company must have an internal audit function.

Shareholder Approval of Equity Compensation Plans

The NYSE rules require that, with certain limited exceptions, shareholders approved all equity-compensation plans and material revisions thereto.[194] An equity compensation plan is a plan or other arrangement that provides for the delivery of equity securities of the listed company to any employee, director or other service provider as compensation for services, other than plans that are made available to shareholders generally, such as a typical dividend reinvestment plan, or plans that merely allow employees, directors or other service providers to elect to buy shares for their current fair market value.

Corporate Governance Guidelines

The NYSE rules require each listed company to adopt and disclose corporate governance guidelines addressing the following:[195]

- director qualification standards, including independence requirements, any policies, limiting the number of boards on which a director may sit and director tenure, retirement and succession matters;
- director responsibilities, including basic duties and responsibilities with respect to attendance at board meetings and advance review of meeting materials;
- director access to management and, as necessary and appropriate, independent advisors;

[194] NYSE Rule 303A.08.
[195] NYSE Rule 303A.09.

- director compensation, including general principles for determining the form and amount of director compensation;
- director orientation and continuing education;
- management succession, including policies and principles for CEO selection and performance review, as well as policies regarding succession in the event of an emergency or the retirement of the CEO; and
- annual performance evaluation of the board of directors.

Each listed company's website must include its corporate governance guidelines and the charters of its most important committees. Its annual report must state that the foregoing information is available on its website, and that the information is available in print to any shareholder who requests it.

Code of Business Conduct and Ethics

Each listed company must adopt and disclose a code of business conduct and ethics for directors, officers and employees, and promptly disclose any waivers of the code for directors or executive officers.[196] The code of business conduct and ethics must require that any waiver of the code for directors and executive officers be made only by the board of directors or a committee of the board of directors and must be promptly disclosed to shareholders.

Each code of business conduct and ethics must contain compliance standards and procedures that facilitate the effective operation of the code and address:

- conflicts of interest, including a policy prohibiting conflicts of interest and providing a means for employees, officers and directors to communicate potential conflicts to the listed company;
- corporate opportunities, including a prohibition on employees, officers and directors from personally taking opportunities that are discovered through the use of corporate property, information or position, using corporate property, information or position for personal gain, and competing with the listed company;
- confidentiality of information entrusted to employees, officers and directors by the listed company or its customers, except when disclosure is authorized or legally mandated;
- fair dealing with the listed company's customers, suppliers, competitors and employees;
- protection and proper use of the listed company's assets;
- compliance with laws, rules and regulations, including insider trading laws; and
- encouraging the reporting of any illegal or unethical behavior, which includes a non-retaliation policy for reports made in good faith.

The listed company's website must include its code of business conduct and ethics. The listed company's annual report filed with the SEC must state that the foregoing information is available on its website and that the information is available to any shareholder who requests it.

[196] NYSE Rule 303A.10.

Certifications of Compliance with Listing Standards

The CEO of each listed company must certify to the NYSE each year that he or she is not aware of any violation by the listed company of the NYSE corporate governance listing standards.[197] An interim affirmation is required to be provided to the NYSE each time a change occurs to the board of directors or any of the committees specified in the corporate governance listing standards. The NYSE expects issuers to file the certification with the NYSE within 30 days after its annual meeting of shareholders. This certification and the certifications of the CEO and the CFO required to be filed by the Sarbanes-Oxley Act must be included in the listed company's annual report distributed to shareholders or, if none, its annual report filed with the SEC. However, if the listed company distributes a "glossy" annual report to shareholders which does not include a complete copy of the Form 10-K or Form 20-F as part of the annual report, the listed company can incorporate the certifications of the CEO and CFO required to be filed by the Sarbanes-Oxley Act rather than including them in the annual report to shareholders.

The CEO of each listed company must promptly notify the NYSE in writing after any executive officer becomes aware of any non-compliance with any applicable provisions of the corporate governance listing standards.

Violations of Listing Standards

The NYSE may issue a public reprimand letter to any listed company that violates an NYSE listing standard.[198] For companies that repeatedly or flagrantly violate NYSE listing standards, suspension or delisting remain the ultimate penalties.

Ceasing to be a Foreign Private Issuer

Within six months of ceasing to qualify as a foreign private issuer, an NYSE listed company must satisfy the majority independent board requirements, satisfy the website posting requirements, have fully independent nominating and compensation committees and have a three person audit committee whose members comply with the applicable independence requirements. By the later of six months after ceasing to qualify as a foreign private issuer and the first annual meeting (but not more than 12 months) after such occurrence, such company would also have to comply with the shareholder approval requirements for equity compensation plans.

NASDAQ

NASDAQ's corporate governance rules are set out in NASDAQ Rule 5600 Series. As is the case with the NYSE's corporate governance rules, a foreign private issuer may follow its home country practice in lieu of the requirements of the NASDAQ Rule 5600 Series, provided that such an issuer must (i) notify NASDAQ in writing promptly after any executive officer becomes aware of any material non-compliance with the requirements of NASDAQ Rule 5600 Series, (ii) must comply with the requirement that voting rights of existing holders of stock registered under Section 12 of the Exchange Act cannot be

[197] NYSE Rule 303A.12.
[198] NYSE Rule 303A.13.

disparately reduced or restricted through any corporate action or issuance and (iii) must comply with Rule 10A-3 under the Exchange Act relating to audit committees and their independence. A foreign private issuer that follows a home country practice in lieu of one of the requirements of NASDAQ Rule 5600 Series must disclose each requirement that it does not follow (and describe the home country practice it follows) in its annual report filed with the SEC or on its website or, in the case of a foreign private issuer making its initial public offering in the United States or its first listing on NASDAQ, in its registration statement filed with the SEC or on its website.

The scope and substance of the NASDAQ's corporate governance requirements are substantially similar to the corporate governance requirements of the NYSE, addressing director independence, nominating and governance committees, compensation committee and audit committee requirements, the need for a code of ethics and compliance certificates. There are certain differences, however, such that the NASDAQ rules require ongoing reviews of related party transactions for conflict-of-interest situations and for such transactions to be approved by the audit committee or other independent body of the board of directors. The NASDAQ rules also do not require adoption of corporate governance guidelines as required by the NYSE, although it may be good practice to do so.

TAX CONSIDERATIONS

[373] When a foreign investor plans to acquire an existing U.S. business, the acquisition can generally be structured one of two ways: (i) the foreign investor can buy the assets of the target business directly or (ii) the foreign investor can buy the stock or other ownership interests in the target. Each of these two methods (discussed in more detail in paragraphs 01–81 above) has different advantages and disadvantages to each of the buyer and the seller of which a foreign investor should be aware. Often, however, a foreign investor may have little discretion in structuring the acquisition due to the seller's tax considerations and the cost of compensating the seller for the incremental tax costs that arise from utilizing the buyer's preferred structure.

BUYER AND SELLER OBJECTIVES

Seller Objectives

[374] As a general matter, a U.S. seller will attempt to maximize its after-tax proceeds on the disposition of its business. In the case of a sale at a gain, that goal generally is achieved by limiting the amount of the gain and, in the case of an individual, maximizing the amount of gain that is taxed at long-term capital gains rates (currently taxed at a maximum federal rate of 20% for assets held for more than one year (plus 3.8% for certain individuals)) rather than ordinary income rates (taxed at a maximum federal rate of 39.6%). If the seller of a U.S. business is a foreign person, the seller's goal is to avoid any U.S. tax on the sale. Generally, a foreign person is not subject to U.S. federal income tax on any capital gains (assuming that such capital gain is not connected with a U.S. trade or business). However, where the disposition is at a loss, limitations on the use of capital losses (except for a small amount permitted to individuals, capital losses can only be used to offset capital gains), and the inability to claim certain losses on the dispositions of members of consolidated groups lead to different considerations.

Foreign Buyer Considerations

[375] A far greater number of U.S. federal income tax considerations will affect the foreign investor than the U.S. seller in an acquisition. The foreign investor will generally try to optimize the post-acquisition tax position of both itself and the acquired entity by (i) stepping-up the basis in the underlying entity's assets to decrease the amount of future income subject to U.S. taxation; (ii) consolidating all U.S. activities in a single, consolidated group; and (iii) removing any foreign operations from the U.S. taxing jurisdiction. These tax considerations affect both the purchase price and the structure of the acquisition.

ASSET ACQUISITION

Tax Considerations of Seller

[376] As noted above, the seller's primary considerations will be (i) to minimize the amount of gain recognized on the sale and (ii), in the case of an individual seller, to maximize the amount of gain taxed as long-term capital gain.[199] An asset sale may not allow the seller to achieve either goal. Assuming the target entity is a corporation, any gain on the disposition of corporate assets may be subject to double taxation. Tax will be due on any gain recognized at the corporate level (corporations are not entitled to preferential rates on capital gains) and then again as the after-tax proceeds are distributed to the shareholders as either a dividend (assuming the corporate seller has earnings and profits)[200] or in liquidation of the corporate seller (assuming the shareholders are not corporations that own at least 80% (by vote and value) of the corporate seller's stock and the amount of the liquidation proceeds exceeds the shareholder's basis in its stock).

[199] Although only individuals are taxed at a lower rate on capital gains, corporations may care about the character of income as capital or ordinary. As noted above, if a corporation has capital losses, those losses will not reduce ordinary income, only capital gain. Thus, if a corporation has capital losses in the year of the sale or has carried over capital losses from earlier periods (corporations can carry over unused capital losses for five years), it will prefer capital gains from the sale of the business rather than ordinary income.

[200] If the shareholder that receives the dividend is taxed as a corporation, the recipient generally would be entitled to: (i) a 70% dividends-received deduction if it owned less than 20% of the stock (by vote or value) of the payor; (ii) an 80% dividends-received deduction if it owned at least 20% (by vote and value) but less than 80% (by vote or value) of the stock of the payor; and (3) a 100% dividends-received deduction if it owned at least 80% (by vote and value) of the stock of the payor (and certain other requirements were met).

[377] This double-tax burden is not applicable on the sale of the assets of a partnership (including entities that are taxed as partnerships, such as limited liability companies with more than one member and that have not elected to be taxed as a "C" corporation) or an "S" corporation,[201] since partnerships and "S" corporations generally do not pay entity-level taxes; rather, any taxable income recognized with respect to the asset sale of a partnership or an "S" corporation is taken into account by the partners or shareholders, as applicable, and such owners must pay any resulting tax liability. However, if the "S" corporation has not been an "S" corporation since its inception, a corporate-level tax (the "built-in gains" tax) may be due on the gains, if any, inherent in the corporate assets at the time of its conversion to an "S" corporation. However, a sale of certain business assets (such as inventory or accounts receivables) may give rise to ordinary income (rather than capital gain), which is recognized by the entity's owners.

[378] A corporate shareholder holding 80% or more of the stock of a subsidiary that joins in the filing of a consolidated tax return with the seller will also not be subject to double taxation on the sale of assets of its subsidiary. However, if the subsidiary being sold was previously acquired by the seller in a transaction treated as a stock purchase, the seller's basis in the stock of the subsidiary may be higher than the subsidiary's basis in its assets. Because, in the case of a corporation, capital gains are taxed at the same rate as ordinary income, the corporate seller still will want to sell stock. If, however, the sale of the stock would give rise to a loss, rules prohibiting the recognition of certain losses on the sale of stock of a subsidiary can sometimes be avoided by selling assets.

[379] Foreign persons who are selling their U.S. business often will have to consider both U.S. tax considerations and tax issues arising out of the country where they are incorporated. From a U.S. tax perspective, the sale of corporate stock (or any other capital asset other than U.S. real property) owned by a foreign person generally will not be subject to U.S. income tax.[202] Thus, they will have a strong incentive to sell stock rather than assets. If they own an interest in a partnership or other pass-through entity and such entity is engaged in a U.S. trade or business, they will be subject to U.S. tax on any gain whether they sell an interest in the pass-through entity or if the entity sells assets and distributes the proceeds to the foreign person.

Tax Considerations of Buyer

[380] In most cases, it will be preferable for the foreign investor to acquire assets rather than stock. However, if the target is a corporation and the aggregate basis

[201] An "S" corporation is a corporation which, unlike a "regular" corporation (known as a "C" corporation), is not generally taxed on its income. Rather, the "S" corporation's items of income, gain, loss, deduction and credit are passed through to the shareholders and reported by them. To qualify as an "S" corporation, an entity must meet certain requirements and must be a U.S. corporation with only one class of stock and with no more than 75 shareholders who must be U.S. residents or certain qualified trusts.

[202] One instance when a foreign person will be subject to U.S. tax on gain from the sale of stock of a U.S. corporation is if the U.S. corporation is a "U.S. real property holding corporation" ("USRPHC"). A USRPHC is a U.S. corporation if at any time during the last five years more than 50% of the value of its assets consisted of U.S. real property interests.

of its assets is higher than the purchase price of the stock, a stock purchase may be preferable since the higher asset basis will remain with the acquired corporation.

Step-Up in Basis of Assets

[381] In the majority of acquisitions, the purchase price will exceed the aggregate adjusted basis of the underlying depreciable or amortizable corporate assets. In this case, a purchase of assets rather than stock will allow a foreign buyer to depreciate or amortize its newly acquired assets for the full purchase price, thereby reducing its taxable income on a going-forward basis. If the purchase price is greater than the aggregate fair market value of the acquired assets, the remainder will be allocated to goodwill, which generally can be amortized over a 15-year period. With a stock acquisition, the adjusted basis of each depreciable asset will be preserved.

Consolidation of U.S. Operations

[382] When considering how to structure an acquisition of a U.S. business, a foreign investor should also analyze its current, if any, U.S. activities and U.S. source income. An optimal structure would allow the foreign investor to integrate all current and proposed U.S. activities in a meaningful manner, both from a business and from a U.S. federal income tax perspective. Considerations in this regard would include ownership requirements for filing returns on a consolidated basis in the United States, as well as tax presence issues. An asset acquisition may allow a foreign purchaser to immediately transfer foreign assets from the U.S. chain of ownership to the foreign buyer's foreign operations with no additional tax cost.

Debt Financing of Acquisition

[383] While the broader issue of the financing of a U.S. acquisition is beyond the scope of this section, some of the U.S. federal income tax issues relating to any debt financing should be mentioned. Generally, a U.S. taxpayer is permitted a deduction for interest on debt used to finance the acquisition of a trade or business. However, because there is generally no similar deduction permitted for a dividend paid with respect to equity used to finance an acquisition of a trade or business, or to finance its operations, special considerations apply where debt from a related person is used to finance the acquisition. First, in order for the intercompany obligation to be treated as debt (rather than equity), it is important to treat the transaction as though it were financed by a third party. This involves not only documenting the intercompany obligation as debt, but also establishing a market rate of interest, giving the related person the standard rights of a creditor upon default and ensuring that interest and other payments are made when due. In addition, while the United States does not have any statutory thin capitalization rules, the case law serves to limit the permissive debt-to-equity ratio from related-party debt and may recharacterize excessive debt as equity. Second, in 2016, the IRS promulgated final and temporary regulations that, if applicable, allow the IRS to treat purported debt as equity, and to treat purported deductible interest payments as nondeductible dividend payments. In general, these rules will apply where (a) a U.S. corporation is at least owned 80% directly or indirectly by a non-U.S. parent, (b) that U.S. corporation issues debt to the non-U.S. parent, and (c) there is no new investment in the U.S. corporation (or any of its controlled subsidiaries) by the non-U.S. parent in connection with the issuance of the debt.

[384] Even if the related-party financing is treated as debt for tax purposes, the deduction of a U.S. corporation may be limited by the "earnings stripping rules" of the U.S. Internal Revenue Code of 1986, as amended (the "Code") if the indebtedness is from or guaranteed directly or indirectly by its foreign parent (for this purpose, guarantees include comfort letters and other nonbinding commitments). The earnings stripping rules only apply if the debt-to-equity ratio exceeds 1.5 to 1 and its net interest expense (*i.e.*, interest expense less interest income) exceeds 50% of the corporation "adjusted taxable income" (*i.e.*, taxable income without reduction for interest expense, depreciation and other miscellaneous items). If these rules apply, the interest expense is only deferred until the net interest expense or debt-to-equity ratio drops to acceptable levels.

Choice of Entity

[385] The rules governing acquisitions of assets generally apply equally regardless of the type of entity that is used to make the acquisition. Thus, the choice of entity to make the acquisition depends on how the foreign investor wishes to be taxed. Although the taxation of foreign persons is discussed in more detail below, as a practical matter, there are two basic choices for an acquisition vehicle.

[386] One possibility is to use a corporation. The corporation would be subject to corporate-level taxation and either a withholding tax on dividends paid (if a U.S. corporation is used and no treaty benefits are available for the owner of the U.S. corporation), or a branch profits tax (if a foreign corporation is used and no treaty benefits are available for the foreign corporation). On the other hand, a partnership is not a taxable entity in the United States, but its partners are subject to tax on their respective proportionate share of U.S. trade or business income of the partnership. Thus, foreign partners generally would be required to file U.S. tax returns to report their respective shares of the income of the partnership and may be subject to a branch profits tax as well.

[387] Foreign investment through entities treated as partnerships for U.S. federal income tax purposes is popular. The use of limited liability companies (LLCs) is becoming increasingly widespread due to its tax treatment as a partnership accompanied with limited liability for state law purposes. Investment through a partnership as opposed to through a corporation can also affect the availability of treaty benefits. However, if an entity that is treated as a partnership for U.S. federal income tax purposes is engaged in, or deemed to be engaged in, a U.S. trade or business, non-U.S. equity investors in an entity would also be deemed to be so engaged by virtue of their ownership of such equity. In that event, a non-U.S. equity investor would be required to file a U.S. federal income tax return for such year and pay tax on its income and gain that is effectively connected with that U.S. trade or business at the tax rates applicable to similarly situated United States persons. In addition, any non-U.S. equity investor that is a corporation for U.S. federal income tax purposes may be required to pay a branch profits tax equal to 30% of its earnings and profits for the taxable year that are not reinvested in the business. The entity treated as a partnership would also be required to withhold taxes on any income and gain effectively connected with a U.S. trade or business that is allocable to a non-U.S. equity investor under Section 1446 of the Code.

State Tax Considerations

[388] Most states conform their corporate income tax provisions to federal income tax law. As a result, the general treatment for federal income tax purposes of an asset sale as a taxable transaction equally applies for state and local tax purposes. However, the federal tax basis for an asset may be different from the state tax basis for the same asset because some state and federal depreciation rules differ. As a result, the amount of taxable gain in some states may differ from the federal amount of gain.

[389] Another state tax concern in an asset purchase is the purchaser's liability for the seller's previously existing state tax liabilities. While a purchaser generally prefers to acquire assets of a business as opposed to stock in order to avoid liability for the seller's pre-existing obligations, many states, unlike Federal tax law, impose liability for the seller's sales tax on the purchaser of the seller's business when the purchaser acquires the assets of the seller's business. States vary considerably in their methods of enforcing the tax liability. Many states that impose the seller's outstanding sales tax liability upon the purchaser also have "bulk sale" notification provisions. Such provisions require a bulk sale notification be given to the state prior to the asset sale and compliance with such provisions can absolve the purchaser of any liabilities.

[390] Almost every state imposes sales and use tax on transfers of tangible personal property for consideration. In an asset transfer, the state sales and use tax would apply to any tangible personal property transferred in the sale. States vary as to whether the sales tax is legally imposed upon the seller or the purchaser. However, most states provide an occasional sale exemption, which exempts the sale of an entire division or other going business from sales and use tax, but the breadth of these provisions vary from state to state, with some states' occasional sales provisions being quite narrow. In addition, many states and localities impose a realty transfer tax on the sale or transfer of real estate or, in some cases, transfers of leases of real property.

STOCK ACQUISITION

Tax Considerations of Seller

[391] Assuming the sellers are individuals, the sale of stock, as opposed to assets, means that the sellers will avoid the imposition of corporate-level tax on the appreciation of the underlying assets, and any gain will be taxed at capital gains rates (assuming the assets are held in an entity that is treated as a corporation for U.S. federal income tax purposes). This tax benefit to the seller should be a point in negotiating the purchase price, especially since the buyer will not be able to step-up the basis of the underlying assets of the business.

[392] The sellers may also prefer to sell stock rather than assets because the foreign entity will be acquiring the legal entity with all of its legal attributes, as well as the going business. Because the corporation will remain intact, the purchaser will assume all of the corporation's existing, contingent and unstated liabilities, including any liabilities for unpaid taxes. The foreign investor's exposure can be mitigated through the negotiation of warranties and indemnification for breach of such warranties and pre-closing taxes to protect the buyer against future unforeseen liabilities. When the seller has substantial other assets or is otherwise creditworthy, these warranties can meaningfully reduce the risk of loss to the foreign investor. In addition, the foreign investor could negotiate some sort of "holdback" or escrow of part of the purchase price until a future date when the buyer has more knowledge of the liabilities to which the target corporation is subject or obtain "representation and warranty" insurance.

Tax Considerations of Buyer

[393] While a stock acquisition, absent a "Section 338 election" (discussed below), will not allow a buyer to fully depreciate the fair market value of the assets of the acquired business to the extent of the purchase price paid for the business, it may preserve net operating loss ("NOLs") carry-forwards and other tax attributes present in the target (although the use of those attributes will be limited). This consideration is especially relevant when a foreign investor intends to acquire a minority or non-controlling stake in the target corporation, but it may be much less important when the foreign investor obtains a majority or controlling stake in the target corporation. Generally, if there is more than a 50% change in ownership of a corporation with NOLs, the corporation can only use NOLs in any year after the change in ownership in an amount equal to the equity value of the corporation multiplied by the "long-term tax-exempt rate" (which varies monthly). Similar rules apply to other tax attributes such as tax credits following an ownership change.

[394] As noted above, in those limited cases where the purchase price for the stock is lower than the aggregate adjusted basis of the corporation's depreciable assets, the foreign investor will consider a stock acquisition to be more tax efficient. This can occur when the value of the corporation and its underlying assets have declined significantly (*e.g.*, because of unforeseen liabilities or in a recessionary business environment) but the depreciable corporate assets still have a high adjusted basis for tax purposes. A stock acquisition will allow the foreign investor to benefit from the high depreciation of the underlying corporate assets.

[395] Additional consideration should also be given to the allocation of part of the purchase price in any acquisition to a covenant not to compete, especially in a stock acquisition. While stock is a nondepreciable asset, the basis of a covenant not to compete generally can be amortized over a 15-year period. An individual seller, on the other hand, will resist an allocation to a covenant not to compete because income from the covenant will be ordinary rather than capital. It is important to document any intended allocation to a covenant not to compete during the negotiations and preferably in the acquisition documentation to forestall any challenge by the U.S. Internal Revenue Service ("IRS").

Section 338 Election

[396] As discussed above, the primary drawback to a stock acquisition is the inability of the foreign investor to fully depreciate the fair market value of the assets of the acquired business to the extent of the purchase price paid for the business, including goodwill and going-concern value. In certain cases, an election under Section 338 of the Code can be used by the foreign corporate buyer to step-up the basis in the assets of a corporate target. It is the functional equivalent of an asset sale for U.S. federal income tax purposes, but a stock sale for all other purposes (*i.e.*, assumption of liabilities and state law benefits).

[397] There are two types of Section 338 elections. In both cases, the target corporation is treated as selling all of its assets to a new corporation and then liquidating. However, in an election under Section 338(g) of the Code, the purchaser bears the tax liability for the deemed asset sale. The seller is not required to join in a Section 338(g) election, unlike a Section 338(h)(10) election which is a joint election by the seller and the purchaser. As a practical matter, a Section 338(g) election will only be made if the target corporation has enough net operating losses to offset any gain on the deemed sale or is a foreign corporation that is not a controlled foreign corporation. In a Section 338(h)(10) election, the tax liability for the deemed asset sale remains with the seller. However, a Section 338(h)(10) election can only be made by a corporation selling an affiliated subsidiary in a consolidated group or by persons selling stock of a subchapter S corporation. In either case, the seller will agree to join in a Section 338(h)(10) election only if he will bear little or no incremental tax cost from making the election. (*See* discussion of seller considerations in asset sales.)

[398] The state tax consequences of making a Section 338 election may differ significantly among the states. Some states do not follow the federal concepts of income, while some states recognize a Section 338(g) election, but not a Section 338(h)(10) election. This raises the potential for incongruous tax consequences at the state and federal levels. For example, if a state taxes gain on subsidiary capital and does not recognize a 338(h)(10) election, the seller will be taxed on its stock sale, and the target (and the buyer) will be taxed on its separate deemed asset sale.

TAX-FREE ACQUISITIONS

Tax-Free Acquisition of a U.S. Target

[399] A foreign corporate buyer may prefer to complete a tax-free acquisition of a target U.S. corporation by tendering its own stock (or, in limited cases, securities) as consideration to the seller. The advantage to the seller is that the seller can defer recognition of any gain, and as a result any income taxes, from the "sale" (but not from the receipt of "boot"—*i.e.*, something other than stock or securities) by taking an equity interest in the buyer. The buyer may be in a position to negotiate a sale on better economic terms because of the tax savings realized by the seller, although at the cost of providing the seller with an equity or other stake in the buyer. However, a tax-free reorganization also would not cause a step-up in the basis of the underlying corporate assets to fair market value.

[400] There are a variety of forms of tax-free transactions under the Code. In a "Section 351" exchange, property (including stock) can be transferred tax free to a corporation in exchange for stock if the persons transferring such property "control" the transferee immediately after the exchange (*i.e.*, the transferors own stock possessing at least 80% of the total combined voting power of all classes of stock entitled to vote and at least 80% of the total number of shares of all other classes of stock of the corporation). This may require the formation of a holding company to which the target's shareholder and the foreign buyer both transfer property. The other tax-free transactions are reorganization provisions under Section 368 of the Code. These transactions include mergers (including foreign law equivalents such as amalgamations) and acquisitions of stock or assets solely for voting stock of the purchaser or its parent. If stock in a foreign corporation is given to a U.S. person in exchange for stock or assets of a target corporation, Section 367 of the Code (discussed below) will generally apply.

Section 367 Complexity

[401] Although both the foreign buyer and the seller may seek to structure an acquisition that would otherwise be tax-free under the Code, Section 367 of the Code may prevent the tax-free treatment of the acquisition involving a foreign corporation. Current regulations under Section 367 of the Code permit the tax-free acquisitions of U.S. corporations by foreign corporations where the U.S. persons own less than 50% of the foreign corporation after the acquisition and if certain other requirements are satisfied. Moreover, a U.S. seller who becomes a 5% or greater shareholder of the foreign investor would have to enter into a gain recognition agreement, whereby it agrees to recognize its gain on the transaction if, among other things, the foreign acquirer disposes of its interest in the target corporation or substantially all of the target corporation's assets within five years.

[402] A foreign acquirer can avoid the complexities and limitations of Section 367, however, if it uses the stock of a U.S. corporation to complete the acquisitive reorganization. As a practical matter, the buyer may be hesitant to accept stock of a U.S. subsidiary of the foreign investor constituting a minority interest in exchange for its stock of the target unless such subsidiary has substantial assets.

State Tax Consequences

[403] Most states do not specifically address corporate reorganizations, and instead such states rely upon their general conformity provisions to federal income tax laws. As such, a transaction that is a tax-free reorganization for federal income tax purposes will also be a tax-free reorganization for state income tax purposes.

[404] In addition, some states provide a sales and use tax exemption for any transfer of tangible personal property pursuant to an income tax-free reorganization described in Section 368 of the Code. If no specific exemption is provided, the state tax consequences will mirror those of an asset or stock sale depending on how the reorganization is structured.

POST-ACQUISITION U.S. FEDERAL INCOME TAXATION OF FOREIGN INVESTOR

Taxation of Foreign Persons

[405] The United States has two methods of taxation applicable to foreign persons depending on the nature of the income and whether or not the foreign person is considered to be engaged in a U.S. trade or business. A foreign person is defined as a foreign corporation, nonresident alien individual, foreign partnership, or a foreign estate or trust. A foreign person whose level of income-producing activity constitutes a U.S. trade or business is subject to tax on its net income effectively connected with that U.S. trade or business at graduated rates in a manner similar to that of a similarly situated U.S. person with trade or business income. Currently, the maximum marginal rate of tax imposed on the net trade or business income of a foreign person is 35%, in the case of a foreign corporation, and 39.6%, in the case of a nonresident alien individual. If such a foreign person is a foreign corporation, such foreign corporation also may be subject to a branch profits tax.

[406] A foreign person not engaged in the conduct of a U.S. trade or business may be subject to tax on the gross amount of fixed and determinable annual or periodical U.S. source income (*e.g.*, dividends, interest, rents and royalties) at a flat tax rate, typically collected through withholding taxes. The flat rate of tax, unless modified by treaty, is 30%. A foreign person can also elect to treat certain passive income from U.S. real property as effectively connected trade or business income and, thereby, be subject to tax on a net, rather than a gross, basis.

U.S. Trade or Business Income

[407] The determination of whether a foreign person is engaged in the conduct of a U.S. trade or business is a question of fact. There is no bright-line test to determine whether a foreign person has sufficient income-producing activities to be considered to be engaged in the conduct of a U.S. trade or business. Generally, the higher the level of contact with the United States, the more likely the foreign person will be treated as being engaged in the conduct of a U.S. trade or business.

[408] The following factors, while not exhaustive, should be taken into account to determine whether a foreign person is engaged in a U.S. trade or business:

- use of a U.S. office or other fixed place of business;
- use of U.S. employees;
- use of a resident agent or other local representative, such person's power to contractually and legally bind the foreign person, and the frequency of such person's use of that power;
- number, frequency and range of U.S.-based activities
- investment through a partnership or trust, trust or other entities that are treated as "pass-through" entities for U.S. federal income tax purposes;
- types of investments; and
- character of the activities.

EFFECTIVELY CONNECTED INCOME

[409] Only income that is "effectively connected" with the conduct of the foreign person's U.S. trade or business will be subject to tax in the United States at graduated rates. U.S. source income that is fixed or determinable annual or periodical income will be regarded as effectively connected U.S. trade or business income if it is derived from U.S. assets or U.S. business activities. U.S. source income that is not fixed or determinable will generally be regarded as effectively connected with a U.S. trade or business. In certain limited cases, foreign source income also may be regarded as effectively connected U.S. trade or business income to the extent that such income is attributable to the foreign person's U.S. office or other fixed place of business.

BRANCH PROFITS TAX

[410] A foreign corporation engaged in the conduct of a U.S. trade or business may also be subject to a branch profits tax on its "effectively connected earnings and profits," as though it repatriated its earnings and profits from the United States in the form of a dividend from a subsidiary entity. The branch profits tax is imposed at a maximum rate of 30%, unless modified by treaty, on any amount that is not reinvested or deemed reinvested in the U.S. trade or business ("dividend equivalent amount") as though the branch distributed a dividend of its earnings and profits for the year. It is intended to equalize the treatment of U.S. branches of foreign corporations with that of the operation of a U.S. trade or business through a U.S. subsidiary.

TREATY MODIFICATIONS

[411] The United States has numerous treaties for the elimination of double taxation with foreign countries in force. A resident of one of these countries may be able to rely on its country's treaty with the United States to prevent the taxation of its business income as U.S. trade or business income, except to the extent that the business income is attributable to a U.S. "permanent establishment" so long as such resident is entitled to claim the benefits of such treaty. Each of these treaties provides a specific definition of permanent establishment. As general matter, a permanent establishment will be found to exist if the foreign person maintains "a fixed place of business" through which the business of an enterprise is wholly or partly carried on. The treaty requirement of a permanent establishment is generally considered to be harder to satisfy than the nontreaty standard of being engaged in a U.S. trade or business. U.S. source income of a passive type (*e.g.*, dividends, interest, royalties) of a foreign person that is not attributable to a permanent establishment is still subject to withholding, albeit at a rate that is generally reduced by treaty. The branch profits tax rate may also be reduced or eliminated by treaty to the maximum permitted rate of withholding on payments of dividends to such country.

STATE TAXATION

[412] Generally, states impose income and franchise taxes upon corporations doing business within the state. If a foreign corporation that was not previously subject to a state's taxing jurisdiction acquires the assets of a target corporation that is doing business in the state, the foreign corporation may now be considered to be doing business in the state and, thus, be subject to the state's taxing jurisdiction. Note that this rule may apply even if an applicable tax treaty would provide that the foreign corporation does not have a permanent establishment in the United States because the treaty generally will not apply to state taxes. If a foreign corporation acquires the stock of a target, instead of the target's assets, then the foreign corporation will not necessarily be considered to be doing business in those states where the target is doing business.

FOREIGN INVESTMENT IN U.S. REAL PROPERTY (FIRPTA)

[413] Generally, a foreign person's capital gains that are not effectively connected to a U.S. trade or business are not subject to U.S. federal income tax. However, with respect to real property, the United States has enacted rules which cause a foreign person to be subject to tax on the disposition of any "U.S. real property interest." A U.S. real property interest (a "USRPI") is defined as any interest in real property located in the United States or the Virgin Islands, and any equity interest in a U.S. real property holding company, but does not generally include a mortgage loan unless the loan provides for contingent payments based upon the income from or value of the real property securing the loan. Subject to certain exceptions, a U.S. real property holding company is any domestic corporation if the fair market value of its U.S. real property interests equals or exceeds the fair market value of all of its assets (except cash or cash equivalents).

[414] Any gain or loss that a foreign person recognizes in connection with the disposition of a USRPI would be generally treated as a gain or loss effectively connected with a U.S. trade or business engaged in by the foreign person, and would be subject to U.S. federal income tax on a net basis. In addition, there would be withholding by the purchaser, currently at a rate of 15%, of the gross proceeds from that disposition. Any such withholding tax may be refundable or creditable against the foreign person's actual U.S. federal income tax liability, provided that the required information is timely furnished to the IRS.

TAXATION OF FOREIGN OPERATIONS

[415] Foreign investors also need to be aware of various U.S. anti-deferral regimes that cause the current U.S. taxation of certain income earned by foreign operations of U.S. shareholders. These rules make the ownership of foreign operations by a foreign investor through a U.S. company often subject to a higher effective rate of taxation (and reporting requirements) than if the same operations were held by a non-U.S. company.

[416] The main U.S. tax regime of which a foreign investor should be aware are the controlled foreign corporation (CFC) provisions. "United States shareholders" (as defined in Section 958(b) of the Code) of a "CFC" are generally subject to current taxation on certain types of income earned by the CFC. For purposes of the CFC provisions, a "U.S. shareholder" is a U.S. person that owns 10% or more of the voting interests in the foreign corporation and a CFC is a foreign corporation that is owned more than 50% (by vote or value) by U.S. shareholders.

[417] These rules can increase the effective tax rate on income of foreign operations if held through a U.S. company in two ways. First, the U.S. corporate tax rate on such income may be higher than that of the foreign operations and of the foreign investor (*e.g.*, 35% U.S. corporate tax rate versus 19% UK corporate tax rate). Second, the earnings will be subject to a withholding tax on their subsequent repatriation up the ownership chain to the foreign investor (*e.g.*, 5% U.S.–UK treaty withholding rate on dividends if the foreign owner owns between 10% and 80% of the payor).

[418] While for business reasons, a foreign investor may desire to hold other investments through its U.S. subsidiary, the increased tax cost from that structure can be significant, depending on the size, revenues and future plans for the foreign operations. Furthermore, the business purposes may be able to be achieved through service agreements among the various entities providing for the desired goods or services and compensation on an arm's-length basis. Actual ownership of the foreign operations by a U.S. company may not be necessary to achieve the business goals.

[419] Some of these costs can be avoided or minimized if a U.S. corporation with CFCs is acquired by a foreign corporation and the "former" U.S. owners of the acquired U.S. corporation own less than 60% of the foreign acquirer after the acquisition. If a foreign acquirer engages in such a transaction, the acquired U.S. corporation may be able to sell its CFC(s) to a foreign affiliate and offset any taxable gain with certain tax attributes (*e.g.*, NOLs or tax credits). As a result of such a sale,

the acquired former CFC should no longer be subject to the CFC rules. Additionally, if the acquired U.S. corporation does not sell its CFCs (as described in the prior sentence) and such CFCs have "unrepatriated" earnings, such CFCs may be able to loan such earnings to the foreign acquirer (a "hopscotch loan") that should not be subject to taxation in the U.S.

TRANSFER PRICING

[420] The United States has rules which allow the IRS to reallocate items of income, gain, and loss among parties under common control "to prevent evasion of taxes." The regulations provide various methods by which goods and services can be priced, including the comparable uncontrolled price method, the resale price method, the cost-plus method, the profit-split method, and the comparable profits method. Because the IRS enjoys a tremendous amount of discretion in this area and its determination can only be overcome if a taxpayer can prove that such determination was unreasonable, arbitrary or capricious, the use of advance pricing agreements is becoming increasingly popular among taxpayers. These agreements can be between the United States and the taxpayer or can also include the government of a foreign jurisdiction as well.

U.S. ANTITRUST AND MERGER CONTROL LAWS

An Overview of U.S. Antitrust Laws

[421] U.S. antitrust law prohibits mergers and acquisitions where the effect may be substantially to lessen competition. U.S. antitrust law also reaches many forms of conduct that is not merger-related, with prohibitions against agreements that unreasonably restrain trade and behavior that monopolizes or attempts to monopolize a market. Companies participating in merger and acquisition activity relating to the United States should have an understanding of the laws governing competitive activities, for at least two reasons. First, acquirers may wish to include compliance with competition law as one element of due diligence, to assure that they are not buying into exposures from past antitrust violations.[203] Second, because the U.S. antitrust laws are extraterritorial in scope and are deemed to apply to conduct outside of the

[203] Certain egregious violations of the antitrust laws can be prosecuted criminally. An individual who authorizes, directs or participates in criminal violations of the antitrust laws commits a felony for which he or she is personally liable for fines of up to US$1 million and/or imprisonment for as long as 10 years for each offense. In recent years numerous business executives have been sentenced to jail for violations that involve price-fixing, bid-rigging, and market allocation. In addition, the company may be subject to fines of up to US$100 million for each violation of The Sherman Act; the government has also employed an alternative standard of the "twice the gain/twice the loss" to obtain fines of up to US$600 million. As a practical matter, mergers and acquisitions themselves will not be treated as criminal violations, but they may involve reviews that bring criminal conduct to light.

United States that affects U.S. commerce,[204] all parties may wish to assure that their U.S. and non-U.S. activities are antitrust-compliant before filing premerger notification under the HSR Act and submitting to review by U.S. authorities.

[422] The federal antitrust laws are enforced by the United States Department of Justice (the "DOJ"), the Federal Trade Commission (the "FTC"), state attorneys general, and private parties who have been injured by antitrust violations. Violations of the antitrust laws can result in treble damages and may expose a company to permanent injunctions that could place it at a severe competitive disadvantage. Even if successfully defended, antitrust litigation is extremely costly, burdensome and may have serious effects on a company's business reputation.

[423] In general, the antitrust laws require companies and their employees to conduct their business affairs and make their commercial decisions unilaterally and independently—for example, not in collaboration with their competitors. Several categories of business conduct are deemed to be egregious violations of the antitrust laws and are often addressed through criminal sanctions: agreements, understandings or arrangements between competitors that have the purpose or effect of establishing or influencing the price of goods or services (price-fixing); bid-rigging; and market allocation. Other categories of business conduct are viewed as less egregious, but can still result in antitrust exposure: group boycotts, tie-ins, exclusive dealing, reciprocal dealing, resale price maintenance, and monopolization.

MERGER REVIEW BY THE ANTITRUST ENFORCEMENT AGENCIES

[424] In the United States, responsibility at the federal level for review of mergers is vested in two agencies, the DOJ and the FTC. The principal statute governing the review of mergers by these agencies is section 7 of the Clayton Act, which prohibits mergers whose effect "may be substantially to lessen competition, or to tend to create a monopoly" in any line of commerce in any section of the country.[205] Mergers also may be challenged under section 1 of the Sherman Act[206] which prohibits contracts, combinations, and conspiracies in restraint of trade, and section 5 of the Federal Trade Commission Act[207] which prohibits unfair methods of competition.[208] Many

[204] *See United States v. Nippon Paper Co.*, 109 F.3d 1 (1st Cir. 1997) ("Sherman Act applies to wholly foreign conduct which has an intended and substantial effect in the United States").

[205] 15 U.S.C. §18.

[206] 15 U.S.C. §1.

[207] 15 U.S.C. §45.

[208] Section 7 of the Clayton Act, under which the majority of mergers and acquisitions are challenged, will prohibit a merger if its effect is substantially to lessen competition. *See Merger Guidelines* §0, n.1; 15 U.S.C. §18. Section 1 of the Sherman Act will prohibit a merger if it constitutes a contract, combination or conspiracy in restraint of trade. *See id.* at §0, n.2; 15 U.S.C. §1. Likewise, Section 5 of the FTC Act will prohibit a merger if it can be found to constitute an "unfair method of competition." *See id.* at §0, n.3; 15 U.S.C. §45. Despite the existence of three different statutes, the courts and the antitrust enforcement agencies generally analyze the competitive effects of a merger using one mode of analysis. *See, e.g., The Bon-Ton Stores, Inc. v. The May Dept. Stores Co.*, 881 F. Supp. 860 (W.D.N.Y. 1994) (action by private party challenging an acquisition under Sections 1 and 2 of the Sherman Act and Section 7 of

U.S. states also have their own antitrust laws, but because these tend to be similar to the federal statutes, they are not treated separately below.

[425] Under U.S. antitrust law, the fundamental question raised by any merger is whether it will create or enhance market power; that is, the power to raise prices above competitive levels or to exclude competitors.[209] In analyzing whether a merger is likely to have this effect, antitrust authorities use the joint DOJ/FTC 2010 Horizontal Merger Guidelines (the "Merger Guidelines" or the "Guidelines"). Under the Guidelines, the analysis focuses on whether a merger creates, enhances, or entrenches market power or facilitates its exercise.[210]

[426] The Merger Guidelines follow a step-by-step approach to analysis, which often begins with market definition.[211] The "relevant market" consists of a product dimension and a geographic dimension.[212]

[427] With respect to product market definition, the government begins by focusing on each product that overlaps between the parties. For each such product, the government then determines whether any other products are sufficiently close substitutes, and therefore, should be included in the product market. This is done by evaluating whether, in response to a "small but significant, nontransitory price increase" in the product or "SSNIP," (often 5%), enough customers would switch to an alternative product to make the price increase unprofitable. If this is the case, the product market will be expanded to include the alternative product. The government will perform this same test on other alternative products until it finds a market in which a price increase will be profitable; this is the relevant product market for purposes of the antitrust analysis.[213]

[428] The government takes into account the geographic dimensions of the market as well. It considers the willingness and ability of customers to substitute to some products and the willingness and ability of suppliers to serve some customers. Both supplier and customer locations are relevant in this analysis. Geographic markets based on the locations of suppliers encompass the region from which sales are made. Competitors in the market are firms with relevant production, sales, or service facilities in that region. The government also considers the location of the customers.[214]

the Clayton Act); *United States v. Long Island Jewish Medical Center*, 983 F. Supp. 121, 135 (E.D.N.Y. 1997) ("While the complaint includes a request for relief under Section 1 of the Sherman Act. the Court will focus its attention on Section 7 of the Clayton Act, as that law applies equally to both statutes.").

[209] *FTC v. Butterworth Health Corp.*, 946 F. Supp. 1285, 1302 (W.D. Mi. 1996) (FTC challenge to a hospital merger not upheld where the FTC failed to show that the market power of the merged firm was likely to be exercised to the detriment of consumers).

[210] Merger Guidelines, §1.0.

[211] Merger Guidelines, §4.0. Historically market definition was the first step in merger analysis, and most U.S. courts continue to follow that practice. The current Guidelines are more flexible, however, and formal market definition is now often deferred until assessment of competitive effect.

[212] *United States v. Englehard Corp.*, 126 F.3d 1302, 1307 (11th Cir. 1997) (finding that the Government's market definition was "flawed," the court upheld the district court's denial of a preliminary injunction); *FTC v. Freeman Hosp.*, 69 F.3d 260, 272 (8th Cir. 1995) ("identification of a relevant market is a "necessary predicate" to a successful challenge under the Clayton Act"; action dismissed without consideration of anticompetitive effects).

[213] Merger Guidelines, §4.1.

[214] Merger Guidelines, §4.2.2.

[429] Once the relevant market has been defined, the next step under the Merger Guidelines is to measure market concentration, by employing the Herfindahl-Hirschman Index ("HHI"). The HHI is calculated by summing the squares of the individual market shares of all market participants. The Guidelines divide the spectrum of market concentration into three regions: unconcentrated (HHI under 1500), moderately concentrated (HHI of 1500–2500), and highly concentrated (HHI above 2500). The Guidelines also provide a number of HHI safe harbors. In general, the government will not challenge a merger that results in (i) an increase in the HHI of less than 100 points, or (ii) an HHI of 1500 or less.[215]

[430] Where a merger falls outside the HHI safe harbors, the government will consider whether it is likely to have any anticompetitive effects.[216] Under the Guidelines, the government focuses on two types of potential anticompetitive effects: (i) whether the merger will allow the merged entity to raise prices or exclude competitors on its own (referred to as "unilateral effects"); and (ii) whether the merger will facilitate collusion between the merged entity and its remaining competitors on prices or other terms of competition (known as "coordinated effects").[217]

[431] To evaluate potential unilateral effects, the government will consider whether, if the merged entity attempted to raise prices above competitive levels, enough customers could and would switch to competitors to defeat the price increase. This includes an analysis of whether the merging parties could be considered each other's closest competitors and the likely supply response by any remaining competitors and whether they could adequately replace the lost competition. A combined market share of less than 30% is unlikely to raise concerns that the merged entity will be able to exercise unilateral market power.[218] With respect to coordinate effects, the government will consider whether factors present in the market would make collusion more or less likely, including whether there has been collusion in the market in the past, and the ease with which the parties could monitor and enforce any agreement on price or other terms of competition.[219]

[432] If the government determines that a merger is likely to have anticompetitive effects in any relevant market, it will consider whether these effects are likely to be ameliorated or defeated by the entry of new competition, either as a result of expansion by existing market participants or entry by new competitors. Under

[215] Merger Guidelines, §5.3; *see also FTC v. Staples*, 970 F. Supp. 1066, 1081 (D.D.C. 1997); *The Bon-Ton Stores, Inc. v. The May Dept. Stores Co.*, 881 F. Supp. 860, 875-6 (W.D.N.Y. 1994); *FTC v. University Health, Inc.*, 938 F.2d 1206, 1211 n.12 (11th Cir. 1991); *United States v. Baker Hughes Inc.*, 908 F.2d 981, 983 n.3 (D.C. Cir. 1990).

[216] In challenging mergers in court, the agencies have enjoyed a presumption by the courts that mergers that fall outside of the safe harbors are presumptively unlawful, and the burden of rebutting such a presumption, through a showing of a lack of adverse effects or inability to exercise market power, is on the merging parties. *See, e.g., FTC v. Butterworth Health Corp.*, 946 F. Supp. 1285, 1302 (W.D. Mi. 1996) ("The FTC has made its prima facie case, creating a presumption of illegality."); *University Health, Inc.*, 938 F.2d at 1218 (court gave a presumption of illegality where the FTC was able to show that the acquisition would produce a firm with an undue market share and would result in a significant increase in concentration).

[217] Merger Guidelines, §1.0, 6.0-7.2.

[218] *See United States v. Philadelphia National Bank*, 374 U.S. 321 (1963).

[219] Merger Guidelines, §7.2.

the Merger Guidelines, in order for potential entry to allay competitive concerns, it must be (i) sufficiently rapid to deter the competitive effects of concern,[220] (ii) sufficiently likely to occur (meaning that it will be profitable, accounting for the assets, capabilities, and capital needed and the risks involved, including the need for the entrant to incur costs that would not be recovered if the entrant later exits),[221] and (iii) sufficient in magnitude, character, and scope to deter or counteract the competitive effects of concern.[222]

[433] If the government determines that a merger is likely to have anticompetitive effects, it also considers whether those effects may be outweighed by procompetitive efficiencies likely to result from the merger, including cost savings and improvements in quality.[223] To be recognized under the Guidelines, efficiencies must be (i) merger specific (*i.e.*, they cannot be achieved through other, less "anticompetitive" means like a joint venture), (ii) net efficiencies that take into account the costs of implementation, (iii) likely to be passed onto consumers in the form of lower prices or higher quality and (iv) an actual motivating factor in the parties entering into the transaction (as evidenced by documents created in the ordinary course of business during consideration of the merger). The greater the competitive concerns raised by a transaction, the greater the magnitude of the efficiencies required to overcome those concerns.

APPLICABILITY OF THE HART-SCOTT-RODINO ACT

[434] For transactions exceeding certain thresholds, the Hart-Scott Rodino Antitrust Improvements Act of 1976[224] (the "HSR Act") and its implementing regulations (the "Rules")[225] require parties to notify U.S. antitrust authorities and to wait a statutorily prescribed period—usually 30 days—before consummating the transaction. The HSR Act is designed to give the federal agencies time to conduct an antitrust review of a proposed transaction and, if deemed appropriate, to challenge the transaction under section 7 of the Clayton Act[226] before the transaction is consummated. The obligations under the HSR Act are procedural, so the fact that a transaction raises no possible antitrust issue does not itself, exempt the transaction from the Act. Any transaction meeting the Act's threshold requirements triggers a filing unless an exemption recognized in the HSR Act or the Rules applies.

[435] The obligations under the HSR Act are not limited to U.S. firms. The HSR Act applies to non-U.S. firms with sufficient sales in or into the U.S. or assets located in

[220] Merger Guidelines, §9.1.
[221] Merger Guidelines, §9.2.
[222] Merger Guidelines, §9.0, 9.3.
[223] *See, e.g., Long Island Jewish Medical Center*, 983 F.2d at 146-47 ("The courts have recognized that 'in certain circumstances, a defendant may rebut the government's prima facie case with evidence that the intended merger would create significant efficiencies in the relevant market.'"); *Butterworth Health Corp.*, 946 F. Supp. at 1300.
[224] 15 U.S.C. §18a (the "HSR Act" or the "Act").
[225] 16 C.F.R. §801 et seq.
[226] 15 U.S.C. §18.

the U.S. It covers transactions between two non-U.S. firms that have sufficient nexus with the U.S. Failure to comply with the requirements of the HSR Act can result in significant civil penalties or injunctive relief.

[436] The HSR Act applies when two tests are satisfied—the "size of the persons" test and the "size of the transaction" test.

[437] First, under the "size of transaction" test, the transaction must result in the acquirer's holding a combination of nonexempt voting securities, noncorporate interests, or assets of the target with a value greater than US$80.8m.[227] Transactions valued at more than US$323m are reportable regardless of the size of the persons.[228] The measurement of transaction value is subject to complex rules.

[438] Assets must be valued at the higher of acquisition price or fair market value.[229] The acquisition price includes the value of any consideration being paid for the assets plus the value of any assumed liabilities.[230] The fair market value must be determined by the board of directors of the acquiring person's ultimate parent, or the board's designee, acting in good faith.[231]

[439] The rules for valuing voting securities vary, depending on whether the securities are publicly traded. If the securities are traded on a national securities exchange or authorized to be quoted on an interdealer quotation system of a national securities association registered with the U.S. Securities and Exchange Commission ("SEC"), they are valued at the higher of the market price or the acquisition price.[232] If the securities are not traded on such exchanges (*e.g.*, for a private, closely held corporation), the voting securities are valued at the acquisition price, if determined, or the fair market value.[233] The acquisition of "nonvoting" securities, that is, securities that do not confer the present right to vote for the board of directors or similar body, are not covered by the HSR Act.

[440] The "result in" element in measuring value looks to the total of the target's assets and voting securities that will be held by the acquirer *after* the transaction has been completed, not necessarily *in* the immediate transaction. Thus, where the acquirer has previously purchased assets or voting securities of the target, those prior

---

[227] 15 U.S.C. §18a(a)(2)(B)(i). On Dec. 21, 2000, President Clinton signed into law significant amendments to the HSR Act, representing the first major changes since the Act's 1976 enactment. The changes made by the amendments, which became effective Feb. 1, 2001, include: (i) increasing the size of the transaction dollar threshold from US$15 million to US$50 million, (ii) eliminating the 15% size of the transaction threshold under which acquisitions of 15% of a persons assets or voting securities were subject to the Act, (iii) making transactions valued at more than US$200 million reportable regardless of the size of the persons involved in the transaction, (iv) instituting a mechanism to adjust the size of the transaction threshold each year beginning in 2005, and (v) implementing a graduated filing fee structure. *See* Pub. L. 106-553, 114 Stat. 2762. This same legislation required the FTC to begin indexing the dollar thresholds in the HSR Act and Rules annually for each fiscal year starting after September 2004 based on changes in the U.S. gross national product. The dollar thresholds in the section reflect the indexed amounts that took effect as of Mar. 2, 2005.

[228] 15 U.S.C. §18a(a)(2)(A).

[229] 16 C.F.R. §801.10.

[230] 16 C.F.R. at §801.10 (c)(2).

[231] 16 C.F.R. at §801.10(c)(3).

[232] *Id.*

[233] *Id.*

holdings must be examined under certain aggregation rules to determine whether the latest transaction exceeds the "size-of-transaction" threshold.

[441] Second, for transactions with value greater than US$80.8m and not more than US$323m, a "size of persons" test also applies—one person involved in the transaction must annual net sales or total assets of at least US$161.5m, and another person must have annual net sales or total assets of at least US$16.2m. Where the acquired person is not engaged in manufacturing, the threshold applicable to that person is US$16.2m in total assets or US$161.5m in annual net sales.[234] The "person" for purposes of this test is the ultimate parent of the entity making the acquisition or the entity whose assets or voting securities are being acquired, together with all other entities controlled, directly or indirectly, by that ultimate parent.[235] Annual net sales of a "person" are those appearing on the ultimate parent's last regularly prepared, consolidated annual statement of income and expense; total assets are those appearing on the ultimate parent's last regularly prepared, consolidated balance sheet.[236]

TRANSACTIONS EXEMPT FROM THE HSR ACT

[442] Under the HSR Act and the Rules, many acquisitions that meet the "size of the persons" and "size of the transaction" tests are nonetheless deemed to be exempt. A number of exemptions are available with respect to acquisitions by or from non-U.S. entities. In general, applicability of these exemptions is determined by the extent to which the transaction has a connection to U.S. commerce.[237] Even where the non-U.S. exemptions do not apply, numerous other acquisitions may be available. The most significant exemptions are set forth below.

[443] *Non-U.S. Assets.* The acquisition of assets located outside the United States is exempt if there are no sales in or into the United States attributable to the assets.[238] If there are U.S. sales attributable to the assets, the acquisition is still exempt if the acquiring person will not hold assets of the acquired person to which more than US$80.8m in U.S. sales are attributable.[239] If the assets have more than US$80.8m in attributable U.S. sales, the acquisition is still exempt if (i) both the acquiring and acquired persons are foreign; (ii) the aggregate sales of the acquiring and acquired persons in or into the U.S. are less than US$161.5m in their respective most recent fiscal year; (iii) the aggregate total assets of the acquiring and acquired persons located in the United States are less than US$161.5m; or (iv) the transaction is not valued at more than US$323m.[240]

[234] *Id.*

[235] For purposes of the Act, "control" is defined as (i) with respect to a corporation or other entity that issues voting securities, holding 50% or more of the outstanding voting securities, or having a contractual right to appoint 50% or more of the board of directors, or (ii) with respect to a partnership or other entity that does not issue voting securities, having the right to 50% or more of its profits or assets upon dissolution. 16 C.F.R. §801.1(b).

[236] 16 C.F.R. §801.11.

[237] *See* 16 C.F.R. 802.50, 802.51.

[238] *Id.* at §802.50(a).

[239] *Id.*

[240] *Id.* at §802.50(b).

[444] *Non-U.S. Voting Securities.* A transaction in which a U.S. person is acquiring voting securities of a non-U.S. issuer is exempt unless the non-U.S. issuer (including all entities it controls) (i) holds assets located in the United States having an aggregate fair market value of over US$80.8m (not counting the value of cash, cash equivalents, instruments evidencing government obligations, and voting or nonvoting securities of another person), or (ii) made aggregate sales in or into the United States of more than US$80.8m in its most recent fiscal year.[241] A transaction in which a non-U.S. person is acquiring voting securities of a non-U.S. issuer is exempt unless the transaction will confer control of an issuer (i) that holds assets located in the United States that have an aggregate fair market value of more than US$80.8m (not counting the value of cash, cash equivalents, instruments evidencing government obligations, and voting or nonvoting securities of another person), or (ii) that made sales in or into the United States totaling more than US$80.8m in its most recent fiscal year.[242] Where an acquisition exceeds the thresholds provided by section 802.51(b)(1), the acquisition is still exempt where: (i) both the acquiring and acquired persons are foreign; (ii) the aggregate sales of the acquiring and acquired persons in or into the U.S. are less than US$161.5m in their respective most recent fiscal year; (iii) the aggregate total assets of the acquiring and acquired persons located in the U.S. are less than US$161.5m; or (iv) the transaction is not valued at more than US$323m.[243]

[445] *Non-U.S. Governments and Banks.* Certain acquisitions to or from non-U.S. governments[244] and certain non-U.S. banking transactions[245] are exempt.

[446] *Investment Purposes.* The acquisition of up to 10% of an issuer's voting securities is exempt if made "solely for the purpose of investment." This exemption applies regardless of the value of the securities being acquired.[246] The exact scope of the exemption is unclear. A shareholder is permitted to vote the shares it holds, but any conduct beyond this may be viewed as going beyond an investment purpose if it is undertaken with the "intention of participating in the formulation, determination, or direction of the basic business decisions of the issuer."[247] In particular, activities likely to be found inconsistent with an "investment only" intent include but are not limited to:

> (i) nominating a candidate for the board of directors of the issuer; (ii) proposing corporate action requiring shareholder approval; (iii) soliciting proxies; (iv) having a controlling shareholder, director, officer or employee simultaneously serving as an officer or director of the issuer; (v) being a competitor of the issuer; or (vi) doing any of the foregoing with respect to any entity directly or indirectly controlling the issuer.[248]

[447] A party may acquire stock subject to the "investment only" exemption and then change its investment intent. No filing would be required for stock acquired

[241] *Id.* at §802.51(a)(1).
[242] *Id.* at §802.51(b)(1).
[243] *Id.* at §802.51(c).
[244] *Id.* at §802.52.
[245] *Id.* at §802.53.
[246] *Id.* at §802.9.
[247] *Id.* at §801.1(i)(1).
[248] 43 Fed. Reg. 33,450, 33,465 (1978).

"prior to the change in intent, but a filing would be required before any further acquisitions could be made.[249]

[448] *Ordinary Course of Business.* The acquisitions of goods or realty transferred in the ordinary course of business is exempt.[250] The rules interpret the exemption as covering (i) new goods; (ii) inventory and supplies held for consumption, resale, or lease; (iii) used durable goods held solely for resale or lease; (iv) used durable goods, where those goods have been or will be replaced by the seller within six months of the transaction; or (v) used durable goods used by the seller to provide management and administrative support services, where the seller has contracted in good faith with another person to obtain services substantially similar to those provided by the goods being sold.[251] Under the rules, the exemption excludes acquisitions of goods as part of an acquisition of all or substantially all the assets of an operating unit.[252] An operating "unit" may be a single store or production facility, and need not be a separate legal entity.[253]

[449] *Real Property.* The rules exempt the acquisition of numerous classes of real property:[254] new facilities, unproductive real property, office and residential property, hotels and motels and related facilities (but not hotel trademarks and management), recreational land, agricultural property, retail rental space, warehouses, and investment rental properties. The definition of each class of covered real estate is set forth in the rules. The rules are also interpreted to exempt acquisitions by Real Estate Investment Trusts ("REITs") that are consistent with a REIT's special tax status under the Internal Revenue Code. Where an acquisition includes both exempt real property and nonexempt assets, the transaction remains exempt if the value of nonexempt assets is less than US$80.8m.

[450] *Carbon-Based Mineral Reserves.* The rules exempt the acquisition of carbon-based mineral reserves below thresholds that are higher than normal,[255] based on the agencies' view that larger transactions in the sector are unlikely to threaten competition. In particular, the acquisition of reserves (or rights to reserves) of oil, natural gas, shale or tar sands are exempt if their value does not exceed US$500m.[256] Similarly, the acquisition of reserves (or rights to reserves) of coal are exempt if their value does not exceed US$200m.[257] The exemption covers associated exploration and production assets, as long as those assets are dedicated to the reserves in question.[258]

[451] *Voting Securities of Issuers Holding Exempt Assets.* Nominally, the exemptions covering carbon-based mineral reserves, real estate, and investment rental property apply only to acquisition of assets. A separate exemption[259] extends the exemption

[249] 43 Fed. Reg. 33,450, 33,466 (1978).
[250] *See* 15 U.S.C. §18a(c)(1).
[251] 16 C.F.R. §802.1.
[252] *Id.* at §802.1(a).
[253] *Id.*
[254] *Id.* at §802.2 and §802.5.
[255] *See id.* at §802.3.
[256] *Id.* at §802.3(a).
[257] *Id.* at §802.3(b).
[258] *See id.* at §802.3(a),(b).
[259] *See* C.F.R. §802.4.

by also exempting the acquisition of the voting securities or noncorporate interests in any entity that holds assets that would be exempt if acquired directly, so long as the entity does not hold more than US$80.8m in nonexempt assets.

[452] *Stock Options, Warrants, and Most Convertibles.* The acquisition of stock options, warrants and convertible voting securities is generally exempt. While options, warrants and convertible voting securities are technically within the definition of "voting securities"[260] their acquisition is exempt so long as they do not confer present voting rights.[261] The exercise of an option or warrant or the conversion of a convertible security is deemed to be an event covered by the HSR Act.[262]

[453] *Securities Underwriting.* The acquisition of voting securities by a securities underwriter is exempt when conducted in the ordinary course of the underwriter's business and in the process of underwriting.[263]

[454] *Acquisitions by Creditors and Insurers.* Certain acquisitions by a creditor, including acquisition of collateral or receivables, foreclosures, loan work-outs, acquisitions upon default, and acquisitions in connection with the establishment of a lease financing are exempt if the acquisition constitutes a bona fide credit transaction entered into in the ordinary course of the creditor's business.[264] Similarly, acquisitions made by an insurer pursuant to a condition in a contract of insurance relating to fidelity, surety or casualty obligations is exempt if made in the insurer's ordinary course of business.[265]

[455] *Acquisitions by Institutional Investors.* Acquisitions of voting securities by certain institutional investors (including to banks, bank holding companies, savings and loans, trust companies, insurance companies, investment companies registered with the SEC, finance companies, broker-dealers, pension trusts, and certain nonprofits) are exempt provided a number of conditions are met. These conditions include a requirement that the acquisitions be made in the ordinary course of business, solely for the purpose of investment, and with the acquiring person holding no more than 15% of the voting securities of the issuer.[266] This exemption does not apply if the acquisition is of the voting securities of an institutional investor of the same type as any included in the acquiring person, or if an entity within the acquiring person that is not an institutional investor holds any voting securities of the issuer whose voting securities are to be acquired.[267]

Content of an HSR Filing

[456] If a premerger filing is required, the buyer and seller each must submit separate HSR filing forms. In a stock acquisition in which the buyer is buying stock from

[260] *Id.* at §801.1(f).
[261] *Id.* at §802.31, 801.1(f), Example 1.
[262] *Id.* at §801.32.
[263] *Id.* at 802.60.
[264] *Id.* at §802.63.
[265] *Id.*
[266] *Id.* at §802.64.
[267] *Id.*

holders other than the issuer (such as a tender offer), the buyer must notify the issuer of the buyer's acquisition plans and of the issuer's obligation to make a filing at the time the buyer makes its filing.[268]

[457] In their respective filings, the parties must provide information about the transaction (including copies of any signed letter of intent or purchase agreement); information about their SEC filings; their most recent annual audit report and most recent regularly prepared balance sheet, consolidated U.S. revenue figures broken down by lines of business using Department of Commerce North American Industry Classification System (NAICS) Codes, information about subsidiaries, minority shareholders, and minority shareholdings in unaffiliated entities; a certain geographic information about lines of business that overlap with the other party, and documents containing competitive analyses prepared for purposes of evaluating the acquisition. Filings are submitted to the FTC and DOJ. The buyer's filing with the FTC must be accompanied by a filing fee, the amount of which depends on the size of the transaction and which currently ranges from US$45 000 to US$280 000. As a matter of practice, the FTC and Justice Department divide responsibility for conducting substantive antitrust reviews.

THE PREMERGER WAITING PERIOD

[458] If stock is being purchased from a party other than the issuer (except cash tender offers), the buyer may not close on the purchase until 30 days after the agencies have received the buyer's filing. If the acquisition is a cash tender offer, the waiting period expires 15 days after the buyer files. In all other transactions (*i.e.*, stock purchased from issuer, mergers or asset acquisitions), a 30-day waiting period begins only when both parties have filed. In all instances, the filing is not perfected until the buyer has paid the appropriate filing fee.[269] If the 30th day falls on a Saturday, Sunday or legal public holiday, the waiting period is extended to the next regular business day.[270]

[459] The 30-day and 15-day waiting periods may be terminated early if both agencies agree to early termination.[271] Early termination of the 30-day period is common where a transaction poses no antitrust concerns and most often occurs between 10 and 20 days after the beginning of the waiting period. The granting of early termination is published in the Federal Register[272] and on the FTC web site. The Federal Register listing includes the names of the ultimate parents of the buyer and seller, the name of the particular entity whose assets or voting securities are being acquired, the transaction number assigned to the acquisition by the FTC, and the date on which early termination was granted. No specific terms of the transaction are made public.

[460] The waiting period is automatically extended if either FTC or DOJ issues a formal request for additional information; when they do so, the transaction may

[268] 16 C.F.R. §803.5.
[269] 16 C.F.R. §803.10.
[270] *See Id.*
[271] *Id.* at §803.11.
[272] *Id.*

not be completed until 30 days from completion of submission of the additional requested information (10 days in the context of a cash tender offer).[273] Second requests generally are very broad, and compliance often requires several months. At the end of the second request period, if the reviewing agency determines that determines that the transaction will violate the antitrust laws, it does not have the unilateral power to bar the parties from proceeding; instead, the agency will need to apply in federal court for an injunction barring consummation of the transaction.

[461] HSR filings are kept confidential. The agencies will not disclose the contents of one party's filing to the other party, and the filings are not subject to release under the Freedom of Information Act.[274] On rare occasions, the agencies may make filings available in response to a request by a Congressional committee or in the course of an administrative or judicial proceeding.[275] In situations where HSR materials are made available in connection with litigation, parties may be able to obtain protective orders from the court to limit disclosure.

HSR ACT COMPLIANCE

[462] Compliance with the statutory requirements of the HSR Act is vigorously enforced by the agencies. This includes not only complying with the requirements for a proper HSR filing, but the observance of the statutorily prescribed waiting periods. Fines of up to US$40 000 per day may be imposed against "any person" who fails to comply with the HSR Act,[276] including both corporate entities and individuals. The DOJ and FTC have obtained multi-million dollar for failing to file under the HSR Act and properly to observe the waiting period. A court may order divestiture of illegally acquired voting securities or assets or "grant other equitable relief as the court in its discretion determines necessary or appropriate."[277]

[463] The power to enforce the HSR Act rests solely with the government. Private parties may complain to the FTC and DOJ about alleged violations, but do not have authority to enforce or obtain damages under the HSR Act.[278]

[273] 15 U.S.C. §18a(e)(2).

[274] Federal courts have held that state attorneys general, as members of the "public," could not obtain information submitted to the FTC and DOJ under the HSR Act. *See Lieberman v. FTC,* 771 F.2d 32 (2d Cir. 1985); *Mattox v. FTC,* 752 F.2d 116 (5th Cir. 1985). As a result, if a state attorney general wants to obtain HSR materials with respect to its own investigation of a merger or acquisition, it must obtain the consent of the merging parties.

[275] 15 U.S.C. §18a(h).

[276] 15 U.S.C. §18a(g).

[277] *Id.*

[278] *See Hammermill Paper Co. v. Icahn,* No. 80-47-B (W.D. Pa. 1980) (Slip. Op.).

Made in the USA
Monee, IL
18 October 2026

66041401R10096